THE MAN WHO LEFT TOO SOON

THE LIFE AND WORKS OF STIEG LARSSON

BARRY FORSHAW

JB
JOHN BLAKE

Published by John Blake Publishing Ltd,
3 Bramber Court, 2 Bramber Road,
London W14 9PB, England

www.johnblakepublishing.co.uk
www.facebook.com/Johnblakepub facebook
twitter.com/johnblakepub twitter

First published in hardback in 2010
Updated paperback published 2011

ISBN: 978 1 84358 370 7

British Library Cataloguing-in-Publication Data:

A catalogue record for this book is available from the British Library.

Design by www.envydesign.co.uk

Printed in Great Britain by CPI Bookmarque, Croydon CRO 4TD

1 3 5 7 9 10 8 6 4 2

Papers used by John Blake Publishing are natural, recyclable products made from wood grown in sustainable forests. The manufacturing processes conform to the environmental regulations of the country of origin.

As this book contains spoilers, it is intended for those already familiar with Stieg Larsson's *Millennium Trilogy*

THE MAN WHO LEFT TOO SOON

CONTENTS

INTRODUCTION

AAs the posthumous success of Stieg Larsson's *Millennium Trilogy* seems to grow to ever-more unprecedented levels, with worldwide sales in the millions, it is an apposite time to celebrate the life and work of an intriguing, courageous – and self-destructive – man. Of course, extremely talented people often possess a certain carelessness with regard to their own health, for a variety of reasons. Leonard Bernstein certainly matched Stieg Larsson in terms of a prodigious nicotine intake, but preferred haute cuisine to the junk food that was another element in Stieg Larsson's own reckless lifestyle.

Bernstein, however, believed he was one of the gods and that the health strictures which ordinary mortals were obliged to take note of simply didn't apply to him – knowing that he was an immortal in terms of his music, he ill-advisedly applied this mindset to his much-abused body. With Stieg Larsson, who died in 2004 aged 50, the scenario was rather different, and the combination of what might be called a Protestant work ethic and a fierce desire to right the wrongs of the world were partly behind the cavalier approach to his own wellbeing. What counted was the work – not maintaining the instrument that carried it out.

It goes without saying that Larsson's early death is a crucial element in the mythic qualities that his life and work have come to possess. But it is the innovation and intelligence of the *Millennium Trilogy* (along with its trenchant and fierce social critiques, so much a part of Larsson's own crusading personality) that are among the real reasons behind the all-conquering acclaim the books have engendered.

Just as Larsson cannily pays out chunks of information to his readers to create a total picture, it seemed to me appropriate to attempt something similar in this book. The approach I have taken is piecemeal, utilising a variety of elements – Stieg's life, his influential journalistic career as a courageous fighter against extremist organisations, his relatives, his publishers, his translators, the successful movies being made from his books – and the acrimonious dispute over his legacy. I've been lucky enough to speak to most of the people concerned, but like virtually all readers of the novels, I never had a chance to meet the author, for whom the phrase 'taken too soon' could have been coined.

Larsson aficionados will be aware that his biography is, to some extent, to be found in his books – hence the concentration here on the three novels of his trilogy, with biographical data built into these sections rather than hived off into separate chapters, though his life is addressed separately. So at the centre of this study (to be read, of course, only after reading the novels themselves) is a thoroughgoing examination of the phenomenally successful novels in the trilogy: *The Girl with the Dragon Tattoo*, *The Girl Who Played with Fire* and *The Girl Who Kicked the*

Hornets' Nest, comprising one of the most striking and innovative trilogies in modern fiction. And for all their faults – discussed here alongside their felicities – the auguries are that the books will join the pantheon of the very finest popular literature, to be read for generations to come.

Barry Forshaw, London 2011

CHAPTER 1

TAKEN TOO SOON

At the prestigious Crime Writers' Association Dagger awards in London's Grosvenor House Hotel in October 2008, there was a 'no-show' for one of the awards. An author had not appeared for a photo opportunity with the other nominees, and the clock was ticking. Where was Stieg Larsson? The Swedish author had been nominated for his astonishingly successful debut novel, *The Girl with the Dragon Tattoo*, and was the only author who could not be found for the photo call. It was a publicity opportunity that Stieg Larsson would never make. He had died before any of his three novels were published in his native Sweden, let alone seeing them become runaway bestsellers, or before they reached other shores in translation, going on to be a worldwide publishing phenomenon. And the fact that not everyone in the UK's top organisation for crime writers knew that the debut award was in fact a posthumous nomination was a measure of the unprecedented speed with which his star had risen. What's more, having died suddenly before writing a will, he left behind a confused situation that has led to a bitter fracas over his considerable literary and financial legacy.

In fact, the Larsson story is even more remarkable: had he not become a bestselling crime writer, he would be remembered as something of a hero, a man who took on some dangerous neo-Nazi opponents, and whose premature death prompted much sinister speculation. How had he died? Was it simply – as the official medical verdict had it – a massive heart attack? Or did his enemies, who often told him that his days were numbered, have a hand in his demise?

Sales of *The Girl with the Dragon Tattoo* had reached the million mark in Sweden (under its original Swedish title *Män som hatar kvinnor* – 'Men who hate women') even before it was discovered by foreign publishers, and Larsson was already celebrated as a courageous, campaigning journalist, taking on far-Right groups. He also fought for the rights of battered women and could add impeccable feminist credentials to his impressive political résumé. He was, however, most celebrated as an authority on extremist organisations, and his battles with them often put him in physical danger – something that seemed not to faze him. He was known in the UK to readers of the British-based international magazine *Searchlight*, which campaigns against racism and fascism, while in Sweden he became founder and editor of its Swedish equivalent, *Expo* – still going strong after his death.

So what was the secret of the unprecedented success of his first novel in the *Millennium Trilogy*? His UK publisher, Quercus, was also responsible for the similarly out-of-the-blue sales triumph of Stef Penney's *The Tenderness of Wolves*, and launched the paperback of *The Girl with the*

Dragon Tattoo with a print run of 200,000 copies; within a short time, the book's sales had reached unprecedented levels. A modestly sized independent, Quercus does not have the advertising spend of bigger publishers and has relied on publishing a judicious choice of outstanding novels – promoted by word-of-mouth recommendation – the latter very much a factor in the success of the Stieg Larsson books.

The protagonists of *Dragon Tattoo* are a trenchantly characterised duo: disgraced journalist Mikael Blomkvist and youthful computer hacker Lisbeth Salander. Salander, in particular, is something completely new in crime fiction: she has an alienating punk appearance (facial jewellery, ill-matched clothes and the dragon tattoo of the title). But despite her forbidding looks, she is immensely vulnerable, struggling with personal demons. As she and her journalist colleague investigate the disappearance of the niece of an ailing tycoon, readers soon realised Salander was an irresistible new character in the genre.

Stieg Larsson was born Karl Stig-Erland Larsson on 15 August 1954 in Skelleftehamn, a small town on the Gulf of Bothnia in the region of Västerbotten, on the northeast coast of Sweden, 400 miles north of Stockholm. He was the scion of a northern Swedish family, but was not, initially, raised by his parents, who for a variety of reasons – including financial ones – felt that his grandparents might better supply that function until he was nine years old. Stieg's grandfather was clearly a significant figure in the author's life. He was a man of political commitment who was prepared to risk going to prison for his beliefs, and in fact he did just that, suffering incarceration during the Second World War for his open opposition to the Nazis. It's not hard to see here a template for Stieg Larsson's similar courage in confronting dangerous right-wing opponents.

When his grandfather died, Stieg took the event very badly, and a period of adjustment was necessary when he moved back to the parental home with his father Erland and his brother Joakim. The two boys shared a bedroom, and I spoke to Joakim about how keen his brother was on the pleasures of narrative and storytelling. His childhood preferences included Enid Blyton (interestingly, at the time the famous children's writer was undergoing a subtle ban in her own country in the broadcasting media, as the BBC disapproved of what they considered to be the poor quality of her writing). The much-loved adventures of children's heroine Pippi Longstocking by Astrid Lindgren were also a favourite, and these were to be an intriguing influence on Larsson's later writing. It is now widely assumed that his tenacious heroine Lisbeth Salander is a radically reworked – and tattooed – modern version of Lindgren's creation, with a polymorphous sex life.

Larsson's father, Erland, now approaching 80, is a youthful-looking and typical northern Swede – modest and low-key. He told me that he remembers buying his young son a typewriter, but the incessant drumming of the keys so upset neighbours that it had to be moved into a basement room in the apartment building.

After national service, Stieg began a 30-year stint as the UK magazine *Searchlight*'s Scandinavian correspondent. He had decided to devote his life to fighting fascism along with religious and racial intolerance in the 1980s and 1990s, writing books on honour killings and the extreme Right in Sweden. This was a dangerous time for a writer of Larsson's stamp, and a car bomb had killed a fellow investigative journalist. But Stieg had a source of strength in his partner, Eva Gabrielsson, an architectural historian who shared his political convictions. Of course, any woman who chooses to live with a man with Larsson's combative lifestyle has to sport a certain toughness herself, and the couple developed strategies for their safety. If they sat in a restaurant or bar together, they would arrange it so both were looking at opposite entrances. Ironically, however, Larsson's real nemesis was to come from an unexpected source – one very close to home.

Larsson was an active member of the Kommunistika Arbetareförbundet, the Communist Workers League. During this period he also worked as a photographer. Further burnishing his Trotskyite credentials, he edited the journal *Fjärde Internationalen.* But his life was not all politically-motivated causes; Larsson was known to be a particularly keen admirer of science fiction, and his knowledge and enthusiasm for the genre was prodigious (it went far beyond being simply a fan: the Anglo-Swedish journalist Dan Lucas, who worked with him, told me that Larsson had a forensic grasp of the entire field and he could talk knowledgeably about all of its best writers). This attention to detail, in which knowledge was vacuumed up without apparent effort, was characteristic of his entire approach to his life and work – if Larsson took an interest in a subject he would acquire (almost by symbiosis) a total grasp of every element involved. Utilising his knowledge of the field, he worked, either as editor or co-editor, on various science fiction fanzines, among them *Fijagh*! and *Sfären*. He also held the position of president of his country's most prestigious science fiction organisation, the Skandinavisk Förening for Science Fiction, popularly known as SFSF. Inheriting his father's talents for the visual arts, from 1977 to 1999 Larsson held down a job as a graphic designer for an important Swedish news agency, Tidningarnas Telegrambyrå.

It was inevitable that with his deeply felt political convictions, organisational skills and journalistic savvy, Larsson would at some point bring together these different strands of experience to forge something that he could feel proud of creating. He decided to found the Swedish Expo Foundation – which was inspired by the similarly motivated Searchlight Foundation in Britain – with a brief to 'counteract the growth of the extreme Right and the white power culture in schools and among young people'. He was, of course, the natural choice as editor for the foundation house magazine, *Expo*, subsequently to become the inspiration for the fictional magazine *Millennium*, which the journalist Mikael Blomkvist works on in Larsson's trilogy.
With a series of lacerating and well researched articles, Larsson took on (in no uncertain terms) Sweden's far Right and the organisations arguing for racial purity. As he was a particularly vocal and unflinching exponent of his views, it was inevitable that he would soon put himself in the firing line for a series of death threats, and this was to affect his mode of living for the rest of his short life.

Before the creation of the Expo Foundation in 1995, a remarkable and controversial phenomenon held sway in Sweden – a phenomenon that may be said to have been the sand in the oyster that created the pearl of its foundation. Despite the country's abiding image of tolerance and liberality, the 'white power' music scene held sway, and enjoyed a surprisingly large following, particularly among the young. It was a caustic, tendentious fusion of punk-inspired rock and crudely white supremacist lyrics – if the noun 'lyrics' might be applicable to the words of these uncompromising anthems, the performers barking out their songs with the same aggressive snarl that Johnny Rotten and others had affected in the UK. And Sweden was, amazingly, the world's most assiduous progenitor of such incendiary material; not even a nascent neo-Nazi movement in Germany could claim to be in this particular musical vanguard.

1995 was a significant year in race relations in Sweden, with seven murders which were related to far-Right extremism. The agenda of such organisations included a targeted provocation of the far Left, and an argument might be made that both groups needed each other as nemeses in order to motivate their followers. Certainly, the Expo Foundation established in that year was designed to counteract the burgeoning influence of the extreme Right which had taken a particular hold in schools and among young people. Apart from Stieg Larsson, the Expo organisers included like-minded journalists, teachers and a variety of motivated young people worried by what they saw as a growing fascist tendency among their peers. Expo, aware of how it might be perceived, attempted to maintain a rigorous distance from links to particular political groups or parties, and its avowed intention was to safeguard 'democracy and freedom of speech against racist, anti-Semitic and totalitarian tendencies throughout society'.

When the first issue of the *Expo* magazine was published it certainly achieved one of its principal aims: to act as an irritant to the far-Right groups it saw as its bitter opponents. The magazine was quickly established as the focus for an intense hate campaign from neo-Nazi organisations, and everyone connected with the publication was obliged to take extra security measures, as they realised that the personal safety which they had taken for granted was no longer guaranteed. There were destructive attacks on the printing factory at which *Expo* was produced, and by 1996 important national newspapers such as *Aftonbladet* were recording the divisive conflicts within Swedish society.

The magazine was bankrolled by funds accrued via lectures, magazine subscriptions and advertising sales, and survived in a turbulent media market. Some of the first, pioneering group of editorial staff stood down in 1998, many of them exhausted from leading a similar lifestyle to that of Stieg Larsson (that is to say: extensive work on anti-Nazi causes funded by punishing full-time work schedules elsewhere). Three of the original staff remained and decided to give the magazine a crucial overhaul, although the basic crusading ethos remained. The magazine is still in rude health, six years after Stieg Larsson's death, and is still staffed by journalists who work on a largely voluntary basis (the current editor-in-chief is Daniel Poohl).

Apart from the magazine itself, a legacy of which Larsson would have been proud, there is the *Expo* archive, the largest individual source of information on the extreme Right in the whole of Scandinavia. *Expo* liaises with the Norwegian magazine *Monitor* and *Searchlight* in the UK, both ploughing similar furrows in long-running battles with extremist groups. However, the influence of the publication extends considerably further, with correspondents and contacts in Russia, Poland and the United States (The Centre for New Community, CNC, is a particularly influential organisation). Larsson and his similarly motivated colleagues have left a legacy that has survived against all the odds.

In 2000 Larsson wrote an article for *Searchlight* called 'Radical Conservatives Shift to Anti-Semitism', a swingeing attack on a new Swedish magazine called *Salt*. The piece began in typically combative Larsson style: 'Sooner or later, Sweden was bound to get its own posh, full-colour, upmarket, bi-monthly, almost intelligent [a particularly cutting dig!], radical-conservative magazine. First published last October as a "conservative ideas magazine", *Salt* is already looking forward to its sixth edition.' Larsson anatomises a magazine which is clearly anathema to him, noting this was to be (according to its published credo) 'no conservative magazine emulating wishy-washy, leftist liberal ideas, but a vehicle to critically target the ideology of power, meaning feminists, gays, multicultural ideas, and so on'.

He noted that the new magazine had utilised a variety of high-profile, respectable conservative writers, including the influential and combative British right-wing philosopher Roger Scruton – not someone Larsson would have enjoyed a companionable discussion with – but also pointed out that most of Sweden's intellectual set had ignored the magazine, except (as he put it) a tiny section of the ultraconservative Right, who gloated that 'Sweden had finally got a voice to shriek at feminism and other allegedly evil forces of modern society'.

As in so much of Larsson's political writing, this broadside against ideologies that he so detested clearly reflects the mindset of the author of the *Millennium Trilogy*. He noted, for instance, that *Salt* had – in his view – given space to people whose sentiments could be regarded as anti-Semitic. Larsson's was, of course, no carefully argued, understated attack on right-wing shibboleths – such an approach, quite simply, was not Stieg Larsson's style. Anger and contempt were his motivating force – as they became for his tattoo-sporting heroine. He ended in typically robust fashion: '*Salt*... will undoubtedly find an appropriate readership among the cultural elitists who would dearly love to rehabilitate the anti-Semitism of the "good old days".'

Needless to say, this was no isolated example of the scorn that Larsson could summon up for his opponents. In 2004, in a piece entitled 'Sweden – National Democrats break up', Larsson claimed, in the process of identifying what he saw as a full-blown split in the organisation, that elements of the National Democrats were, in his perception, racist. With some relish, he wrote that the party, which had begun in 2001 as a 'unified nationalist movement', lasted a mere three years before falling prey to the squabbles of Sweden's fractious nationalist fringe. Larsson's main thesis was that a party which had a skinhead image ('harbouring uniformed and violent loonies') would not be able to win the populist vote needed to make serious electoral inroads. It needed to attract (as he characterised them) 'the pseudo-respectable, suit-and-tie racists' – an observation that has an application beyond the boundaries of Sweden. The late writer would now be highly exercised by the unprecedented gains of the far Right in the 2010 elections.

When Larsson died in 2004, Graeme Atkinson of *Searchlight*, in a piece entitled 'A dedicated anti-fascist and good friend: Stieg Larsson 1954 – 2004', extolled the virtues of his late colleague. Atkinson described the writer's poor upbringing in the forests of northern Sweden, his (somewhat surprising) enthusiastically undertaken military service and wide travels in Africa, where he witnessed bloody civil war in Eritrea at first hand. (Regarding the latter, some unexpected facts were to emerge in 2010 concerning the extent of Larsson's involvement with the actual nitty-gritty of combat training – to be addressed later in this book.)

For Atkinson, Larsson's most commendable achievement was how he had put his talents at the disposal of the antifascist movement as a writer and illustrator, but most notably as a researcher whose knowledge of the Swedish and international far Right could only be described as encyclopaedic.

Larsson's sense of humour is remarked upon in this obituary – how Stieg ('an incarnation of internationalism') never allowed the seriousness of his work to cause him to lose his ability to smile or to bury the sense of humour that fired his endless collection of hilarious stories and anecdotes. This was a theme that appeared again and again when I spoke to those who knew him – and a welcome corrective to the image of the writer as a grim-faced, humourless activist, a picture that some people cherish. Atkinson mentions Larsson's modesty, but also points out that the writer made big financial and health sacrifices for the antifascist cause, to which 'he gave everything and asked almost nothing in return. For him it was results which led to a better world that made making sacrifices worthwhile.'

Interestingly, Atkinson's tribute suggests that Stieg's advice to those he left behind might well have been that of his famous fellow radical Swede, Joe Hill – 'Don't mourn, organise!' – though with the added down-to-earth injunction 'but have some fun doing so!'

Atkinson observed that barely a day passes without his thinking about Stieg Larsson. It is his belief that the writer's pronounced concern for issues relating to racism and extremism may be traced back to his childhood, growing up with his grandparents in Skelleftea. Atkinson noted that from his conversations with Stieg, the latter's grandfather

Severin Boström, with whom the boy had a very close relationship, was a key influence on his thinking. In the 1930s, Severin had been a vocal critic of the rise of Nazism in Germany and its progenitor, Adolf Hitler; Atkinson also comments that Stieg's passionate desire for the betterment of society was also a product of this close relationship with his grandfather. Intriguingly, Atkinson has also said that he was not aware that Stieg had a brother, and that there was no mention of a sibling, which appears to tie in with the estrangement from his family noted elsewhere.

How separate were the identities of Larsson the campaigning journalist and Larsson the novelist? In a paper that the writer gave at a conference for OSCE (Organization for Security and Co-operation in Europe) in Paris in June 2004, he used a telling phrase about how slander, innuendo or rumour was utilised by hate groups 'to legitimise the actions' that follow – i.e. retributional violence. In some ways, a metaphor for his novels might be adduced from this statement – one that Larsson himself might not have liked.

Analysing the structure of all the Larsson novels we can see that the reader is presented with the elements of 'slander, innuendo or rumour' (via their use against the beleaguered Lisbeth Salander) – along with extreme violence, sexual or otherwise – to 'legitimise the actions that follow', i.e. Lisbeth's use of massive force to rout and destroy her enemies. The legitimising process is both a function of Salander's action-generating rationale and ours as complicit readers – we are persuaded of the loathsome tactics of her opponents, and, accordingly) her violent reaction has a moral justification, a sort of brass-knuckle version of the equal and opposite reactions of Newton's laws of motion.

In a paper called 'The Nature and Extent of the Relationship Between Racist, Xenophobic and Anti-Semitic Propaganda on the internet and Hate Crimes', Larsson (credited as part of the 'Expo Foundation, Sweden') invokes the British journal *Searchlight* (of which, of course, he was a foreign luminary) specifically, an editorial which posited that racist violence follows racist agitation, 'as sure as night follows day'.

Larsson said that he would like to make 'a small point', continuing: 'It seems to be a foregone conclusion that violence follows hate propaganda.' But while agreeing with this argument, Larsson had a slightly more nuanced position.

'We have seen this all through recorded history,' he went on. 'When a nation or a clan or a paramilitary outfit – or whatever – is about to go and do something fundamentally evil to other people, there will be a period of slander, innuendo or rumour-mongering that is meant to legitimise the actions that will follow. The best-known case in world history of hate propaganda leading to violence is perhaps *Mein Kampf* by Adolf Hitler, who outlined [in that book] the core of his political philosophy – that Jews were the ultimate evil and had to be purged. We all know the result of this.'

But Larsson observed that when addressing the research on the subject as he prepared for the paper he was to give, it struck him that although a large number of websites across the world took on the subject of hate propaganda, there was little actual scientific research being quoted on such sites.

'I couldn't find a single scientific paper,' Larsson lamented, 'mapping out the relationship between agitation and action. At the same time, it would perhaps seem superfluous to point out that propaganda is the tool of any lobby group or political group from right to left, from good to evil. I rather doubt that any group would spend time, effort and money on propaganda if it didn't have a proven effect.'

Larsson's attitude to the propaganda that bombards us daily was relatively benign – he noted, for instance, its acceptable legal status. After the end of the Second World War, he observed, race biology and obviously anti-Semitic sentiments didn't make much of an impact on everyday life among Europeans. 'Although there were an abundance of groups producing hate propaganda, a Nazi magazine or a leaflet was actually very hard to come by for the average member of the public. You really had to make an effort to be able to read any of the rather tatty Mimeographed editions making the rounds in the political sub-vegetation.

'The arrival of the internet has changed all that. And to tell the truth, we who monitor such things have been slow to catch on. For the racist groups, cyberspace is a dream. It is no accident that today the first item on the agenda for any racist or ultra-nationalist group is the creation of a home page. Nazis were among the first to realise the potential of the internet. This is clearly worded in their own internal strategies.'

Larsson, always *au fait* with the exigencies of disseminating information, posited that compared with the production of books or magazines, the internet was cost-reductive: it is cheap and easy to maintain.

'An internet homepage of the smallest racist group of three or four people has the same circulation and availability as *Der Spiegel* or a CNN broadcast. It is in everybody's computer, just the click of a mouse away. And – perhaps most importantly – it offers a brand new way of organising, merchandising, fundraising and communication.'

In a conclusion with obvious ramifications for his later

fiction, Larsson pointed out that on the internet you can find absolutely anything you are looking for – a proposition even truer today than when Larsson made it.

'Experts in terrorism,' he continued, 'will tell you that every group that has ever taken violent action has done so following a period – sometimes years – of active propaganda. In many ways this stage is the process of dehumanizing the target of your propaganda... first you joke about the Holocaust, and then you claim it is a forgery – it never happened.'

Interestingly, though, Larsson was keen to broaden out the discussion from attacks on minority ethnic groups by pointing out that propaganda often has another underlying theme (one with considerable resonance in the US with its survivalist movements): fostering suspicion against democratic society, democratic politicians and democracy itself.

'My personal opinion', he said, 'one which some of my partners and associates will agree with, while others will disagree, is that legislation alone cannot solve the challenge of internet hate propaganda. Indeed, I would even counsel caution against relying too much on legislation. Please don't misunderstand me. We have laws separating right from wrong according to our social standards. If we have a law against incitement of racial hatred, then let us by all means use it as a tool to prosecute offenders.

'But the reality of the problem is that we are now facing thousands and thousands of racist pages from all over the world. The reality of the situation is that we haven't even got enough police officers to investigate, let alone enough prosecutors to take action. For that reason, the judicial process in any country will only skim the surface and make examples of a few of the worst offenders, while letting most of the offensive material slide.'

Larsson had saved his most telling salvoes till the end of his address, noting that the radical Right had become a significant political movement, whereas many years ago it had been a small fringe, netting at best a handful of votes in elections. It was to become an even more telling observation after the author's death. Recently, a crime-fiction-writing team, comprising a journalist and criminologist and a reformed criminal, has enjoyed massive success in Sweden. The duo goes simply by their two surnames: Roslund and Hellström. I spoke to Anders Roslund, an articulate, award-winning journalist, about Larsson's comment a few days after the Swedish far Right's electoral success in 2010, asking when Sweden became the broken society that Stieg Larsson depicts. 'Last week at the elections,' he replied dryly. Roslund and Hellström are among the heirs apparent to Larsson. Their novel *Three Seconds* (translated into English by Kari Dickson) is a book that invites comparison with *The Girl with the Dragon Tattoo*: there is the same obsessive piling on of detail, the same endemic corruption of the authorities (police force, Ministry of Justice), and there's even Larsson's tactic of the slow, challenging introductory chapters that suddenly shift into higher gear.

Larsson's comments also included this observation: 'Today the same groups have moved out of the basement hideouts they could be found in during the 1960s and 1970s. In some countries they are polling 10% to 15% of the vote. In other words, we have a shift of the political winds in which sentiments which were almost taboo 30 years ago are again becoming a real political option. The internet has become one of the most important tools in the revival of race-hate politics. This is the challenge offered to democracy by racism.'

His conclusion was a rational but perhaps over-hopeful one,

given the straitened budgets of most governments, along with the rise of confrontational religious extremism, since his death: 'We cannot wish that they will go away. We cannot legislate the problem away. We can only defeat them in a process where democratic society will rise to this challenge. And to do that we need more research, more knowledge, more funding, more democratic groups responding to these movements.'

CHAPTER 2

THE RELATIVES

Stieg Larsson's father and brother, Erland and Joakim, are very different: on the occasions when I spoke to them, I found two very distinct personalities. While Erland gives the impression of being slightly less worldly than either of his sons, he has clearly learnt how to deal with the astonishing media sensation that Stieg's life became after his death. But, controversially, Erland is, perhaps to his credit, not the kind of personality to play the sort of role that might be expected of him, that's to say, a sober-voiced, judicious custodian of the flame. What is crystal clear is his immense pride, uncomplicatedly expressed, in his late son's achievement, not to mention a continuing surprise at just how jaw-droppingly global the success has become. Erland has learned to enjoy that acclaim, but he remains intrigued to hear people discuss Stieg's individual achievements as a writer, as if some of the praise is new to him and being heard for the first time. This is no pose – while artistically talented, Erland is not an intellectual in the sense that his late son was. The father's artistic skills lie in the visual realm; he is a strikingly talented artist, a skill that he has maintained over the years and he has made a particularly charming and understated drawing of his own late son. He is also, as we shall see, a man who has vigorously divided opinion in the posthumous battle over his son's legacy.

In London, a month before the UK release of Stieg Larsson's second novel, *The Girl Who Played with Fire*, Erland Larsson spoke about the author's childhood. Inevitably, he was asked about Stieg's early reading, and he pointed out that both he and his wife were keen that Stieg should have a close relationship with books. By the age of 13 or 14, Stieg had consumed Selma Lagerlöf's *The Ring of the Löwenskölds*, a book which also captivated Stieg's brother Joakim, despite the fact that it was not something that Erland had himself read. This novel is interesting for its parallels with Larsson – like him, Selma Lagerlöf was holding down a full-time job (in her case as a teacher in a high school for girls in Sweden) while she was writing her first book. A particular concern for her was the folklore and historic traditions of Sweden – not concerns of Larsson – but the attempt to anatomise the soul of the country in fiction is not dissimilar. And *The Ring of the Löwenskölds* is a trilogy, in which we are allowed to know more about the characters as the books progress – a technique utilised by Larsson.

Erland pointed out that he and his wife were admirers of the highly influential crime novels of Maj Sjöwall and Per Wahlöö, which contain clearly expressed socialist agendas, as well as (in total contrast) the right-wing, bone-crunching detective fiction of Mickey Spillane. Erland remarked that he wasn't sure that these parental tastes had been taken up by his son, but it might be argued that elements in these very different writers are in fact freighted into the *Millennium Trilogy*: the political elements that were such a key factor of the remarkable series of novels by Maj Sjöwall and Per Wahlöö, and the unabashedly grisly violence of Mickey Spillane's Mike Hammer books – even though the violence is used to very different ends in the *Millennium Trilogy* than in *I, The Jury* or *Kiss Me Deadly*.

While always polite and friendly, I found Erland Larsson to be guarded around English writers such as myself – understandably so, perhaps, given the growing waves of journalistic disapproval that were beginning to engulf him because of the contentious issue of his late son's legacy. But as I shared with him an interest in art and illustration, he relaxed after a few minutes and gave frank answers to my questions about his son. While noting with regret that children today spend far more time on computers than they do reading, he speculated that Stieg's interest in journalism may have been prompted – as it was in so many young people of his generation – by the Vietnam War. But this early politicisation went along with the dedicated work ethic that was to prove so central to his life, and, possibly, so injurious to his health when combined with his excessive lifestyle.

'When Stieg was 12,' said Erland, 'I read a novel he had written in a notebook. It was then that we gave him a typewriter – it was for his thirteenth birthday and I remember it was very expensive at the time. It was also very noisy, so we had to make space for him in the cellar. He would write in the cellar and come up for meals, but at least we could sleep at night.'

According to his father, Stieg's interest in journalism, and the possibility that he might make a living from it, came at the same time as his growing involvement in Vietnam issues.

'Stieg was young and leaning towards the Left. In Sweden at the time, in every town in Sweden, on every Saturday, young people would be marching shouting "Out of Vietnam!" Stieg was one of those young people, and he started writing about the Vietnam War.

'His grandfather was a communist and I worked with him at a factory, and soon I became a Communist too. In those days you had to be a Communist to survive. It was a dark place, like a Nazi camp. Today the factory is better, but then it was a terrible place. Stieg was never a Communist. His mother became a very well-known Social Democrat – perhaps Stieg became fascinated with politics because we were a political family.'

In his early teenage years, Stieg seemed to take more of an interest in politics than writing fiction, according to his father. 'At the beginning, we discussed politics at some length at the dinner table. When Stieg was 14 I found myself losing an argument in a discussion with him. He just had better arguments than his mother or I. The young back then were learning to argue about the Vietnam War. But he wasn't writing fiction during those days – at least he didn't discuss such things with his mother and me. It would be years later before we had such conversations.'

And while, later, he did discuss the *Millennium* novels with Stieg, he didn't know if Stieg had such conversations with anyone else. 'He told me about them, and sent me the manuscript. For the first book, he asked for my opinion and I told him I felt that there was too much violence and sex in the books. But he replied that sex was what sold books! Some time after that he sent me the second manuscript.

'His talent was very evident, but, hey, I saw his talent when he was a boy – that is why we bought him the typewriter. For the next two years he continued writing the books in the *Millennium Trilogy*, but he was also working to expose the dangers of the Nazis in our midst. He used to come to London often, and even speak to Scotland Yard, as well as speaking on the subject in Germany and Sweden – even discussing these matters with ministers and politicians.'

Possible origins of the books' characters Mikael Blomkvist and Lisbeth Salander have been much discussed in Sweden, and Erland Larsson suggested that one inspiration for Salander may have been Stieg's niece, Therese, who had been very close to the author and they often visited each other. Therese suffered from anorexia nervosa, and sported a tattoo – so the parallels with Salander are not difficult to discern. Whenever Therese travelled to Stockholm she would visit Stieg and the two used to socialise with via e-mail. This electronic correspondence might have made instructive reading for Salander aficionados, but a recent crash of Therese's computer regrettably erased all their e-mails.

Like Salander, Therese 'certainly knew her way around computers,' said Erland. 'She is a little dyslexic, but she manages well in her job and can read, and works hard. But she fights for her existence, if you understand what I mean. Once, in a Swedish newspaper, they ran a story saying "Therese is actually Salander", but in reality Salander is a mixture of different people.'

Erland has been, to put it mildly, bemused by the unprecedented international success of the books. He observed, 'I thought it was wonderful when editors wanted to publish Stieg's novels. Then I thought it was wonderful seeing the books selling so well. And then I thought it was wonderful that the film people wanted to make them into movies. So now nothing relating to Stieg's books surprises me...'

Of course, the Holy Grail for Stieg Larsson admirers is the fabled fourth book: the next stage in the lives of Mikael Blomkvist and Lisbeth Salander that would make the *Millennium Trilogy* into a quartet. Does it exist? It's a topic of conversation that often comes up when admirers of the author and his work get together, and it's hardly surprising that people would dearly like to believe that the fourth book exists – possibly in a form that needs heavy editing, perhaps, but nevertheless a book which was largely finished before the author's untimely death. So what is the truth of the matter? Is there a fourth book which some day we will be allowed to see? The answer is at the heart of an acrimonious falling-out between the family and Larsson's partner, Eva Gabrielsson, and new claims and counter-claims on the issue surface on an almost weekly basis.

'When Stieg died,' said Erland, 'they called me from Stockholm and I went to the hospital, heartbroken. Then we went to Stieg's apartment [which he shared with Eva] and found about 250 pages of the manuscript for the fourth book.' Asked if there were plans to publish it, Erland replied, 'No. We have the rights, but there are problems, as Eva has the manuscript and she does not wish to share it. In fact, there are family problems.' The truth about the fourth book was to be revealed later.

Joakim, Stieg's brother, is a complex and intriguing figure; a man who, like his father, has been obliged to learn to live with the immense celebrity of his late sibling, and has risen (with some difficulty, as he admits) to the challenge. As I learned from conversations with him, Joakim is a confirmed Anglophile, keen to demonstrate to British listeners such as myself his very good English – more idiomatic than his father's, but this is a generational skill. Among a variety of English enthusiasms, Joakim has a particular predilection for the world-conquering popular music produced in the UK in the 1960s, notably Ray Davies, composer and front man of the Kinks. Joakim is a particular admirer of Davies's song-writing skills, and continues to follow his work to this day, catching concerts in London. Like many Swedes of his generation, his adolescent years were lived to the soundtrack of British rock music – the aforementioned Kinks, the Beatles, the Rolling Stones. The anti-establishment and rebellious stance of these musicians was a key influence on him in terms of his attitude to society, and remains so to this day. When I tried to draw the conversation around to his late brother, Joakim politely addressed the issues he has had to talk about a million times, but he was more interested in talking to me about growing up in the Beatles' Britain of the 1960s. Joakim told me, with some feeling, that he envied me this: 'Your country in the 1960s was where things were happening.'

Like his father, Erland, he is becoming accustomed to dealing with the sometimes smothering (and often deeply negative) attention paid to them because of their relationship with Stieg, but Joakim – as becomes clear to anyone who spends a little time with him – is very much his own man, and there is a quiet determination not to be subsumed by the celebrity of his dead brother. This impulse manifests itself in a quietly sardonic, distancing sense of humour about the whole phenomenon, but Joakim is well aware that this attitude has to be held in check to some degree – and that most of the people who speak to him will expect a certain reverential tone, which he is prepared to adopt, up to a point. But like Stieg, he is rightly concerned with being true to himself and remains an interesting and intriguing personality in his own right, leaving aside the relationship with his late brother.

Stieg Larsson was 18 when he met Eva Gabrielsson at – unsurprisingly – a rally against the Vietnam War, and the couple soon decided to move in together. Theirs was to be – at times – an almost symbiotic relationship, despite their differing characters. Eva made her mark as an architectural historian, and her more pronounced financial acumen helped when it came to supporting them if Larsson's crusading journalistic work proved insufficiently remunerative.

Eva Gabrielsson is a fascinating, complex figure in her own right, leaving aside the long association she had with Stieg. The literary editor of the *Independent*, Boyd Tonkin, for whom I have covered much Scandinavian fiction, spoke to her for the newspaper in October 2009 and obtained some intriguing insights into both Eva herself and the man with whom she shared her life. Gabrielsson, who lived with Stieg Larsson for more than 30 years, remembered long discussions with Larsson concerning his nascent career as a novelist – and also recalled a conversation with her sister who had returned to Sweden in the mid-1990s, finding the country very changed. 'She did not recognise the politics, mentality or how society worked,' Eva told Tonkin. Regarding this disillusionment, Eva continued, 'Stieg and I had long talks with her about this,' noting that to them and to many other Swedes, 'a nation that for so long prized its civic ideals of compassion and community had somehow lost its soul.'

'The developments in the 1990s,' Eva went on, 'revealed greed, bonus systems, golden parachutes and corruption beyond imagination... all in all, a total disrespect for the traditional Swedish values of honesty, equality and the common good. This was shocking, especially since nobody turned out to be responsible or held accountable... you could say that the veil of naivety about a dream-castle country fell with a bang, not with a whimper.'

At the time of Tonkin's interview, Niels Arden Oplev's Swedish film of the first book, *The Girl with the Dragon Tattoo,* was drawing large audiences throughout Europe, but the news media were still transfixed by the acrimonious disagreements over Larsson's estate and the passionate campaign being waged in Sweden to obtain for Gabrielsson the rights which many felt she was entitled to.

Tonkin noted that leaving aside the sheer readability of the *Millennium Trilogy*, in the books, Larsson and Lisbeth Salander had channelled 'An underground stream of fury and hurt among readers, in Sweden and far beyond. It seems to have much to do with grief over a shared loss of innocence, and the withering of belief in a fair society. Individually, Salander emerges as a victim of multiple abuse, betrayed by psychiatry and social "care"'. 'Collectively,' according to Tonkin, 'Sweden comes across as a nation undermined from the top by a cabal of thugs and spies whose responsibility for her ordeal gradually unfolds.'

Eva Gabrielsson countered that readers of the novels recognise their own anger and frustration about everyday injustices and corruptions. 'This is also a frustration with the lameness of politicians... the books clearly state that individual people do matter and may not be abused, lied to, misled or deceived for money, power or anyone's prestige.'

On the author's disgust at male violence and at 'the official indifference that allows misogynistic cruelty free rein,' Tonkin noted that, 'Blomkvist has a kind of mission statement: this story is not primarily about spies and secret government agencies; it's about violence against women and the men who enable it. Typically, Larsson interrupts the galloping plot to show how a good woman cop spontaneously takes revenge on an un-prosecuted wife-beater when "something snapped in her"; with Salander active and dangerous (even when confined to a hospital bed with only a customised PDA for company), we get to hear that snap a lot.'

Regarding the gender-based abuse that so exercised Larsson, Gabrielsson told Tonkin that: 'In his mind it was a question which was constantly ignored, everywhere, and a systematic flaw in all our societies... Stieg had a deep mistrust of social workers and psychologists, given their power in times of need and weakness.' She continued that Stieg was, 'Especially furious with a certain small group of expert witnesses in Swedish paedophile cases, who for some reason too often landed on the side of the bad guys, calling the abused girl or boy disturbed and not trustworthy.'

Tonkin ended his discussion with Larsson's partner with a melancholy regret that we will not encounter Lisbeth again. 'So, like some legendary woman warrior, Salander disappears into her twilight of the tattooed, hi-tech gods. The novels as a whole mix this near-mythical dimension with a hothouse domestic atmosphere among tight-knit cliques. Larsson has made the literary moods of saga and soap opera converge – with suspense as the adhesive. And behind the quick-fire action, those great chords of moral and political witness continue to resonate.'

In a 2010 interview for the *Observer* newspaper, Eva

Gabrielsson spoke frankly to Rachel Cooke about her life with Stieg Larsson – and also made clear what she felt the dispute with Stieg's family over his estate had cost her. Remembering their days of relative impoverishment as journalists, Gabrielsson talked about the modest ambitions that she and Larsson had for the first book. They had principally envisioned sales in Scandinavia and Germany, with any possible profits helping them to pay off loans and purchase a summer hideaway in the archipelago. And demonstrating a commitment to the social issues that had been so important to the couple, she talked about plans to donate profits of any future books in the sequence to their chosen causes.

Interestingly, Gabrielsson appears to have had a relatively fatalistic view of the couple's future (perhaps the result of their cautious lifestyles avoiding possibly violent enemies), but her various misgivings involved Gabrielsson herself rather than her partner – although both were in the habit of phoning each other at every possible opportunity to reassure the other about their safe arrival at destinations.

But, of course, the dual hammer blows of fate that were to leave their mark on Gabrielsson were the premature death of her partner and the subsequent brouhaha over the estate. Regarding Larsson's death, Gabrielsson attempted (rather optimistically) to scotch one particular rumour – that Larsson was a workaholic – and noted that if he'd kept the regime of punishing workloads and minimal sleep so widely reported, she would probably have noticed this – although, tellingly, she does not discuss the famous chain-smoking, commonly felt to be a key factor in his early demise. Gabrielsson tells Rachel Cooke that her principal concern in terms of her partner's legacy was the treatment of his work; would translations do justice to his prose? Would any possible future film adaptations compromise the work and smooth out the rough edges? (The latter misgiving, in fact, so far confounded.) These, of course, are issues that Gabrielsson deals with in the book she has written about her relationship with the late author.

The book is in two parts: the first addresses the incendiary issues concerning the bitter battle between Gabrielsson and Larsson's surviving relatives – she is keen, she says, to correct the way in which she has been portrayed, notably as 'an impossible person with psychological problems'. The second part of the book is the one that she has laboured over longest; it is a study of loss – the loss of someone with whom you have spent a good proportion of your life. Gabrielsson wanted to discuss the strategy she has utilised to get through the 'hell' of this kind of experience – by, it seems, embracing the primal nature of such experiences, however lacerating they can be. Movingly, she talks about the agony of getting over Larsson's death, and suggests that the perception of Swedish women as always capable does not tell the whole truth. A nurturing network of friends offered a lifeline – as well as supplying, she wryly notes, a great deal of food and drink. This support, she says, was invaluable, and carried her through a fraught period. Gabrielsson's book is more even-handed than one might expect, making her points and arguing her corner (she is dignified in defending herself against criticism of her behaviour in the dispute over the estate) but although she is not attempting to demonise her late partner's relatives, her anger is palpable.

The description that Eva Gabrielsson gives of her meeting with Erland, Larsson's father, immediately after her partner's death has a novelistic richness – although, of course, we are being given one side of the story (and by an articulate writer at that, rather than the less sophisticated, non-bookish Erland Larsson). Gabrielsson describes how she felt that Erland's behaviour was 'odd', and appeared to her to be inappropriate; he was, she says, apparently formulating the words for the pending obituary and talking about how he had been 'boasting to everyone that his son had a crime novel coming out, that he'd promised a local newspaper an interview with him...'. Gabrielsson's sister had noticed Eva's distressed reaction to this, and took Erland Larsson out for a walk.

On this day, in what may now be seen as a very significant action, Eva Gabrielsson gave her sister Stieg Larsson's backpack, which contained his diary and his laptop – she was keen that they should be taken to the offices of *Expo*, so that some of his colleagues might work on his material. She was concerned, she points out, about the survival of the magazine – and she notes that a degree of chaos followed his death. The repercussions of this day's events – principally because of the contents of the laptop in the backpack – have continued long after the author's death.

Initially, it appears that Gabrielsson had no idea just how contentious the battle over the author's estate would be. She alone attended the legal meeting at which it was affirmed that Stieg had left behind no testament (in order, as is now widely known, to protect his partner from possible attacks), and that Larsson's father and brother would inherit the estate. As events moved towards their current impasse, Gabrielsson was not primarily concerned with financial matters. Erland Larsson had told her, Gabrielsson informed Rachel Cooke, that he, Erland, would not be inheriting anything. In her distress, Gabrielsson was, in fact, trying to find a therapist – in vain, as all available therapists were working with the Swedes who had suffered following the Asian tsunami.

Gabrielsson rehearses the bitter details of the succeeding dispute, and adds that she feels that the current custodians of her partner's work are not doing it justice. She disputes several changes that have been made to the books, and also disagrees with the perception that Larsson had a workaholic nature – he was, apparently, 'The most laid-back person, lying on his back, reading or thinking, watching spaghetti westerns.'

Intriguingly, Gabrielsson records another painful ambiguity relating to the success of her late partner's novels, leaving aside the financial battles. She is pleased that readers are absorbing Larsson's passionate response to corruption, barbarism and misogyny (not to mention the craven nature of most of the media – a key theme of the books), and that Larsson's readers – by their enthusiastic devotion to his work – are 'voting for Stieg's ideal'. However, in a telling phrase she says sees the books as 'whoring him out' and regards their success in the marketplace as rather like having your children sold (a recurrent theme of Gabrielsson's discussions of the books is her symbiotic involvement in their creation).

She is, finally, grateful for the time she had with Larsson, but is convinced that, if they had married, and had their address revealed, he would have been murdered. She discusses the tearfulness that overtakes her at times, but is comforted by the fact that an idea will occur to her that she then simply has 'to get on with'. Her view of the dispute with the Larsson family is fatalistic, and she is aware that her options are running out. But she has confidence in the fact that – as she puts it – 'the truth will win out in the end'. And the real revelation of the interview is that what exists of the fabled fourth book on the closely guarded laptop is 200 pages long.

CHAPTER 3
DEATH AND DISPUTES

Larsson knew the great crime novels of the American hard-boiled masters Raymond Chandler and Dashiell Hammett, and, consciously or otherwise, shared the American writers' careless attitude to their own health. And when, after submitting his manuscripts to his editor Eva Gedin at the Swedish publisher Norstedts, he undertook a punishing walk up seven flights of stairs because of a broken lift, his lengthy abuse of his body's own resources finally took its toll with the heart attack that was to claim his life.

Larsson's British publisher, Christopher MacLehose, has long been the doyen of foreign crime fiction in translation. He has had another Swedish talent, Henning Mankell, under his belt, and was the discoverer of a key Scandinavian crime breakthrough, Peter Høeg's *Miss Smilla's Feeling for Snow*. In his understated manner, MacLehose is proud of Larsson's success. A distinguished and quietly-spoken publisher of the old school, he spoke to me about Larsson with regret for the premature loss of such a remarkable author, and is frank about the fact that Larsson appeared to be oblivious to all warnings about his health. 'He smoked over 60 cigarettes a day and was a classic workaholic,' says MacLehose. 'To say that he didn't give his body a chance almost understates the case. And like many driven men, he tended not to listen to the counsel of those around him – he was warned again and again that he should look after himself, but all such advice fell on deaf ears.'

The suggestion that Stieg Larsson did not talk to his brother and father for many years is disputed, but it is certainly true that he never married his partner Eva Gabrielsson – and by the diktats of the Swedish legal system, she, accordingly, did not inherit his estate or literary legacy (which is principally, of course, the three novels of the *Millennium Trilogy*). The legatees were, in fact, his father Erland and his brother Joakim. The reason why Stieg and Eva did not marry is now (as previously discussed) common knowledge: he considered that his well-known battles with extremist groups put him in some considerable danger, and he felt that he would to some extent shield Eva from some of this danger by avoiding marriage. She has said that Stieg was under the impression that the Swedish special cohabitation act for unmarried couples would cover rights of inheritance – which, in fact, it does not. Had he realised the uproar that would ensue – a bitter dispute in which his legacy, both artistic and financial, would be fought over – it is entirely possible that he might have rethought this strategy to obviate the pain and acrimony that would follow his death; given his character, it is hardly likely that '*après moi, le deluge*' would have been his philosophy. The situation that has arisen regarding his royalties, with claims and counterclaims, is further complicated by Swedish laws regarding intestate deaths, in which the state takes 50% of the deceased's earnings before relatives can make a claim.

There was considerable press coverage, both in Sweden and the UK, in November 2009 when Stieg's father and brother spoke to Swedish newspapers. They had decided that they would be offering Eva a compensatory sum which would have no corollary conditions for her. Controversially, Joakim told one newspaper that she would be obliged to ring them and say 'Yes, please', and Stieg Larsson readers (many of whom have closely followed this un-illuminating saga) might not have been surprised that – after such an approach – Eva's response was not immediately forthcoming. She gave no public pronouncement on the family's suggestion, but made it clear that she was unhappy with the concept of discussing such matters via the press.

Cynics pointed to the offer as being part of an attempt to reclaim one of the most precious jewels in the crown in the Stieg Larsson legacy – the laptop which remained in the possession of Eva Gabrielsson – and which apparently contains what Larsson had written of the fourth, unfinished, novel (which, as mentioned earlier, Gabrielsson has said consists of a few hundred pages). The laptop was, at this point, safely squirreled away in a safe by Eva – and if all this sounds rather like the plot strand in one of the Larsson novels, that is surely only appropriate.

There had, in fact, already been a variety of attempts to support Eva in the campaign to gain access to the monies which she felt to be her due, having been an integral part of Larsson's creative process when he was writing the three novels of the *Millennium Trilogy*, and various campaigns were mounted by such people as the Norwegian publisher

Jan Moberg. So incendiary is the situation involving the dispute that there have even been movements to bring about change in Sweden's inheritance laws.

At the time of this latest twist in the dispute, the estate had been valued at more than £20 million, and more was accruing all the time – particularly as a successful series of movies have been completed in Sweden, with the possibility of American remakes now confirmed – and the further fact that the paperback of the third book in the trilogy had not (at the time that the offer was made) appeared in the UK. And the inevitability of that paperback matching the phenomenal sale of its predecessors could hardly be gainsaid.

Ironically, the only will that Stieg Larsson had made was one written under the spell of a youthful enthusiasm: he had left all that he might have to the Communist party (despite his father's claim 'Stieg was never a communist'). This will, however, was never officially witnessed, ensuring that the estate became the joint property of his family and the Swedish state. Despite Eva's claim that, as the late author's common-law wife she was the natural legatee, under existing Swedish laws her position has no legal justification. She has pointed out that Stieg's father and brother had negotiated with her for the laptop containing what was written of the fourth novel, but the lawyer had advised her that this was not a proposition that she should entertain. The latest offer of 20 million kronor (nearly £2 million) from Larsson's father and brother was an attempt at a reconciliation, with Erland and Joakim telling the press that this was evidence of their desire to move on the stalled negotiations.

Eva, at the time of these developments, was writing her own memoir describing her times with Stieg, and the fact that Eva had said Stieg had effectively cut himself off from his family, suggested that the book would pull no punches. And whatever text had been written of Eva's memoir, it was very obviously in a state of flux – changing, perhaps, as these bitter divisions continued.

The Stieg saga has some time to run, however. In January 2010 there were two heated debates in Sweden, one focusing on whether or not Stieg Larsson had actually written his three *Millennium* novels. The controversy began when a former colleague from the Swedish news agency TT (Tidningarnas Telegrambyrå) seemed to claim that Larsson was an exemplary researcher but a maladroit writer who could never have produced a readable novel, suggesting that Stieg's partner Eva Gabrielsson was the actual writer. This claim was immediately rejected by others who knew him. The accusation – like a more acerbic version of the questions of authorship concerning the novels of the late Dick Francis, whose wife Mary was widely believed to be an essential creative part of the franchise – was detonated in the newspaper *Dagens Nyheter* by the reporter Anders Hellberg, who claimed that Larsson 'could not write'. Hellberg, however, does not exactly offer up a concrete alternative.

Anders Hellberg had worked with Larsson at TT in the late Seventies and early Eighties. Reporting on these events was Sofia Curman of the Swedish news daily *dn.se* (with Oliver Grassmann). Hellberg's incendiary comments included the following: 'The language was weak, the word order was often incorrect, sentence constructions were simple and the syntax was sometimes completely mad' – in other words, Larsson was not the kind of writer who could have produced the *Millennium Trilogy*.

Hellberg indirectly supported the view that the novels may

have been partly the product of Larsson's long-term partner Eva Gabrielsson, noting that she was 'a very good writer', but Gabrielsson herself was quick to scotch the idea in a statement given to the Swedish daily *Expressen*.

Similarly, and unsurprisingly, Larsson's Swedish publisher, Eva Gedin of Norstedts, also gave short shrift to the assertion. (She was one of the first people I spoke to in my Larsson odyssey, interviewing her for *The Times*.) 'To claim that Stieg did not write the *Millennium Trilogy* is just nonsense.' Gedin said. 'I can only comment on Stieg as a crime novelist. When he came to our publishing house he was a very mature writer and his scripts were thoroughly worked through.'

In a rare concordance between the warring factions in the estate squabble, Larsson's brother Joakim also criticised the *Dagens Nyheter* piece, saying that he was 'angry' but 'not surprised', adding: 'It's just another nonsense article about Stieg that I won't waste my energy on. Nowadays, my brother is a national icon and there are many claiming to have known him who try to live off his reputation.'

Hellberg has been subsequently deluged with negative responses from passionate Larsson admirers – and Sweden has more than its share of those. The writer Kurdo Baksi, whose book *Stieg Larsson, My Friend* gives his account of a working relationship with the author at *Tidningarnas Telegrambyrå*, was quoted in the contentious piece, but had some caveats about the views attributed to him. However, his aspect of the dispute, as repeated in *The Local*, a Swedish news source, has had a life of its own. Eva Gabrielsson criticised Baksi's book, which was interpreted as describing Larsson as a 'mediocre journalist who lacked objectivity'. Kurdo Baksi, it was said, makes the claim that Larsson 'wrote biased articles and even invented material'.

Gabrielsson was unsparing in her response when speaking to the Swedish television channel SVT: 'Kurdo is trying to perform a character assassination of Stieg as a journalist. This is pure slander.' She noted that Larsson only worked with Baksi for a brief time on a magazine and some political pieces in the 1990s – and that Baksi was not that well acquainted with the late writer.

Kurdo Baksi's remarks to SVT that Larsson was a 'mediocre' journalist who lacked objectivity in his work at the news agency also produced a stinging response from Larsson's former boss at TT, Kenneth Ahlborn, who described the assertions as false, and said that they were essentially 'an attempt to grab the media spotlight'. He continued: 'I was Stieg's boss. We worked in the same room every day. If anyone should speak about his relationship to TT it should be me. The assertion that he could make up biased, objectionable articles is so bizarre. We don't work like that at TT and Stieg was not like that.'

Against this mounting wave of criticism, Baksi, in his own defence, commented on Hellberg's piece.

'I have not been quoted correctly,' he said. 'First of all, I never said I was a better writer than Stieg. Maybe I was better than him at handling quick, short journalistic texts, but I am absolutely not a better writer. Anders Hellberg has used our conversation to create a perspective that I just can't accept.'

However, this defence drew a swift and uncompromising reply from Hellberg, who maintained that there had been no misinterpretation: 'Sadly,' he said, 'I was unable to record the conversation, but I have written down exactly what Kurdo Baksi said. If he doesn't want to stand by it now, that's his business.'

Meanwhile, Baksi commented on Larsson's alleged

journalistic shortcomings: 'I still say Stieg Larsson wasn't a brilliant journalist, but he was a brilliant author. He showed it both in his non-fiction books and in his novels.' When I talked to the writer Dan Lucas (who worked with Larsson in Sweden), he also spoke well of Larsson's journalistic accomplishments.

Sofia Curman of *dn.se* also quoted writer/journalist Anna-Lena Lodenius, author in tandem with Larsson of *Extremhögern* ('The Extreme Right'). Lodenius points out that she never acted as an editor on any of Larsson's journalistic pieces. She noted: 'It's possible that the dry style of TT wasn't his thing. But of course he could write.' Lodenius remarked that she feared it would be painful for her to read the *Millennium* books. 'When I did read the *Millennium Trilogy*,' she said, 'I clearly heard his voice. I recognised his language and I found some of his favourite words in the books, the same words that I always crossed out when we wrote together. Like everyone else he had certain expressions that were characteristic of his writing. There is no doubt that it's the same Stieg that I used to work with.'

Kurdo Baksi had a final salvo about the dual authorship dispute that evokes the Shakespeare/Francis Bacon theory: 'Shakespeare's works were written nearly 400 years ago, and the discussion as to who the real author was is still there. Many say [sic] it was his wife. But in Stieg's case, he was the actual writer. His very special style, which is apparent in everything he ever wrote, is clearly there in all of the *Millennium* books. My only point regarding his style was that it was better suited for novels than for news articles.'

In the *Expressen* pieces, Eva Gabrielsson noted that her interaction with her partner in the writing of the *Millennium* sequence was a matter of 'proofreading and discussions'.

CHAPTER 4

PUBLISHING LARSSON

'He was a difficult man, but brilliant and multifaceted,' according to his Swedish publisher, Eva Gedin of Norstedts. 'Many Swedes were aware of his bravery in tackling extremist organisations,' she told me. 'He could be infuriating – and he certainly wasn't afraid of making enemies. But most of his enemies were well chosen; as for his friends and associates, frustration with him might result from the fact that he was clearly asking his body to do more than it could cope with.'

Gedin speaks with a mixture of admiration and regret regarding the late author. 'He came to my attention via the recommendation of another journalist, who rang me up and said, "You may know about Stieg as an antifascist journalist – but did you know he is also an amazing novelist? You have to read this book!" And so we discovered *The Girl with the Dragon Tattoo*.

'When I read it, I told him – on the spot – that we wanted to sign him to a three-book contract. His response was a quiet one; generally speaking, he was a surprisingly quiet, shy person – except in one area. He was boastful about himself only in respect of his amazing work ethic. You were always told – in great detail – how he'd copy-edited his magazine, fired off myriad letters, written several chapters, and generally crammed a week of activity into 24 hours. One could always forgive him all this, as he wasn't really self-aggrandising.'

In a radio interview for PRI's *The World*, Eva Gedin gave some interesting responses concerning the life and death of Stieg Larsson. She talked about first encountering the unpublished manuscripts: 'We were very excited because we needed a new crime writer, and we could see that we had something really good in our hands.' Remarking on the steadily growing, viral word of mouth on the books, she noted that, 'You could sort of hear people talking about Stieg's book almost everywhere we went – when we went to buy groceries, you could hear people saying "Hey, have you read this new writer Stieg Larsson?"' Acknowledging that the success of the books was in great part due to the groundbreaking character of Lisbeth Salander, Gedin anatomised the success of this innovative creation: 'She's a superhero, something you haven't seen in crime fiction. She's such an extraordinary person. Smart... and revengeful.'

Larsson had in fact told Eva Gedin that he had conceived Salander (as mentioned earlier) as a grown-up version of the classic Swedish children's heroine Pippi Longstocking.

So was Larsson – to those who knew him – a heroic figure? 'He was the best kind of hero,' according to Gedin. 'He simply got on with the job, and never seemed to be after any kind of personal glory. Perhaps some might call taking on some sinister organisations foolhardy but I – and many others

– had only admiration for him. Of course, it was obvious that something had to give in terms of his health. Which is not to say that he was self-destructive. Outwardly, even before the success of *Dragon Tattoo*, he was a man of influence and importance; he charmed the ex-minister of immigration, Mona Sahlin – a woman many considered to be a possible future prime minister of Sweden. And, of course, he lectured on the tactics of far-Right groups in France, Germany – and at Scotland Yard.'

His Swedish and English publishers are agreed that one myth should be squashed: the notion that Larsson barely lived to see the success of his books, albeit not the sales success. 'He knew he was a success as a writer,' says Gedin. 'It was pleasing to those around him to see him quietly savouring the fact that he had made such a success of the second career.'

But, I asked Gedin, what about the other oft-repeated part of the legend concerning Larsson: that his death was somehow suspicious? That the failure of his health was due to some sinister chemical assistance, like the poisoning of the former Russian intelligence officer, Alexander Litvinenko, in London? On this, Eva Gedin is emphatic. 'Absolutely not! It might help Stieg's legend if it were true that he was the victim of some kind of poisoning, but frankly there was this almost casually self-destructive element: the massive self-imposed workload, the heavy smoking and so forth. But the fact that his death was not a homicide doesn't make him any less of a hero. That is exactly what he was.'

Before becoming Editorial Director at Chatto & Windus, Larsson's UK publisher Christopher MacLehose – who publishes the *Millennium* books through his own imprint within the Quercus publishing company – was Literary Editor of the *Scotsman*. He also held down the position of Editor-in-Chief at the publisher William Collins, but his most significant role, and the one in which he produced some of the great literary glories of an illustrious career, was as publisher at Harvill Press. (For the last seven years of his time with the company, the imprint became part of the powerful conglomerate Random House.) Under MacLehose's authoritative stewardship, Harvill became synonymous with the very best writing from other shores than those of the UK, customarily translated with the greatest skill and sensitivity. Important modern writers published by MacLehose included George Perec, W G Sebald and José Saramago, but particularly innovative were his crime fiction acquisitions, notably Henning Mankell, Fred Vargas and Arnaldur Indridason. These authors represented some of the most intelligent and innovative writing in the field and beautifully complemented such literary giants in the Harvill list as Raymond Carver, Richard Ford and Peter Matthieson.

While maintaining a consistent standard of literary excellence, MacLehose never forgot that the Harvill imprint was founded in the 1940s by Manya Harari and Marjorie Villiers with a view to inaugurating a healthy cultural exchange between the countries of Europe after the Second World War.

The publishing passion which MacLehose demonstrated will not surprise those who have met him: the single-mindedness with which he fights for the authors he believes in has fewer precedents in the publishing world than one might wish, on either side of the Atlantic, and has inspired both gratitude and loyalty from the authors for whom MacLehose has gone in to bat. Concerning Harvill's continuing success, he said: 'We left HarperCollins with a substantial part of our backlist intact. So the fuel was there to keep the motor running, as it were. There was also a broad acceptance among young booksellers – and among the public that bought books – that Harvill stood for something: first-class works in whatever language in the world translated into English.' Speaking to him over the years (which involves looking upwards – he is dauntingly tall), MacLehose has always given me the impression that he provides the best possible advocacy for the authors who have been lucky enough to be published by him.

In an interview for the internet crime fiction website *The Rap Sheet*, the journalist Ali Karim asked MacLehose how he had discovered Larsson's work. 'The English translation of the *Millennium Trilogy* came from Norstedts, the Swedish publisher,' MacLehose explained, 'via a very experienced American translator who was asked [by Norstedts] to translate all three books for a film company, which he did in the remarkable time of 11 months.

'It needed a certain amount of editorial work, inevitably. And as the translator Steven Murray [working under the pseudonym of Reg Keeland] was now involved in another project, he didn't have time to do this. It should be said that the trilogy came to me many months after the translator had finished it. Why? Because it needed a great deal of editorial work, but also because there was this feeling "what can you do commercially with a writer who has died?" This I felt was ludicrous – as was: "Come on, what can we do with this? We haven't got an author!" It is a tragedy in one sense that Stieg Larsson did not see his work published in English, nor see *The Girl with the Dragon Tattoo* reach number four in the *New York Times* bestseller lists. This is an astonishing achievement for a translated novel. Incidentally, Knopf, who published it in the US, did so brilliantly. I'm frankly grateful it came to us in the form that it did, needing a certain degree of editorial work; otherwise, it would have been bought by somebody else.'

Asked about the Swedish film adaptations, MacLehose drew for comparison on the success of the film adaptations of the work of Ian Fleming. 'Salander will leave James Bond in her wake. Salander is just so interesting, and she is much more intellectually stimulating than James Bond ever was. She is a woman of so many facets and aspects: the physical, emotional, the history of mental illness, where she stands in Swedish society. And then there are her computer skills, her professional skills as an analyst. She is, of course, not a complete human being, because of her emotional wreckage, but she is utterly fascinating.'

The *Millennium Trilogy* has been a massive success in the UK for the British independent publisher Quercus, founded by the legendary UK publisher Anthony Cheetham and now run by the energetic and savvy Mark Smith. Christopher MacLehose runs his own imprint within the company, and continues to bring the same innovative publishing skills to bear as he did in his days running the Harvill Press. But how does he compare his current publishing incarnation with the glories of his past career?

'Nothing will quite compare with my years at Harvill Press, as that was an imprint that was devoted to the translation of pure literature. But we did publish Peter Høeg, Henning Mankell, Fred Vargas and many others who are also considered as European crime writers. However, there is no one quite like the Quercus team. They are young, work flat out all day and all night. I'll tell you what it's like: when I left Chatto & Windus and went to Collins, who were then a tremendously vigorous young publishing house, I described it like free-falling downwards, without a parachute. Working with Quercus is like getting out of the aeroplane and suddenly you are moving very fast, very fast indeed, and there is no parachute.'

MacLehose has talked about other much-acclaimed crime novels he has published, such as *Death in Breslau* by Marek Krajewski, and while books such as this will no doubt add lustre to his legacy, there is absolutely no question that the particular jewel in the MacLehose publishing crown will be Stieg Larsson's *Millennium Trilogy*.

In a *New Statesman* interview, MacLehose made an observation that has remained apposite: 'The process by which very good books are well translated and published is so arduous that it will wear down those who do it. I don't think this is sufficiently understood. But fortunately there are young, idealistic, knowledgeable people who continue to throw their lives into it.'

MacLehose himself may no longer be young, but shows not the slightest dimming of the energy and commitment that he has demonstrated with regard to fiction in translation for so many years. The relatively recent phenomenon of Stieg Larsson and the *Millennium Trilogy* may be consuming his energies at present, but it is actually only a staging post in a long and fruitful career.

Stieg Larsson's publisher in the US, Sonny Mehta – a name spoken of with reverence in the world of books – is a publisher for whom the sobriquet 'legendary' might have been coined. He is in charge of the Random House US division Knopf

Doubleday, an imprint which publishes both highly respectable serious writing and cash-cow blockbusters. It is his skill for publishing highly commercial and ambitious literary fiction that has made Mehta one of the most celebrated publishers in the world.

Sonny Mehta (born Ajai Singh Mehta) is the son of an Indian diplomat who was brought up in India and Switzerland before moving to England to study at Cambridge. His first impulse was to be a writer, but when (as publisher) he created something of a literary sensation, at the London publisher Paladin, with Germaine Greer's fiery feminist polemic *The Female Eunuch*, it appeared that he had found his métier. (He had, in fact, studied with Germaine Greer at Cambridge). By the early 1970s Mehta was in charge of the important UK paperback publisher Pan Books, a job he held for over 15 years, and his reputation as one of the most perspicacious of bookmen grew apace. When Random House US chairman Si Newhouse contacted him about the possibility of moving to New York to take over Knopf (senior editor Robert Gottlieb had taken over William Shawn's job as editor of the *New Yorker*, creating a gap), Mehta said yes, and made the momentous move to the US.

By all accounts his early days in the States for Mehta were decidedly tricky, as he struggled to come to terms with a very different publishing scene and (in the evenings) made the most of the city's distractions (even, according to some sources, risking dismissal). But soon his unparalleled skills as a publisher ensured that he made his mark, and the already prestigious reputation of Knopf has been further burnished under his stewardship. He also transformed the company's imprint Vintage (which he took charge of in 1989) into a particularly esteemed trade paperback institution.

While celebrated for such much-lauded literary writers as Gabriel Garcia Marquez, Toni Morrison, Kazuo Ishiguro and V S Naipaul, Mehta's ventures into the world of high-quality crime and thriller writing have been particularly successful. While, for instance, Bret Easton Ellis's *American Psycho* (which frightened off certain UK publishers) was published as a literary novel, its mixture of extreme violence and a canny, modish analysis of the zeitgeist looked forward to Mehta's major success with Stieg Larsson, who moved in something like similar territory. And Mehta – who also coaxed work out of the famously recalcitrant British author Douglas Adams, locking him into a hotel room until a book was complete – is now particularly noteworthy for facilitating the US association with the phenomenal success of the *Millennium Trilogy*. Interestingly, the publisher's own heavy-duty lifestyle (which has led to triple heart bypass surgery) may have given him a particular sympathy for the similarly heavy-smoking Stieg Larsson. Sonny Mehta has, however, outlived his Swedish star author.

Mehta has remarked that the extraordinary success of the books in the Scandinavian countries was unprecedented, and he points out that the three top spots on the bestseller lists were at one time taken up by all three books of the trilogy. 'And this has happened,' he says, 'in France, Germany and Italy – with America being one of the last in a long queue of people to catch up with the phenomenon.'

This delay was not necessarily a bad thing, according to Mehta, as it generated a considerable build-up of anticipation for the appearance of the books in America. 'Readers were aware that something extraordinary was happening abroad,' he says. Mehta regards any comparisons with Larsson's Scandinavian contemporaries (such as

Henning Mankell) as specious. 'Larsson,' he says, 'is totally different from other Swedish crime writers. He paints on a bigger canvas... I find that the social commentary and the social analysis reminds me of John Grisham. Larsson also shares some of the social preoccupations of Sara Paretsky, Michael Connelly and George Pelecanos. But an interesting thing about Larsson... is the fact that he was also a book reviewer; his passion was crime writing, and his trilogy is peppered with references to his peers in the crime writing community. He read crime fiction voraciously. There are references to Agatha Christie and Dorothy Sayers, but he also mentions scenes by contemporary authors, both Americans and Brits. He's like a magpie that way, and that to me is part of the pleasure of reading him. And I think other readers will share this pleasure at the references.'

When talking to me about the translation of *The Girl with the Dragon Tattoo*, Mexico-based Steven Murray (aka Reg Keeland) said that he found it the most fun and engrossing translation task he had ever faced. 'I could tell as I worked on the books that they would be hits,' he said, 'but no one could imagine how big... What strikes me most about Stieg Larsson is the way he kept his prose moving, even when in the midst of arcane digressions on any topic under the Swedish sun. Part of it is creating characters that seem like real people, with all their talents, contradictions and faults.'

Steven Murray dates his days as a translator of Scandinavian crime fiction to when he ran a small press called Fjord Press, which started in the Bay Area then moved to Seattle. 'We published a lot of Danish classics, which in those days sold better than contemporary titles,' he says. 'My interest in Scandinavian fiction began when I studied at

Stanford, and then went to a campus in Germany near Stuttgart. I met a group of people from Scandinavia, and moved around with them – I was impressed with the fact that they could speak whatever language was appropriate for wherever they were. I remember thinking "That's pretty good!" I knew American students were speaking German, but I decided to raise my game.'

I asked Murray how he felt about the fact that signed editions of Stieg Larsson books now have an extra cachet in the collectors' market if they are signed by Murray as translator; his reply to this was modest: 'Oh, I think that's just because the author is dead, and he's not around to sign it. I'm the only one around to sign it – but Christopher MacLehose, his UK publisher, has a connection too – he could sign them!'

But people are more conscious of translators these days, surely? Most literary editors when reviewing foreign fiction rendered into English now expect the reviewer to comment on the translation. 'Actually, we don't always get a mention – quite often, even these days, we are ignored. But translators like me have been working on that very issue for at least 25 years, and perhaps our status has risen somewhat. We do usually get a royalty, even though it's minuscule.

'William Weaver's translation of Umberto Eco's *The Name of the Rose* achieved some recognition in its day as an exemplary translation, and in the 1960s attention was definitely paid to the art of the translator, but perhaps only among those interested in world literature. It may be different in the UK, but frankly most Americans are not sympathetic to translated fiction – in fact, they are a little afraid of it. This might also be based on the fact that (it has to be admitted) there have been bad translations in the past.

But the standard really has risen, without doubt. For instance, most people doing translations of crime fiction these days are top-notch.'

Murray told me that he first encountered Stieg Larsson and the *Millennium Trilogy* when the publisher Norstedts contacted him. 'I was told this would be a rush job – an important one – and that there would be three books. Little did I know how long those three books would be – and how much of a challenge it would be to do really good work on them in a really short time. They said to me, "We have this excellent writer, who unfortunately has passed away, and we need the books doing very quickly." This was, I think, in 2005, shortly after Larsson had died. The translation was also needed for purposes of possible films with the company Yellow Bird, which is why they said to me, "How quickly can you do this?" I would normally quote six months for a volume (as I have to leave room for other things). But I buckled down and managed to do each volume in three months, which really was quite a struggle, take it from me. I didn't exactly give up sleep, but I certainly did give up vacations. It was a very intense working period. But I'm a night owl anyway so I'm happy to go on working in the wee small hours when most people are sound asleep.'

Of course, Steven Murray's current celebrity has really been achieved since his secret identity was discovered; most readers understandably thought that somebody called 'Reg Keeland' – the name that appears in the books – had translated Stieg Larsson's novels, but now the secret is out as to who that pseudonymous translator is.

'Yes, now that people know who I am, I find myself being asked to do far more events and talks – and even interviews such as this one. But I didn't entirely make a secret of my dual writing names. I did, in fact, leave clues on my blogs. In the end, I was outed by the London *Times* – I guess the copies they had received for review had my real name on.'

I asked Murray if, when he was first translating the books, he had any notion that he was working on what was to become a publishing phenomenon. 'Oh yes, that was perfectly clear to me, which was why I insisted that if the books were sold to an English language publisher, I would have to have a separate contract and royalties. Although I have to admit that I really had no idea quite how big the books would be in terms of sales. It seems that barely a week passes without a sales record being broken somewhere. And there are the films – the Swedish ones that have already been made, with Hollywood, inevitably, calling.

'Talking about films of the books, I remember discussing with my wife in the early days the possibility of movie adaptations (even before the Swedish films were made); we would indulge in fantasy casting for the American versions – who would be cast as Lisbeth Salander, for instance. I have to say that I was very happy with the casting of Lisbeth in the Swedish version – the actress Noomi Rapace is really spot-on.

'I was less happy, though, with the actor playing Blomkvist – he was a little too old and worn-out looking. And it was certainly hard to see why he was such a babe magnet, which Blomkvist certainly is in the books!'

Murray is also known for his translations of other respected authors. 'I've been lucky enough to meet several of the authors that I've translated in the past – such as another important Swede, Henning Mankell, for whom I translated *Sidetracked*, among other books. I met him twice at the Göteborg Book Fair – and although one isn't necessarily looking for praise, it's always nice to hear that an author is happy with what you've done. That, of course, is a satisfaction I will never get from Stieg Larsson, and I have to confess that it's a source of regret for me.

'Translation, of course, has some very specific problems; the translator has to render in another language things which simply cannot be rendered – idioms, for example. You cannot simply translate an idiom. A certain amount of subtle rewriting is sometimes necessary, but you can't really do that with the exposition – it's possible, to some extent, with the dialogue.

'I suppose I do a lot of work which might be called mid-Atlantic translation, but I often put in British spellings – and then the publisher takes it from there, changing as they see fit. Interestingly, though, spoken British English is, in some ways, getting close to American. Reading Ian Rankin, these days, I'm surprised by how much sounds American. The phraseology, for instance.'

Murray is still in touch with Eva Gabrielsson, and had dinner with her in Stockholm while she was working on her own memoir of her time with Stieg Larsson. He points out that she does not speak much about the dispute over the estate, and now prefers to leave matters to the lawyers. Her principal concern, as Murray sees it, is for the literary legacy of her late partner's work – that it is treated with respect, and that the right decisions are made concerning adaptations into other media.

Steven Murray nominates Camilla Läckberg as another Scandinavian author he is working on these days whose work inspires him. 'Camilla Läckberg is a wonderful writer, and her book *The Stonecutter* is as impressive as the earlier novel of hers that got really good reviews, *The Ice Princess*.

Stieg Larsson may be dead but Scandinavian crime fiction really is in rude health.'

While the publication of more posthumous novels from Stieg Larsson remains unlikely, there are still some intriguing written items making an appearance – such as a fascinating collection of communications between the author and his Swedish publisher Eva Gedin that offer a host of fresh insights. 'The Last Letters of Stieg Larsson' are in fact the e-mails (with interpolations) which were sent between Larsson and his publisher during the months prior to the publication of his first novel in Sweden. The Swedish tabloids published extracts from them when Larsson's third novel came out, and the e-mails are also available online at a website Norstedts has set up – www.stieglarsson.se – under the heading FÖRFATTAREN (The Author). A hard copy edition has been made available (translated into Italian) by Jacopo De Michelis of Marsilio Editori. They are also available in a deluxe edition of the Trilogy published in the UK by MacLehose Press.

The Marsilio Editori booklet begins with a résumé of the author's career (journalist, war correspondent, international expert in far-Right movements, adviser to the Swedish justice ministry, adviser to Scotland Yard) and we are reminded of Larsson's devotion to defending democracy, whether that involved showing solidarity with Vietnam or supporting the prime minister of Grenada, Maurice Bishop. There is also an encomium for *Expo*, pointing out that it is a research foundation with a very simple aim: to defend democracy and freedom of speech against racist, anti-Semitic, extreme Right and totalitarian movements.

Unsurprisingly, given the radical agenda sometimes

exercised, *Expo* is described as being free from links to political parties. There is a description of volunteers which has relevance to Larsson: people involved in the work of the foundation come from very different backgrounds, from young moderates to ex-Communists. Anyone who works at *Expo* has to leave their personal political baggage outside the door.

Before the quotes from the author, Larsson's status as the creator of a variety of pieces on the theme of democracy and far-Right movements is established, including *Extremhögern*, with Anna-Lena Lodenius, and *Sverigedemokraterna: den nationella rörelsen* ('Swedish Democrats: The National Movement') with Mikael Ekman, along with his massive enthusiasm for science fiction. But the most revealing material begins with a direct quotation from Larsson, telling how he started writing in 2001. At first, he says, it was just a pleasurable hobby, writing a text based on the vintage series *Tvillingdetektiverna* ('Twin Detectives'), the sequence of children's books from the 1950s with his former boss Kenneth Ahlbon at TT. It was a fun pursuit for the two colleagues – they calculated that by the time of writing, the fictional heroes would have been 45 and they were about to undertake their last mystery.

Tvillingdetektiverna was a lengthy series of novels for children inaugurated in 1944 which lasted right up to 1974. Nearly 50 books were published, all featuring the youthful Klas and Göran Bergendahl, identical twins. All the titles incorporated the word '*mysteriet*' (mystery), e.g. *Tunnelbane-mysteriet* ('The Tube Mystery') or *Miljon-mysteriet* ('The Million Mystery') or *Tåg-mysteriet* ('The Train Mystery'). The author's name, Sivar Ahlrud, was a pseudonym for two writers, Ivar Ahlstedt and Sid Roland Rommerud.

This extrapolation into the present, according to Larsson (talking to Lasse Winkler in *Svensk Bokhandel* in October 2004) started him thinking about Pippi Longstocking. How would she behave today? What sort of an adult had she become? How would one define her – as a sociopath, a child-woman? Larsson construed that Pippi might have an alternative view of society and transmogrified her into Lisbeth Salander, making her about 25, a girl completely alienated from society. She doesn't know anyone; she has no ability to socialise.

When planning the trilogy, Larsson decided that he needed a counterbalance to the Lisbeth character, and that was to be Mikael 'Kalle' Blomkvist, a 43-year-old journalist who works on his own magazine, *Millennium*. The action was to revolve around the editorial offices of the magazine and around Lisbeth, who doesn't have a very active life. Larsson decided that the narrative should involve a variety of people, of all types. He opted to work with three distinct groups of characters. One group focused on *Millennium*, which has six employees. The secondary characters would not appear just to swell a scene: they would act and influence the plot; Larsson did not want a closed universe. Then there would be a group centred on Milton Security, a firm run by a Croatian. Finally, inevitably, there would be the police, characters who act independently. The author's game plan was that in the third novel of the planned sequence, all the pieces of the puzzle fall into place so the reader could understand what has happened. But he wanted the books to be about 'something else' as well. Usually, in crime novels, the reader is not shown the consequences of what has happened in the preceding novel in a sequence. His plan was that this would not be the case – there would be a synchronicity and intertextuality.

The creation of crime fiction was something of a nocturnal activity for the author; few were party to this secret pleasure in Larsson's life. He stated his aim clearly: more than being tendentious or aspiring to be classic literature, he considered that the primary function of a detective story narrative was to entertain the reader (though he acknowledged that – having transfixed the reader – Larsson might be able to freight in his own concerns about serious issues).

In November 2004, after Larsson's precipitate death and the dispatch of his final manuscript, his colleague Kurdo Baksi, who makes an appearance in *The Girl Who Kicked the Hornets' Nest*, was obliged to undertake on his own something he customarily shared with Larsson – Baksi was to hold a meeting to commemorate Kristalnacht, the night of anti-Semitic violence in Nazi Germany. Larsson describes Baksi as being 'like a little brother' to him, and speculates that he'll find it amusing that Baksi has a part in his novel.

Larsson, with a journalist's thoroughness, was exercised over such issues as how many printed pages corresponded to a million letters, and wondered if there was a formula or a limit for the thickness of a book. He discussed with Eva Gedin the details of the shape of the final book, demonstrating a willingness to readily submit to the editorial process, and – to those who felt the books needed more rigorous editing – that he would have been more than flexible concerning such issues. He told Eva Gedin that he would be delivering a manuscript in which the story would be complete, the dialogue would not be polished or individual details sorted out. Pointing out that he would need more time for this, Larsson remarked (poignantly, in the light of his brief mortality): 'We've got enough time before the book is due to be printed.' But he was happy for Eva Gedin to intervene with her red pencil at this stage, and said he would revise the whole thing after having received her comments.

Larsson's commercial canniness, which might surprise those who see him as primarily an ideological campaigner, extended as far as the promotion of *The Girl with the Dragon Tattoo*: he mentioned an idea he'd been entertaining for a year about creating a website focusing on *Millennium*, and asked some pertinent questions – a marketing idea such as this for an internet-based sequence is, of course, appropriate.

In reply to both of these points, Eva Gedin reassured Larsson that she wouldn't yet make any changes with a red pencil – but talked about meeting up to discuss the more substantial corrections that may have been needed to be made in book one. She praised the construction of the books, but counselled interventions to be made on the level of line editing – and approved the notion of a website.

All of this, of course, is proof of the careful and fastidious editing process that Larsson would have been able to avail himself of had he lived.

CHAPTER 5

WHAT I WANT TO SAY

On 30 April 2004, an e-mail from Larsson to his editor Eva Gedin offered an unusual insight into the journalist's life as a manager at the *Expo* offices. He notes that he has just discovered that it is Walpurgis Day and that his colleagues in the editorial office are complaining and are keen to go home – or to vacate the offices for a few beers. He says he has promised to let them go after 9 o'clock that evening – a reminder of the managerial status of a man we perhaps think of as a lone investigative journo. Arranging holidays, time off, dealing with staff sicknesses – these everyday problems do not sit easily with the romantic image that people may nurture of the solitary reporter, but they are the quotidian reality for those who run magazines – as Stieg Larsson did. In fact, it's one of the elements that the three Swedish films of the *Millennium Trilogy* succeed in transferring very persuasively from page to film; *Millennium* looks like a real, functioning magazine, with all its attendant problems.

Larsson mentions that the editorial secretary has been

obliged to sleep in the offices of *Expo* for the last two weeks – and that his colleagues are even starting to talk about a trade union (amusing, given the left-wing sympathies of everyone on the magazine!). Revealingly, Larsson communicates his own lack of faith in his abilities as a writer, and acknowledges that his articles improve markedly after an editor has got to work on them – an insight with a possible bearing on the posthumous disagreement over his skills in this area. He is used to making revisions and having them made; in other words, he notes, he is not hypersensitive about such matters. In perhaps the most striking revelation in these exchanges, he talks about the 'obsessions' he nourishes that he won't give up on easily, and that will feature in the books. He thinks (he says) that the first chapters of Book One are long-winded and that it takes some time for the story to exert a grip, but his aim was primarily to fashion a strongly realised *dramatis personae* and vivid locales before the narrative gets into gear. Even Larsson admirers might concede these reservations – the first book, by general consent, could have done with some judicious editorial tightening.

Those same Larsson admirers will, of course, be intrigued by his discussion with his editor about what he wanted to say with these books. It's clear that he was keen to shake up the tropes of detective fiction in as many ways as he could. The introduction of Mikael Blomkvist in the narrative, for example, takes place exclusively via the investigation carried out by Lisbeth Salander.

'I tried to create protagonists who are radically different from the usual characters in detective fiction,' Larsson states. 'That's why Mikael Blomkvist doesn't have ulcers or problems with alcoholism or existential anguish. He doesn't listen to opera or dedicate himself to some strange hobby like model aeroplanes or something similar. In general he doesn't have any problems and his main characteristic is that he behaves like a stereotypical "whore", something that he himself recognises. I also consciously inverted the gender roles: in many ways Blomkvist plays the part of the "bimbo" while Lisbeth Salander has ways of behaving and qualities that are characteristically "male".

'A fundamental rule was never to idealise crime and criminals, nor to make the victims stereotypes. In the first book I created the serial killer by merging three real cases. Everything that is described one can therefore find in real police inquiries. The description of the rape of Lisbeth Salander is based on a case that happened in Östermalm three years ago... I wanted to avoid the victims being anonymous people; because of this, I dedicate a lot of time introducing Dag Svensson and Mia Johansson before [their] murder.

'I hate crime novels where the protagonist can behave however he likes or do things that normal people can't do without consequences. If Mikael Blomkvist shoots someone, even if he does it in self-defence, he ends up in court.

'Lisbeth is an exception simply because she is a sociopath with psychotic traits and she doesn't function like normal people. She therefore doesn't have the same perception of what is "right" or "wrong" as normal people, but she also suffers the consequences.'

Larsson goes on to say that he wanted to fashion a realistic cast of characters surrounding his main protagonists, for instance by granting Dragan Armansky a lengthy introduction in *The Girl with the Dragon Tattoo* to establish that he will be a recurring figure. In *The Girl Who*

Played with Fire, the cadre of coppers working around Bublanski and Sonja Modig are foregrounded. And in the final book, Blomkvist's lawyer sister Annika Giannini and his colleague/lover Erika Berger are brought centre stage. It's interesting to note the problems he mentions with Lisbeth's sometime-lover Miriam Wu: 'I don't know exactly what to do with her,' he writes – and it might be argued that she is one of the least successful characterisations in the sequence. Larsson is aware that his solitary heroine can't have strong friendships and simultaneously maintain her marginalisation.

These valuable documents became available in English in 2010 as part of a handsome *Millennium Trilogy* box set (published by MacLehose Press). Gedin talks about Larsson's 'marvellous mix of humility and self-assurance' – and confirms that the first three books he planned to write were always conceived as an organic trilogy. It was also clear, according to Gedin, that Larsson had every intention of becoming a successful crime writer, and that his publisher could expect much more such work from him. Gedin also provides a nicely balanced view of the much-rehearsed dispute between the author's partner Eva Gabrielsson and his father and brother, and makes the telling comment that there is one voice signally missing from the continuing discussion of Larsson's work and legacy: that of Stieg Larsson himself. Gedin reveals her thoughts about publishing the e-mails between herself and the late author, wondering if there might be something in them to interest readers – surely an unwarranted modesty on her part, given the immense and all-consuming interest in the author and his books since his sudden death. She explains that she had not looked at the e-mails even once since Larsson's demise, but that looking at them again reminded her of his voice, his manner, and the enthusiasm they both shared when bringing to fruition the three projects that had so engaged them – and she notes how unusual it was for a three-book deal to be offered to a first-time writer. She also discusses how obdurate Larsson became when she expressed her reservations about his original title for the first book, *Men Who Hate Women*, pointing out how this sounded off-putting, resembling a dour non-fiction title. Larsson promised to think about changing the title, but decided to stick to his guns and claimed that several friends he had spoken to had agreed with him that the original was the perfect title. Larsson, as we now know, got his way in Sweden, but the title was changed elsewhere (and, frankly, few would argue with the fact that the change was a particularly perspicacious decision).

Gedin also notes that Larsson paid great attention to detail when discussing the minutiae of the books – something that will hardly come as a surprise to admirers of his habit of luxuriating in his infinitely detailed and information-packed narratives. But he also makes a point – in no uncertain terms – about how much he wishes to avoid all the paraphernalia involved in promoting a book (signings, television chat shows, etc) – and states that the idea of becoming a commodity to be sold in this fashion really does not appeal to him. Of course, the author's precipitate death spared him this particular ordeal, but, nevertheless, it is clear that Larsson was not a writer who lived in an ivory tower, attempting to ignore the realities of selling a book in a crowded marketplace. He was well aware that specific 'hooks' needed to be found to exploit the commercial potentialities of his books; ironically, of course, he was not to know that one of those hooks would be his own mortality. Gedin ends her discussion of these now-celebrated e-mails with an especially poignant comment: Larsson had told her that he felt comfortable and nourished in the extremely sympathetic author/editor relationship he found at Norstedts, and confidently believed that his publishers would do their very best for him. But he fully realised that work needed to be done on the books. After their final exchange, Larsson wrote that he was waiting to hear Eva Gedin's reservations about the manuscripts – reservations he was never to hear. Two weeks later, she was to receive the telephone call telling her that the author with whom she was enjoying working and for whom she foresaw such a shining future was dead. She knew that her job – to publish the books in a form that would have pleased him – was just beginning.

CHAPTER 6

STIEG LARSSON TODAY:
Developments and Discoveries

The books of such notable thriller writers as Ian Fleming and John le Carré have become highly collectable – particularly in good condition first editions – and it is salutary to note the speed with which Stieg Larsson has joined this august company. The Rare Book Guide states that by 2009 the British first edition of *The Girl with the Dragon Tattoo* was selling for about £400, while the relatively common US first edition could be obtained for a little under $100. UK first editions have apparently been changing hands on eBay, with a copy in near fine condition fetching £425 ($710). Already, internet sellers are pricing their books at £500 and more, promoting them heavily as investments. Leaving aside any discussion of simple evaluation versus exploitation, this sounds prescient – Larsson is showing every sign of becoming one of the most collectable of authors.

There is, intriguingly, another incentive for purchasing first editions – those copies signed by the translator 'Reg

Keeland' (the *nom de plume* of Steven Murray) – are, as mentioned earlier, sought-after in their own right. And the auguries for future price hikes in the first edition market of Larsson are either good or bad, depending on your point of view: good if you're a dealer, watching the value of your stock rise, and bad if you're a Stieg Larsson aficionado wanting to replace your second edition paperback with a glossy, un-foxed first edition.

Inevitably, with any phenomenon such as the posthumous success of Stieg Larsson there is something of a backlash, and as sales records continue to be broken by the *Millennium Trilogy* on an almost daily basis, it was perhaps inevitable that the naysayers would become more vocal. In fact, almost from the beginning, that is to say, from the publication outside Sweden of *The Girl with the Dragon Tattoo*, there have been those who have opposed the enthusiastic chorus of approval the work of the late author has enjoyed. Interestingly, the bursts of negativity are very different from those accorded to other highly successful but not critically highly regarded authors such as Dan Brown and Jeffrey Archer; with these writers, it is almost a badge of honour among clued-in readers to bring up how maladroit the writing often is when discussing their impressive sales. No such knee-jerk reaction is to be found in most book club, or other literary conversations about Stieg Larsson. His reputation as a 'literary' writer – along with that as a popular thriller writer – persists, possibly due to two factors. First, most readers continue to regard translated Scandinavian fiction as being more worthwhile or ambitious than more obviously mass-market fare; and second, the fact that Larsson is published in the UK by the highly respected literary publisher Christopher MacLehose lends his work a certain cachet. Nevertheless, any admirer of Larsson will have found that discussions of the *Millennium Trilogy* often include a remark from at least one participant along the lines of: 'But don't you think he's rather overrated?'. It is interesting that those looking to dent the late writer's reputation rarely use his borrowings from other writers as ammunition for their campaigns. A few anti-Larsson bullets might be found from a perusal of Daniel Pennac's *Write to Kill* (translated from the French in 1999 by Ian Monk and published by Harvill Press), which boasts a bushel of Larssonian central ideas: a protagonist with a bullet lodged in the brain, a coma, a publisher/journalist/writer character, a wizard with computers, malign and corrupt authorities – perhaps it's a book that found its way onto Stieg's bedside table. Other pre-echoes of the *Millennium Trilogy* include a female character using revamped passports, fake identity cards, wigs and make-up so that she can adopt a succession of different identities – a character, in fact, described as being 'about as mortal as a hero in a comic book'. The superhuman survival abilities here may ring some bells for Larsson readers. She also boasts phenomenal Asperger's syndrome-style skills at calculation, makes a fortune and exacts revenge on a slew of enemies.

Such dissenting voices, however, are showing not the slightest sign of diminishing the author's ever-growing posthumous popularity, and certainly the details of his life and the disputes over his estate seem to throw up new stories and revelations at least once a week. What's more, these stories are reported in the national press of most western countries – and on the news pages, rather than being consigned to the ghetto of the books pages.

One of the most intriguing stories to appear in 2010 concerned an aspect of the author's life beyond the word processor: we were to learn about Larsson's involvement with real-life revolutionaries – Eritrean guerrillas, no less. In the pages of the London newspaper *The Guardian*, journalist Homa Khaleeli filled in some fascinating information that had emerged via one of the author's friends, John Henri Holmberg. Suggesting that Lisbeth Salander's expertise with weaponry had some antecedents in her creator's own life, readers were told that Larsson had instructed Eritrean women in how to use grenade launchers. The details concerning this (not widely known before 2010) were sketchy, but – according to Holmberg – in 1977 Larsson had travelled to Eritrea and had contacted individuals he knew in the Eritrean People's Liberation Front (EPLF), a revolutionary Marxist organisation that was using violent means to bring about their country's independence from Ethiopia. Larsson's hands-on engagement with the dispensing of death (in however laudable a cause) was abruptly cut short when he began to suffer from a kidney inflammation and was obliged to leave Eritrea. This startling story was corroborated by Graeme Atkinson, European editor of *Searchlight* magazine (for which, of course, Larsson had acted as Swedish correspondent) and a close friend of the author. Atkinson acknowledged that Larsson had indeed made this trip to Eritrea, saying: 'Stieg was a revolutionary socialist and believed in a better life and equality for all.' Atkinson went on to speak about how disturbed Stieg Larsson was by the continuing crushing poverty in Africa. Significantly, Atkinson added that Larsson had travelled the country to take part in the armed struggle – which meant becoming part of the fighting and even facing live bullets.

The effect of the story was seismic, proving to some that Larsson was no armchair revolutionary but was prepared to put his beliefs to the test on the most dangerous of front lines. But others voiced the opinion that his passionate desire to change society throughout the world was best conducted through his pioneering investigative journalism, rather than by becoming directly involved in violent action. There was no doubting, however, that the story added some lustre to Larsson's reputation, although the image of him handling a grenade launcher seemed a touch unlikely.

There were other revelations concerning Stieg Larsson in 2010. According to Susan Donaldson James of ABC News, one of the most unsettling incidents in *The Girl Who Played with Fire* had an equally disturbing real-life antecedent. Readers who remember the scene in which two men bind and rape a young prostitute who has been co-opted into a sex trafficking ring will have seen it as an example of the author's rigorous and unsparing attitude towards a certain kind of male sexuality. But Kurdo Baksi (who worked with Larsson) revealed the fact that, at the age of 15, the author witnessed a gang rape committed by people he knew, and he failed to intervene. Sometime later, Larsson, suffering agonies of guilt, pleaded with the girl to forgive him for his inaction, but she declined. Larsson's reading of American fiction was prodigious, and if this is a truthful recollection of an incident that really happened in the author's life, it is nevertheless strongly reminiscent of a similarly gruelling scene in the classic novel by the American writer Nelson Algren, *Never Come Morning*, in which the too-pliable hero allows a gang rape by friends to take place without doing anything to stop it. The incident in which Larsson was involved has elements that were to leave a mark on him for the rest of his life. These elements begin with the fact that the girl was named Lisbeth. According to Baksi, Larsson's moral cowardice over the incident scarred him psychologically, and was one of the reasons behind him writing the novels. Baksi has apparently been making attempts to track down the real victim of the rape and has his own passionate desire to avenge the incident in some way. He accounts for Larsson's inability to act at the time by noting that he was both young and insecure, and believes that his loyalty to his friends was a key factor in stopping him from doing what he knew he should have done. Obviously, his shameful reluctance to intervene would come to be one of the most painful and guilt-inducing aspects of the whole incident.

Baksi and Larsson met in 1992. They shared an interest in socialist politics, and both were engaged in journalistic editorial duties; Baksi (working on the magazine *Black and White*, which, as the name suggests, dealt with racial issues) has said that he was involved in helping Larsson put together the latter's magazine *Expo*. These magazines later became one, and the two men worked together, enjoying – according to Baksi – an unconditional friendship. As for the *Millennium Trilogy*'s Blomkvist being a surrogate for the author himself, Baksi has another view – he regards Blomkvist, with his impressive list of sexual conquests, as very much a wish-fulfilment figure for his creator; he points out that Larsson was, in fact, more like Salander, sharing her taste for junk food and a deep suspicion of the police. The other element shared between Larsson and his heroine, according to Baksi, was a strong reluctance to discuss the past. Unlike Lisbeth, however, Larsson was not a naturally gifted organiser, and his financial improvidence had the effect of nearly bankrupting *Expo*. Baksi was of the opinion that Larsson had hoped that the future sales of his books would help to fund the magazine. Perhaps most significantly, Baksi reports that the late author had told him that he had 'ten books in his head' – more proof that death stilled what could have been a very productive authorial voice.

At a mere 140 or so pages, Baksi's memoir, *Stieg Larsson, My Friend*, is nothing if not concise, but it throws some illumination on aspects of the author's life not otherwise available to readers. Baksi was the first person to view Larsson's body in hospital after his death, and he briskly dismisses the idea that anything other than the author's lack of attention to his health was the cause of his death. He described how beautiful Larsson looked in his best clothes, and wearing a smile. 'He looked so young,' said Baksi wistfully.

Beginning with the painful process of acknowledging that Larsson had passed out of his life, Baksi decides to investigate – in the manner of a detective story writer – the answer to a question: who was Stieg? Discovering that the late writer had worked as a dishwasher at a restaurant, he looked further into his career, deciding that it was not hard to imagine Larsson as an infantryman (the latter had, in fact, completed two years of national service), not to mention the even more unlikely profession of manager at a pulp mill. After a relatively brief run-through of the facts of Larsson's early life, Baksi moves on to their first conversation – by phone – in 1992, when he had been working on the 21 February Committee in the Kungsholmen district of Stockholm, a political group that had called a strike after the shooting of 11 people by a man described by newspapers as 'The Laser Man', a disturbed individual who had been wandering the city aiming a rifle at non-white immigrants.

Baksi, recalling how Stockholm had felt like a city under siege, noted how his mysterious caller (he did not know it was Larsson) had asked why only immigrants (Baksi is a Kurd) were allowed to take part in the strike – suggesting that others, such as the caller himself, might like to have taken part. The caller pointed out – in no uncertain terms – that racism was not just an immigrant problem, but a problem for the country as a whole. And as he began to suggest new initiatives, Baksi became aware that he was talking to Stieg Larsson, a man he remembered encountering at various left-wing demonstrations and rallies, as well as being the author of a groundbreaking book on anti-democratic movements.

It was nearly a year before the two like-minded individuals were to meet, and in *Stieg Larsson, My Friend*, Baksi paints an intriguing picture of a passionately committed figure prepared to put his life on the line for his beliefs while barely looking after his own well-being. We are given a picture – now familiar to Larsson enthusiasts – of the uninspiring food that was the late author's staple diet. There are revealing insiders' views of life at the struggling magazine *Expo*, always on the brink of bankruptcy but powered by the commitment of its staff. And we encounter, in situ, Baksi's controversial critical remarks about Larsson's journalistic standards, so widely reported before the UK publication of the former's book.

Baksi reminds us that life was not safe for those working in left-wing journalism and taking on extremists, mentioning that a group of neo-Nazis had obtained photographs and current addresses of Larsson, Eva Gabrielsson and Baksi himself – deeply worrying for all three. Despite these potential threats to his life, Larsson continued to discuss such issues as the possibility of infiltrating extremist groups before being warned off by a nervous Baksi. With a certain pride, Baksi relates how he was name-checked and featured as a character in *The Girl Who Kicked the Hornets' Nest*, but remembers that in this memoir his principal duty is to supply personal information about Larsson. He mentions several writers numbered among Larsson's favourites, including such female crime writers as Minette Walters and Sara Paretsky, as well as talking about an interview Larsson conducted with a favourite science fiction writer, Harlan Ellison. The book ends with a discussion of health – ironically, not Larsson's but Baksi's own. He had told Larsson that he felt his own health was deteriorating because of overwork, and that he was spending more time in hospital than in the office – in fact, Baksi's doctors said that he was showing the symptoms of burnout. According to Baksi, he told the sympathetic Larsson that both men were not 20-year-olds any more, and that they should start thinking about their health – advice that Larsson signally did not take. The book ends with a talk that Baksi gives at a seminar, packed – to his dismay – with neo-Nazis, and a subsequent trip to the offices of *Expo* where he learns of the death of his friend. His own book, as he points out, was not intended as a blind tribute to Larsson – and it was certainly not received that way. It is a portrait of Larsson, Cromwell-style: warts and all.

But what about current thinking on Stieg Larsson in Sweden? Sitting in a room on the fifteenth floor of a hotel and talking to the journalist Dan Lucas, correspondent for the Swedish newspaper *Dagens Nyheter* in Britain, among other countries, is a pleasurable experience for me – not just because of the lively, informed conversation, but also because Lucas is a direct link to Stieg Larsson, and to be cherished as such; the journalist did agency work with the author between 1989 and 2000.

'I remember him doing work as a researcher and designer of graphs,' said Lucas. 'He was an extremely private person. Certainly, I would have to say that he was not someone that you really got close to. However, I learnt to both respect and like him for his encyclopaedic knowledge in certain areas – areas that are also of interest to me: mainly modern history and European politics... especially, I have to say, of the more unsavoury kind.'

As Lucas gazes out on the cityscape below, I ask what his dealings were with Larsson. 'I was a Stockholm-based EU correspondent during the 1990s,' he replies, 'and saw the steady rise of right-wing populism in several countries. Stieg was a great help in dissecting and analysing these movements.

'For me, the relationship with him was exclusively professional. I did not consider myself his friend, but his colleague. I would go to his "office" (frankly, it was a bit of a dump!) and we would talk about and examine different aspects of politics as well as European history. Now and then, I'd ask him to fix a diagram for a story I was working on.'

Lucas is bemused by the amazing response to Larsson in Britain – and as he (Lucas) is someone who straddles both countries – personally and professionally – I ask why he thinks Larsson has enjoyed this unprecedented success, even more than such other popular Scandinavian writers as Henning Mankell.

'I wish I knew!' is Lucas's rueful answer. 'I think perhaps

it's because Lisbeth Salander is so... how shall I put it? ... alien, different from any character we've ever come across in any thriller. And, let's face it, one can't deny the immense skill of the storytelling. But you also find that skill in Henning Mankell; and as for the latter's success, I can't help thinking that showing both the Swedish and the [Kenneth Branagh] UK versions of the *Wallander* series on TV helps a lot. But with Stieg, I think it's similar to the Björn Borg effect in Sweden... When he triumphed several times at Wimbledon, tennis players flourished all over the country. The same syndrome is now happening with crime writers.'

Time for a tricky question: where does Lucas stand in the contentious debate about whether Larsson was a good or a bad journalist? His answer is uncompromising. He said about Larsson, 'I didn't see a good journalist in action while I worked at the agency. However, I think he was quite different when he was working at *Expo*. That magazine was, after all, the unarguable love of his professional life. I think Stieg saw the agency as his bread-and-butter job, and I sensed he wasn't all that interested in it. He saved his real passion for *Expo*.'

Regarding the current Swedish attitude to the acrimonious struggle between Larsson's partner and his family, Lucas said that the general response was that they were all worthy of some criticism. 'There is absolutely no question what the tabloids think,' he said. 'The attitude among Swedes in general is probably more along the lines of: why don't you people get your act together? Surely there's enough money to go round?'

I ask Lucas whether or not, as a journalist, he considers that Larsson's sometimes negative picture of Sweden (massive governmental corruption, etc) has made the foreign view of the country more jaundiced. 'Perhaps. If those views that non-Swedes used to hold were naive, seeing Sweden as being something of a role model with clean politics and a decent, caring business community, then perhaps the Larsson novels can help readers to get a more balanced, realistic view of the country. However, in the final analysis, these are, after all, thrillers – they are popular entertainment. I'd be very careful of reading them as a valid social commentary on contemporary Swedish society. After all, Larsson didn't live to see recent political developments in Sweden [i.e. the much-reported far-Right party successes]. I think – regarding those developments – he'd be both horrified and a little bit thrilled – as any investigative reporter worth his salt should be. If he were still with us, Stieg would have been right up there exposing the foibles of the far-Right members of parliament.

'I am sorry for Stieg's sake that he couldn't enjoy his success. But I hope that Larsson and Mankell open the door for other Swedish crime writers that I personally think are greater authors: Håkan Nesser, to mention just one.'

As 2010 progressed, Larsson-related material began to appear in newspapers throughout the world on a regular basis, often providing information that had appeared previously elsewhere, but sometimes revealing fascinating new nuggets. For instance, two unpublished manuscripts came to light in Sweden, and this revelation was presented in several news stories as if to suggest – initially at least – that the tantalising possibility of further adventures for Lisbeth Salander were being dangled in front of the reader. But these new Larsson finds were, in fact, nothing to do with the *Millennium Trilogy*. The National Library of Sweden revealed in June that it had located in its files two stories sent by a teenage Larsson in an attempt to break into publication. These tyro efforts, however, were in Larsson's beloved science fiction genre, and were given very short shrift by the *Jules Verne* magazine that they had been submitted to originally. The stories ('The Flies' and 'The Crystal Balls') were subsequently donated to the National Library as part of an archive submitted by the magazine. But will they ever be published? Needless to say, the most insignificant scrap from Larsson's work desk – whenever it was written – would now glean immense interest. Magdalena Gram, the deputy national librarian of Sweden, told the English newspaper *The Independent* that the library would be contacting Larsson's father and brother in regard to the short stories, but the late author's publisher Eva Gedin had no assurances to give that they would ever see the light of day. She pointed out that she had been discussing with Larsson's brother the possibility of publishing articles from the magazine *Expo*, but that these science fiction pieces were a different issue altogether. Larsson's partner Eva Gabrielsson was guarded in her discussion of the stories – but then she had been thrown into the spotlight once again when further revelations were made concerning the fabled 'fourth manuscript'...

Larsson's friend John Henri Holmberg revealed that he had received an e-mail about this much-discussed fourth entry in the *Millennium* sequence from the author less than a month before the latter's death in November 2004. According to Holmberg, whose friendship with the author dated back to the time when the two had met at a science fiction convention in the 1970s, he had been told that Larsson had written 320 pages of the fourth book and intended to complete it by December of that year. According to the synopsis, the finished manuscript would have been 440 pages long. Holmberg's comments about the possible continuation of the saga created considerable interest, and his insistence that publication (or completion) of the manuscript should be a matter of urgency was echoed by many observers. Larsson had talked about elements in connection with this fourth book, notably concerning the sparse population of the location of the book – the isolated Sachs Harbour in the Northwest Territories of Canada (134 people, whose only contact with the outside world was a mail plane that made a landing when weather permitted). Holmberg was not able to expand on this promising set-up, but noted that he (Holmberg) understood that the book would continue the recurrent theme concerning the treatment of women in modern Swedish society.

Another biography, due to be published in 2011 by Larsson's UK publisher MacLehose Press, makes available Jan-Erik Pettersson's study *Stieg* (translated by Tom Geddes), which describes Stieg Larsson's political activism and research from his youth to his work on the magazine *Expo* (the model for *Millennium*). A focal point of the book is Larsson's tireless campaign against the racism and neo-Nazi tendencies of the far Right in Sweden. Pettersson's picture of extremist politics in Sweden is both wide-ranging and detailed, covering the various fringe parties, street demonstrations and acts of violence; he outlines Stieg's persistent efforts to expose those historical and current European connections that are often hidden by extremists in their attempt to present themselves as acceptable and electable. Pettersson's viewpoint is that of a fellow journalist fully conversant with Larsson's work and with contemporary socio-political developments in Sweden.

It was perhaps inevitable that the *Millennium Trilogy* would be adapted into media other than the cinema (the films are discussed here later). The first theatrical appearance of Lisbeth Salander had Larsson's heroine muttering her few carefully chosen words in Danish rather than Swedish – or English. The world premiere of the stage adaptation of *The Girl with the Dragon Tattoo* took place in Copenhagen's Nørrebro Theatre in November 2010. The play was developed in collaboration with Eva Gabrielsson, who may have lost control of the film rights of her late partner's work but was able to secure this first version for the stage. Anna Beck Laulund, speaking at the theatre, stated how keen everyone involved was to be faithful to the spirit of the books, but acknowledged that the films could, inevitably, be more successful at depicting the action elements of the plots. The aim of the theatrical adaptation, she explained, was to concentrate on the themes of misogyny and violence in society. Salander was played by Signe Egholm Olsen, a young actress whose career has been in the ascendant, principally through her appearances in the Danish television series *Borgen* (she also appeared in the 2007 Sean Penn film *Into the Wild*). In the UK, the news quickly prompted speculation about the possibilities of a theatrical adaptation in London.

Not all the examples of Larssoniana have taken the books and their creator quite so seriously. Nora Ephron produced a brief and witty parody in *The New Yorker* ('The Girl Who Fixed the Umlaut'), riffing on Lisbeth's computer skills and her inability to smile. And another Larsson *jeu d'esprit* appeared in 2010 – Adam Roberts' fantasy *The Dragon with the Girl Tattoo*, with the heroine Lizbreath Salamander sporting scales, wings, and a tattoo on her back of a mythical creature: a girl. There are gloomy Nordic dragons, conspiracies and IKEA-style home furnishing (in this novel, fireproofed!).

CHAPTER 7

THE BOOKS: *The Girl with the Dragon Tattoo*

What is the secret of Larsson's astonishing posthumous success in Sweden? Is it a corollary of his heroic status? Whatever the reason, that success was to be repeated in the United Kingdom – and throughout the world. The following discussion of the novels assumes that the reader is already familiar with the trilogy.

At the start of this weighty, first novel of the trilogy, Larsson appears to be testing his readers. He has up his sleeve two extremely engaging protagonists – and once these characters have appeared, our surrender to the novel is guaranteed. Before that, however, we are subjected to lengthy, and at times impenetrable, details of financial scams in which the reader, like the characters, seems to be being told – sharply – to pay attention. But just as our patience is being tested, Larsson finally allows us to luxuriate in some impeccable plotting involving disgraced journalist Mikael Blomkvist and computer hacker Lisbeth Salander. The former is cut from a familiar cloth – the tenacious reporter who has taken on a dangerous enemy (like Larsson himself) – but Salander is that *rara avis*, something new in crime fiction (though she does have antecedents).

Salander, much esteemed by her financial investigator boss, who is fighting his own inappropriately lustful impulses towards her, belies her professional expertise as investigator by an off-putting punk appearance: facial jewellery, outlandish clothes and the eponymous dragon tattoo. One of her subjects is Mikael Blomkvist, sacked after a disastrous legal defeat over a contentious article. Unaware of Salander's report on him, Blomkvist is hired by an ailing magnate to investigate the disappearance (and possible murder) of his niece on an island several years ago. The island was cut off from the mainland by an unlikely accident involving a blocked bridge, isolating a group of suspects – and before the reader can cry 'Ah ha! Locked room scenario!', Larsson beats us to the punch, with his characters noting that this is classic English mystery territory. But not for the first time in the novel we're being wrong-footed: what follows is much darker and bloodier than we seem to be being prepared for – more Thomas Harris than Dorothy Sayers.

Reading the *Millennium Trilogy* is in fact a bittersweet experience, as we are constantly reminded that an accomplished writing voice has been stilled even before his work reached these shores. For instance, just as we are worrying that such an extreme-looking anti-heroine as Salander might alienate the very people she is plugging for information, Larsson has her remove her face metal and don conventional clothes – she has, in fact, a secret identity. She is also – despite her insolent manner – vulnerable, tying in to a feminist undercurrent here, one that would have pleased the fierce Andrea Dworkin (one of the novel's superscriptions is '18% of the women in Sweden have at one time been threatened by a man'). But if this suggests a vitiating political correctness quality, the unsparing horror and torture the novel deals out banishes any such notions.

The prologue for *The Girl with the Dragon Tattoo* begins with a ritual, involving the delivery of a flower to a man – whose identity is not immediately revealed to us – who has reached his 82nd birthday. He takes off the wrapping for a flower he has received through the post then picks up the phone to contact a police friend, retired Detective Superintendent Morrell. The flower has arrived without a note, postmarked Stockholm. Neither man speaks much about the mystery on this occasion, for it is a topic that they have both discussed endlessly over the years. This time, the flower is identified as coming from a plant native to the Australian bush, according to a botanist who was consulted. It is a very rare flower, but the source of this particular specimen is proving impossible to trace. The bloom itself is just the latest in a long line: these mystifying flowers have arrived each year in winter, pressed on watercolour paper in a frame. Neither man has ever reported the matter to the newspapers, and 'The Case of the Pressed Flowers' has nagged at the attention of Morrell, the policeman, for years. It has every appearance of being his last case, forever to be unsolved. This intriguing prologue ends with the old man weeping over the flower, before setting it on the wall above his desk with the 43 other flowers that he has received over the years.

Right from the start of the novel it is clear that Stieg Larsson is determined to come up with original, innovative situations that owe little to his predecessors – even though these very predecessors are name-checked in the book. The latter action, which might have been a hostage to fortune on the part of lesser writers, is confronted with confidence by Larsson – and firmly dealt with. We will, he conveys to us, be reading something new.

The journalist Mikael Blomkvist has lost almost everything. He has been thoroughly trounced by his opponent, the industrialist Wennerström, and is surrounded by fellow journalists, some who have come to gloat (even using a derisory nickname, 'Kalle', based on a character from Astrid Lindgren – the first example of a reference to another writer found in the *Millennium Trilogy*). A 26-page judgement finds Blomkvist guilty of a variety of counts of aggravated libel against Wennerström. And Blomkvist will be going to jail as well as paying a hefty fine, not to mention the court costs and his lawyer's fee. It is, of course, clear to see where this plot device is coming from in terms of Stieg Larsson's own life – it was always an occupational hazard that he would be arraigned by one of the opponents against whom he was making an accusation, and what better way to characterise his hero than utilise something that Larsson was apprehensive about? He realises that he may have to sell his beloved apartment and that *Millennium*, the magazine he works for, may now be in trouble. He asks himself how things have gone so catastrophically wrong.

What follows is a lengthy discussion of the Wennerström case, and the detail with which the various pieces of financial chicanery are set out is discussed forensically. This is, to some degree, a test of the reader's stamina. It is perhaps the 'Proust point' for many new readers of Stieg Larsson, the section in which the less hardy of heart fall down (rather as many readers do not get beyond *Swann's Way*). But such is Larsson's skill at detailing this complicated scam that those who persist will be rewarded – and, to some degree, it is important to pay attention to clarify things that develop later in the book. There are those who have regretted that *The Girl with the Dragon Tattoo* begins with this section, rather than introducing the charismatic (and disturbed) Lisbeth Salander earlier, but Larsson might be said to have a strategy: the delayed introduction of his ace-in-the-hole is a clever device, and making us wait for her will pay dividends.

Chapter 2 begins with the life history of Dragan Armansky, an Armenian Jew from Belarus who in appearance resembles the popular image of the mob boss in an American crime movie, but is actually a talented financial director who began his career in the firm of Milton Security in the 1970s. His nickname is 'The Arab', although he is not of Arabic extraction. One part of the business (which grows under Armansky's stewardship) was described in internal memos as 'pinders', standing for personal investigations. This is not Armansky's favourite part of the business, but he finds it extremely useful when checking on adulterers, unsuitable fiancées and blackmailers. He always keeps a close personal watch on this particular area of his activities.

It is during this section of the book that we are introduced to one of Armansky's employees, who has been conducting a personal investigation for him: it is our first meeting with Lisbeth Salander, 32 years younger than him. While Armansky regards her as the most adroit and efficient of his employees (with her astonishingly detailed and informative reports), he is well aware that many of those who are the targets of her investigations are in for a very bad time. She has managed to identify a paedophile who had used child prostitutes in Tallinn, and the single-mindedness with which she pursues this particular individual is above and beyond the call of duty – as her employer sees it. We are, of course, in our initial encounter with Salander, being introduced to a key theme of the novel: the sexual abuse of women and children.

But what particularly nonplusses Armansky is Salander's appearance. She is a white-faced young woman of anorexic appearance with facial piercings and a wasp tattoo on her neck. The bicep of her left arm is similarly festooned, and Armansky has noticed, when she is wearing a short-sleeved top, that she has on her left shoulder blade a dragon tattoo. He knows that she is a redhead but her hair is dyed a deep black, and he describes her as looking like she has emerged from a lengthy orgy. Interestingly, despite her anorexic appearance, she seems able to vacuum up massive quantities of junk food. She is 24, but with her small breasts she sometimes appears to be about 14.

While initially being hired for whatever jobs are available, Armansky realises that this is a woman of amazing abilities, and he is quickly using her to work full-time on the most ambitious jobs – despite the fact that her findings are often extremely uncomfortable for him, and he is acutely aware that they may lead to libel suits. Every so often she reads the riot act to him, rather than the other way round, and points out that her talents are not being utilised to the full. She notes, for instance, that the security routines in the office are not up to scratch – and she can improve such things. She also notes that the girlfriend of one of her targets has been obliged to go to a women's crisis centre after she has been savagely beaten by him (a key Larsson motif). Armansky's response is to tell her to prove it in three days, and if the allegations are unsubstantiated by Friday afternoon, she will be fired. Needless to say, she delivers the proof, and Armansky is forced to realise that he has someone very special indeed on his staff, despite her unpromising appearance. The fact that he had regarded her as possibly retarded was a misjudgement he is not likely to make again; he begins to give her more challenging assignments and continues to put up with more strong-willed disagreement than he would accept from anyone else.

All of this is handled by Stieg Larsson with total assurance, and the rather uninvolving opening of the book (which has alienated many readers, who have not felt able to persist) seems a distant memory as we realise that we are in the presence of one of the key protagonists – and a highly memorable one at that. Another theme that is to be recurrent for the author occurs when Armansky finds himself having inappropriate daydreams about Salander, even though, as he sees it, she hardly conforms to the image of women that he finds attractive. This aspect of Salander – the fact that her off-putting appearance does not alienate men, as might be supposed – is something that seems designed to confuse the reader's response: is this some kind of insight into Stieg Larsson's own psyche? Or is it the author challenging the reader's expectations in this very fraught area?

At a Christmas party, Armansky makes a clumsy pass, which Salander struggles away from. She does not return to the office or answer her phone, but then, arbitrarily it seems, she reappears in the office at night and asks him if he would like some coffee. She then confronts him about his sexual attraction for her, and makes it ruthlessly clear that nothing will ever happen between them. The dialogue in this discussion has the skilfulness that (as the trilogy progresses) is one of the real strengths of the narrative, particularly as rendered in Reg Keeland/Steven Murray's utilitarian translation. But the upshot of this strange conversation is that Armansky and Salander arrive at a new working relationship in which she will do freelance assignments for him, and for which she will receive a monthly stipend. If she comes up trumps with an investigation, she will be paid more. The arrangement is satisfactory for everyone involved, and Armansky makes only one stipulation – that she does not meet the clients. He is fully aware just how she will be received by most people, and reasons that her talents are best kept under cover.

After the striking introduction of Lisbeth Salander, Larsson does not waste much time in introducing us to the character who will share the narrative with her, and who is in many ways a surrogate figure for the author himself. Arriving at work one day in a T-shirt with a picture of Steven Spielberg's *ET* transformed into a fanged monster, Salander is to attend a meeting with a client, Dirch Frode, a lawyer who has made a point of meeting the member of the firm who has prepared a report he requested. Despite Armansky's best attempts, the meeting takes place, with Frode (a man in his late sixties) looking at Lisbeth Salander with undisguised surprise. She has placed a folder labelled 'Carl Mikael Blomkvist' on Armansky's desk.

It is in this chapter that Larsson introduces another element that is to be a leitmotif throughout the novel: the difficulty which people with more 'normal' lives find in dealing with Lisbeth Salander. This can be read in two ways: firstly, that she does not care how she affects people – which is certainly the rationale we are most likely to accept – but, secondly, it may be pointed out that she is far too intelligent not to know how people will react to her appearance, and this could all be part of a strategy for gaining a kind of advantage in a world that she sees as threatening and unsympathetic. Salander begins a dispassionate account of her findings with regard to Blomkvist, and readers who pick up the novel knowing that it is the first part of a trilogy will be intrigued by her cool response to the man who we know will be the most important ally she is to have. She points out that it has not been a particularly complicated assignment, finding out things about him, such as the fact that he is 43, being born in 1960, and that both his parents are dead. He has a sister some years younger than him who is a lawyer. He graduated from Blomma with decent marks, and played bass in a rock band (even putting out a single) before travelling abroad, hitching his way around India and Thailand before finding his way to Australia. He had begun to study to be a journalist in Stockholm in his twenties but then did military service in Lapland. Since then he has completed his journalism degree.

As the client listens attentively, Salander compares him to Practical Pig in the 'Three Little Pigs': he is an excellent journalist, with many temporary jobs, and his first big, attention-grabbing story was about bank robbers he identified, the Bear Gang. It was here that he got the nickname that he so hates, 'Kalle' Blomkvist (the name, from the children's books of Astrid Lindgren, leads to another reference – the first in the book – to Pippi Longstocking. Salander says she would greet such nicknames with violence).

Armansky is thinking at that moment that Pippi Longstocking is exactly how he has always thought of Salander. Blomkvist's original intention was to be a crime reporter, but he seems to have ended up as a political and financial specialist. He now works for a monthly magazine called *Millennium*, with its editorial offices a few blocks from Armansky's company. It is a left-wing magazine; Salander says it is generally viewed as critical of society, but is held in contempt by anarchists, who do not take it seriously, while more moderate students regard it as a Bolshevist mouthpiece. Salander points out that there are no indications that Blomkvist himself has ever been politically active, even during his secondary school phase when such affiliations were *de rigueur*. He has always, it seems, been devoted to journalism, even when living with a girl who was active in the Syndicalists, who today is a member of parliament on the Left. Salander points out that he has been identified as left-wing simply because his prime targets are corruption and double-dealing in the corporate world, with some of those in his sights being among the most prestigious names in politics and business – and that drawing attention to such matters is hardly an indication of left-wing political sympathies. She also notes that he has written two books and is not rich but is relatively comfortably off.

At this juncture in the novel, not for the last time, art imitates life. Salander notes that Blomkvist is part owner of the magazine *Millennium*, and that any money he is obliged to pay out because of various settlements will cripple him – it is impossible not to see echoes of Larsson's own sometimes parlous state when working for *Expo*, which similarly took on unpopular causes. After the legal judgement against him, Salander decides that Blomkvist has really made a fool of himself, and then she allows herself a direct comment on the Wennerström affair, noting that she has followed the trial and is surprised that Blomkvist published something that was so ill-advised and, as she puts it, off the wall. She believes that Blomkvist was set up.

Those who have re-read the *Millennium Trilogy* after their first acquaintance with this initial book will be struck by the phrase 'set up' – almost a game plan for all three books, with Salander being comprehensively set up again and again. At this point, however, she is standing outside events, and commenting coolly on the luckless Blomkvist. Her reason for believing him to be innocent is the extreme care with which she treats each case, which leads her to suppose that he may be right about Wennerström, who has acted, it seems, dishonestly. So far, Larsson has not revealed the interest of the client Frode in the affair, but the latter now asks if the trio are speaking in confidence. After Armansky nods assent, Frode says that he knows that without any shadow of a doubt Wennerström has acted dishonestly in certain other circumstances, and he, Frode, has a pronounced interest in the legal judgement against Blomkvist.

This strikes Armansky as slightly alarming, as his company is being required to look into a case that has already been concluded. He knows perfectly well that Wennerström has an army of solicitors who will descend on him en masse, and he is particularly aware that utilising Salander (who is, to put it mildly, the loosest of cannons) in such a scenario could potentially be disastrous. On the other hand, she has said that she requires no special treatment or protection, and was not to be given any special privileges. However, Armansky replies that such an investigation could become very expensive, but Frode is already, it seems, convinced of Salander's competence.

She agrees, without much enthusiasm, to look into Blomkvist's case. She notes that his private life is unexceptional. He was married with a daughter, but the couple were divorced and the daughter hardly ever sees her father. However, Frode learns something more about Blomkvist from Salander: she tells him that he is something of a ladies' man, with a succession of love affairs and many one-night stands. There is one particular relationship that seems to be a steady presence: Erika Berger, who is the editor-in-chief at *Millennium*. She is an upper-crust woman (with a Belgian father and Swedish mother). The two met while studying journalism, and have enjoyed a casual relationship over the years. She, however, is married to an artist who appears complacent about the relationship and the affair appears to be a contributing factor to the ending of Blomkvist's marriage.

Readers encountering Stieg Larsson for the first time with *The Girl with the Dragon Tattoo* will have realised by Chapter 3 that one of his specialities is to pay out chunks of information which are then expanded on when appropriate. And having introduced Erika Berger in the text, Larsson presents us with the woman herself in the third chapter. Blomkvist, shivering from cold, enters the editorial offices of *Millennium*, and talks to her. We learn that he is not in a good place. Leaving aside the legal disaster which has just befallen him, we discover that the magazine is living beyond its means, and that the rent on its offices (in the fashionable district of Götgatan above the offices of Greenpeace) is a little too steep for the magazine. The couple glumly discuss the bad news of the judgement which has gone against Blomkvist, and Erika mentions someone else involved: Christer, the art director and designer of *Millennium*, is also a part-owner of the magazine, along with Erika and Blomkvist.

Blomkvist suggests that Christer may have to take over as

publisher, and again we are reminded of the real-life decisions that Larsson himself would have had to have made, working on the staff of a magazine which risked legal entanglements. Erika persuades Blomkvist that he needs to stay on, as he is essential to the running of the magazine, and it's difficult not to see a certain wish fulfilment on Larsson's own part (in the sense that he would desire to be similarly missed from any magazine he might be involved in).

The couple end their discussion by deciding to forget their problems in a relaxing sexual encounter. After they have made love, Blomkvist finds himself thinking about this unconventional relationship that he is part of, not the old-fashioned kind which leads to love, a home shared together, children, and so forth. Once again, it is clear to see that the life that the author chose for himself is reflected in his protagonist. Erika, however, is a sympathiser with this point of view, which possibly echoes Larsson's relationship with Eva Gabrielsson, and as *Millennium* is their mutual creation, it might be read as something of a surrogate child for the couple. Certainly, they lavish a great deal of love and dedication on the magazine. A press release is prepared in which it is pointed out that the journalist Mikael Blomkvist will be leaving his post as publisher of the magazine *Millennium*. Erika feels that the magazine will survive and not be affected by his voluntary stepping down. He persuades her that it is time to take a step backwards, but promises that some day they will be able to prove their allegations about Wennerström – and they will create a furore on Wall Street.

By now we have the classic scenario of the protagonist somewhat cut adrift and on the receiving end of an unjust accusation. The stage is set for Blomkvist to be handed the most significant assignment of his career. And it happens while he is cleaning out his desk at the office of *Millennium*. The phone rings and it is the lawyer Dirch Frode who tells Blomkvist that he is representing a client who is anxious to contact him for a talk. Unusual conditions are given. It is pointed out to Blomkvist that the client would like to be visited in Hedestad, which is three hours away by train. Blomkvist begins to be suspicious and makes it clear that he is not interested. But then he is told the name of Frode's client: no one less than Henrik Vanger. This information takes Blomkvist by surprise, as it is the name of a powerful industrialist with a massive portfolio of interests in a family-owned company. His interest aroused, Blomkvist asks why Vanger wants a meeting – is a press secretary required, perhaps? He is told that he will hear more when he visits Hedestad, with (naturally) all expenses paid. Blomkvist decides that it is necessary to tell the lawyer something that he is not sure the latter knows: the disgrace that has followed the decision in the Wennerström affair. But rather than being a disincentive, this, according to Frode, is precisely the reason why Herr Vanger has contacted him.

At this stage, Larsson has intrigued the reader sufficiently with narrative possibilities for his male protagonist, so that we are now able to move to the company of Lisbeth Salander who is spending Christmas Eve at a nursing home in Upplands–Väsby. She is gazing at the woman she knows as her mother, thinking (not for the first time) that they bear no physical resemblance to each other. The woman, confused and ill-focused after being given a present, says, 'Thank you, Camilla.' To which Salander replies, 'Lisbeth. I'm Lisbeth.'

Blomkvist similarly spends time with his family, who

largely avoid discussing the verdict which has gone against him, but he is now intrigued by his meeting with Frode, even though he has considered cancelling it. He asks Frode if the invitation bears any relation to Wennerström, to which he receives the reply that Herr Vanger is most definitely not a friend of the man who has won the judgement against Blomkvist. Frode drives Blomkvist along frozen roads for his meeting with Vanger, which lead to an isolated island.

Henrik Vanger lives in the family's stone-built farmhouse, and on entering, Blomkvist encounters a remarkably youthful-looking 82-year-old man with a weathered face and thick grey hair. He is made to feel welcome and Frode takes his leave. Blomkvist, the eternal journalist, reaches into his pocket as his new acquaintance begins to talk and turns on a tape recorder. He has not formed a conception of what Vanger wants, but has learnt to be ultra-cautious on such occasions. Vanger assures him after the preliminaries that he will get to the point, and the couple move to a massive, imposing office lined with a remarkable collection of books. Vanger shows him a picture of a strikingly attractive young woman with dark hair, and asks (using Blomkvist's first name) whether he remembers her. And, for that matter whether he remembers being in this room before.

Blomkvist replies that he doesn't, and is told that the photograph is that of Harriet Vanger, the granddaughter of his host's brother Richard. She looked after him when he was two years old and she was 13. Blomkvist admits to having no idea whether this is the truth or not. But more photographs are produced, showing Blomkvist's parents (he is struck by the fact that his mother is clearly pregnant – with his sister). It becomes clear that Vanger knows much about Blomkvist and his family and has followed his career as a journalist on

Millennium, which he claims to read. Blomkvist decides that it is time to ask him what it is that he requires.

This is the moment where the novel most resembles one of the authors that Stieg Larsson read (and who so impressed him) – the American master of the detective novel, Raymond Chandler. This meeting with an elderly client is reminiscent of (among other books) *The Big Sleep*, and if Larsson lacks Chandler's nonpareil skills at evoking character, there is no question that he has the reader comprehensively engaged at this point. Vanger points out that he would like to make an agreement with Blomkvist. He says that he will tell him a story in two parts, the first about the Vanger family and the second part will address his objective. Blomkvist will be surprised at what he hears and may even doubt the sanity of what he is being told. But by this point the journalist is thoroughly engaged. What he says, however, is designed to expedite matters. He points out that he has been in the house for 20 minutes and says that he will allow 30 minutes more before calling a taxi and going home.

Vanger is not fooled; he is aware that the journalist is without a job and undoubtedly in dire financial straits. He talks about Martin Vanger, who currently runs the Vanger Corporation – and sums him up in relatively unenthusiastic terms. It's a family company, but the 30 family members are (as Vanger perceives it) both the strength and the weakness of the organisation. He makes it clear that he particularly despises most of the members of his family – and regards them as crooks, bullies and incompetents.

Then Vanger gets to the main issue: the assignment he wants Blomkvist to take on. Vanger tells Blomkvist that he wants to commission him to write a biography of the Vanger family (which may be called his own autobiography, that is to say Henrik Vanger's), and for this he will put all his journals and archives at Blomkvist's disposal. He also makes it clear that there is to be no whitewash. All skeletons in closets may be dragged into the light. Blomkvist is intrigued by the fact that his host is not concerned with ultimate publication. He says that his motive is a simple one: revenge. Vanger explains that his name is synonymous with honour. He is a man who is true to his word, and he is particularly disgusted by the behaviour of his relatives, which is, as he perceives it, one of the reasons the company is experiencing such difficulties in the present. Blomkvist says he is not interested, pointing out that it would take many months and that he lacks either the impetus or the physical resources, but Vanger is not prepared to give up and suggests that he approaches the assignment with the unforgiving eyes of a journalist. But then he drops the bombshell.

Vanger's clandestine agenda is the solving of a mystery, which is Blomkvist's real mission. This particular plot point has been reserved by Larsson till nearly a sixth of the way into the book, and is rather similar to the sleight of hand displayed by such detective story masters as Raymond Chandler and Dashiell Hammett: that is to say, introduce what appears to be the principal plot of the novel, but withhold the revelation of the real plot until somewhat later. Larsson is a master of this, and uses the tactic repeatedly throughout the three books of the *Millennium Trilogy*.

Vanger talks about his brother, the unpleasant Richard, who – at the age of 17 – was a fervent nationalist and an anti-Semite. He joined the Swedish National Socialist Freedom League, which was one of the first attempts in Sweden to move into neo-Nazi territory. For those who read this book unaware of Stieg Larsson's background, presumably this would have come across as simply a way of establishing a character's negative aspects, but as many of Larsson's readers are by now familiar with his days as an anti-Nazi journalist, it's not hard to see the personal impulse behind this particular authorial choice.

Blomkvist is shown pictures of Richard with a variety of prominent Nazis, and Vanger remarks how (against the wishes of their father) he made contact with the Nazi groups in the country. Vanger enquires of Blomkvist how much he knows about the history of Swedish Nazism. The latter replies that he is not a historian but has read a few books – and what follows is a lengthy and fascinating discussion of some of the more ignoble aspects of Sweden's involvement with Nazism (tied in, of course, to the fictional story of Richard Vanger). One of the strengths of the *Millennium Trilogy* is, of course, the way it ties in so specifically with the author's own particular preoccupations, principally a combative engagement with the far Right, and it is intriguing to speculate how the ten-book sequence he was apparently planning might have progressed.

Certainly, within the confines of the trilogy, there is only intermittently a sense that Larsson is repeating himself in what might be described as his various hobbyhorses (the exploitation of women, extremist groups, etc), but it is probably true that had he lived, further books featuring Lisbeth Salander and Mikael Blomkvist would have had to move into new territory to sustain the energy – rather in the fashion that the cult American TV series *The Wire* moved into such areas as politics and education to keep fresh for the writers and directors what had inspired them to create something innovative in the first place.

Vanger extrapolates the less pleasant aspects of his story, filling in the background of the enigmatic Harriet, before he glances at the clock and tells Blomkvist that the 30 minutes are almost up – but that he is nearing the end of his story. Needless to say, Blomkvist asks him to go on. Vanger says that unlike his brothers and other family members he was childless, and that he took in the children Martin and Harriet (thereby rescuing them from the less-than-loving care of their parents), allowing them to become, in a way, his own children. Martin, who initially appeared weak and introverted, was able to achieve sufficient strength of will after university to become CEO of the Vanger Corporation. Blomkvist enquires: 'And Harriet?' Vanger replies that she was his special favourite and that he looked upon her as his own daughter. She was intelligent and talented, unlike her brother or her mediocre cousins, nephews and other relatives. As yet, of course, neither the reader nor Blomkvist know what has happened to Harriet. Vanger then delivers a telling sentence: 'I want you to find out who in the family murdered Harriet and who since then has spent almost 40 years trying to drive me insane.'

Stieg Larsson's reading of the great crime writers from a variety of countries bore fruit in an intriguing variety of fashions. In Chapter 5 he describes a great family reunion in 1966, when Harriet was 16 and had just begun her second year at secondary school. Vanger describes the reunion as a loathsome annual dinner and a tradition which had long turned into deeply unpleasant affairs. This is perhaps one of the first times when we are reminded that among Larsson's prodigious crime fiction reading were the novels of Agatha Christie. It's particularly interesting to discern her shade whenever it appears, as the graphic sexuality and violence of the books is a million miles away from the discreet British queen of crime. But for those who know their genres, she is actually rarely far away, notably in the careful attention to ingenious (and surprising) plotting.

Blomkvist at this point asks about the murder of Harriet and becomes impatient with the steady parcelling out of facts. But Vanger has decided to make him (and, *inter alios*, the reader) wait. He talks about a children's day parade arranged by the sports club at Hedestad. She has gone into town and returns to the island after 2 o'clock with dinner due later in the afternoon. At this point Vanger takes Blomkvist over to the window and points to the bridge. He tells him that at 2.15, some moments after Harriet arrived home, an accident happened on the bridge. The brother of a farmer whose name was Aronsson drove onto the bridge and collided head-on with an oil lorry. Both men were going fast; the tanker turned over and ended up lying across the bridge with its trailer dangling over the edge. Aronsson was trapped in his car, and unable to scramble out as the tanker driver managed to. As Vanger says, the accident had nothing to do with Harriet, but what happened later was highly significant.

As people scrambled to try to help, attempting to pull the farmer from the wreckage, they were all aware of the danger they were in if the oil issuing from the tanker caused an explosion. At this point, Blomkvist mentally notes that the old man is a good storyteller (pointing up for the reader that we are in the hands of a pretty capable storyteller ourselves). But Vanger concludes that what really matters about the accident is that the bridge was blocked for 24 hours – and there was no way to reach the outside world. This, of course, leads Blomkvist to conclude that something happened to

Harriet on the island and that the list of suspects may be drawn from those trapped there.

It's at this point that Stieg Larsson decides to pull what might be described as a post-modern literary trick. He is drawing our attention to something that readers of Agatha Christie and co. [as noted earlier] will have noticed: we have the set-up for a 'locked room mystery' format, set on an island. Vanger smiles at the observation and says that the journalist is correct, adding, 'Even I have read my Dorothy Sayers.'

There were 64 people on the island. Harriet had lived in a house across the road but had moved into Vanger's house – an arrangement that was perfectly acceptable to her irresponsible mother Isabella. It is known that Harriet came home that day and met and had a conversation in the courtyard before coming upstairs to say hello to Vanger. She had told him that she wished to talk to him about a certain matter, but he was too busy at the time. At this point Blomkvist enquires how the girl died, but again Vanger will not be hurried and points out that the story must be told in chronological fashion.

Several people have remarked on seeing Harriet on the bridge during the confusion that followed the accident, but the possibility of an explosion had obliged Vanger to clear everyone from the area, apart from five people working to rescue the trapped man (one of whom was Vanger's brother Harald). Just before 3 o'clock she was seen crossing the courtyard by her mother and she was known to have spoken to Otto Falk, the local pastor. He, it appears, was the last person to see her alive. Nobody knew how she died. When the injured man was pulled from the car at 5 o'clock, the threat of a fire had been contained. It was 8 o'clock in the evening before it was discovered that Harriet was missing. And from that day onward she has never been seen again.

Blomkvist points out that there is no way of knowing from these facts that she was murdered, but Vanger has a reason for thinking that someone took her life – it is, he says, the only reasonable conclusion. She has vanished so comprehensively, without a social security card or any other means of surviving. And then Vanger makes a striking observation. He considers that her body must be somewhere in the limited area of the island, even though the most thorough of searches had been conducted. Blomkvist suggests that she might have drowned (either accidentally or on purpose) but Vanger regards this as not a real probability. All the areas where she might have been drowned have been dragged and have revealed no trace. He is convinced that she was murdered and that her body was somehow mysteriously disposed of.

We are now nearly 100 pages into the book and it appears that Larsson has set up (in leisurely fashion) for us what will be the basic premise of the plot: the missing girl, the elderly industrialist with the unpleasant family, the compromised hero who (by solving the mystery) will possibly have reclaimed his former position in society. But this is not quite Stieg Larsson's strategy, and when we are reintroduced to Lisbeth Salander on page 90 – she is spending Christmas morning reading Blomkvist's book about financial journalism, *The Knights Templar: A Cautionary Tale for Financial Reporters* – we are forcibly reminded that Blomkvist is not the only protagonist here and that another assignment has already been handed out: Lisbeth is to investigate *him*.

Taking time out to look at Blomkvist's character, we can

see that he is a journalist of rigorous ethics, intolerant of those who are not able to approach their assignments with either true objectivity or incisiveness. He is, it seems, particularly disposed to be impatient with those who take the facts they are given at face value, something that he will never do, and is keen to establish that he is different from all these other reporters. Once again we are reminded that Blomkvist is something of an identification figure for Larsson himself, possibly in the way that James Bond was for Ian Fleming. It was much more likely, however, that Larsson could lead the same life as his journalist hero, acted out on a slightly more realistic stage than the globe-hopping antics of 007, although Blomkvist's sexual attractiveness to a variety of women still ties in with the wish fulfilment of the author's theme.

Salander finishes Blomkvist's book and demonstrates her own intelligence by completely – and effortlessly – assimilating its tactics and findings. But (not for the last time) she maintains a distance from the man with whom she is soon to have a close relationship by saying to herself: 'Hello Kalle Blomkvist, you are pretty pleased with yourself, aren't you?' The reader might perhaps think that in Blomkvist and Salander we have an emblematic version of Freud's ego and super ego, the two being in fruitful symbiosis with each other to achieve a particular end – although as neither has met at this point of the book, such a thesis might be a bit premature. (The two also shift in 'controlling' terms, so this metaphor is a loose one.)

It's worth noting at this point that Larsson is also well aware of the strategy of keeping us intrigued about one of the characters. In the same way that Mikael Blomkvist might be said to be a surrogate or identification figure for the author himself, Blomkvist also fulfils this function for the reader. Right from the start of the book we are placed firmly within his consciousness and are party to most of his thoughts and motivations – not to mention the fact that we are given a fairly extensive itinerary of his days. The same is not true of Lisbeth Salander, although we are told a lot about her. She nevertheless remains something of an enigma and the reader looks upon her with a degree of wonder in rather the same way that those who have already dealt with her have done – and Blomkvist will come to do. It is this maintaining of a character's mystique at which Larsson is particularly adroit, and his particular skill is to maintain this element of mystery about his female protagonist throughout all three books, however extreme the situations he puts her in (and the situations are certainly going to become extreme).

Salander boots up her iBook and sends an e-mail, after utilising an encryption programme. We are reminded of her computer expertise – this is not a woman who would struggle for long with the computer problems that bedevil most of us. But then she performs a rather surprising action – one that gives us a new insight into her as a character. She puts on black jeans, a polo shirt, a jacket and matching knitted gloves. She also takes the rings from her eyebrows and nostril, applies a pale pink lipstick and, by these actions, transforms herself into an ordinary-looking woman simply out for an afternoon walk. This, we are told, is appropriate camouflage and we realise that there is much more to Lisbeth – literally – than meets the eye. She makes her way to the apartment block at which one of the residents is Wennerström.

Chapter 6 utilises a mini version of the ticking clock so

beloved of many crime novelists. Blomkvist has set himself the task of catching the evening train at 9.30 pm. He has looked at the scrapbook that Vanger has given him and has absorbed the available information. There has been a certain amount of interest in the missing girl for a while, but then no new facts were forthcoming, and the interest has waned. More than three decades later, the issue of what happened to Harriet Vanger appears to be of little or no interest. One explanation has been accepted: that she was drowned and lost in the sea.

Vanger asks Blomkvist what he thinks has happened to her, and the latter gives a summing up which would have done Agatha Christie proud: the island normally had some 20-odd residents, but the family reunion had meant that there were 60 on Hedeby Island on the occasion that the girl went missing, and Blomkvist discounts most of them. He suggests that the most likely solution was that a member of the family murdered Harriet and concealed her body. But Vanger is having none of this, and raises a host of objections, principally relating to the timing of the girl's disappearance. There is a photograph, taken during the Children's Day parade which appears to show Harriet two hours before she disappears. And there is an even more intriguing photograph: Vanger finds a picture of his brother Harald, who is seen pointing at something behind the wreckage of the car.

The evidence suggests that Harald spent the afternoon on the bridge. But then Blomkvist is shown a picture of a house, and it is pointed out to him that a window on the second floor is Harriet's room. In the preceding pictures in the sequence it is open, then closed, and now it is open. Somebody has been in the girl's room. Blomkvist, however, is not convinced that this is important evidence, and the conclusion is that although the whereabouts of certain people can be identified at certain times, those who were not in the photographs should be placed in the line of fire regarding suspects. A theory is advanced: the killer opened the boot of a car and put the body of the murdered girl inside. Despite all the assiduous checking of shorelines, etc, nobody was checking cars. And by the next night it would have been possible to spirit the body away. Blomkvist points out that this would have been the action of a 'cold-blooded bastard', to which Vanger replies that this is a fairly accurate description of several members of his family. As Vanger continues his entreaties that Blomkvist track down the killer of Harriet, it's clear that Larsson is prepared to take his time – and risk straining reader's patience – with regard to this piece of exposition.

A basic situation that might have been set out by other authors in a much shorter time is still being treated at length. But such is Larsson's skill that we remain gripped, even though the narrative is not advancing in any significant way. There is, of course, the issue of Salander and the other investigation being undertaken – Larsson is well aware that we will not have forgotten that. He takes us back to his female protagonist, parking a car by a railway station in Sundbyberg. It's a car she's borrowed from her employers, Milton Securities' fleet of vehicles and (true to form) for which she has not requested permission.

She is calling on a contact. The door opens on a darkened apartment and she greets its occupant, saying, 'Hi, Plague.' The reply is 'Wasp,' with a sardonic remark that she only calls when she needs something. She is visiting a man three years older than herself, and consistent with her lack of social graces she points out his lack of physical freshness, commenting that the apartment smells like a monkey house. His reply that he is socially incompetent amuses her, but she hands him 5000 kronor and explains the reason she is there: she's after an electronic cuff that he mentioned some months ago. She examines the cuff and the author knows we will be wondering what this strange object is for.

Larsson then cuts back to the island and Blomkvist's interrogation by Vanger who tells him that in 1967, a year after Harriet disappeared, he received a flower on his birthday – a violet, which arrived in a padded envelope with no return address or message, adding that the same strange gesture has happened on his birthday every year since.

Vanger then delivers his ace-in-the-hole for persuading Blomkvist to investigate the disappearance of Harriet by offering something that the journalist wants more than anything else. He tells Blomkvist he can deliver to him his nemesis, Hans-Erik Wennerström, and points out that he can prove that he is a swindler if Blomkvist is prepared to solve the mystery of the disappearance. It's a measure of Larsson's skill that when he next cuts to Erika and Christer Malm discussing the future of the magazine *Millennium* with an unhappy Blomkvist present, this acrimonious discussion is as interesting as the two principal plot engines. Blomkvist is repeating that he has not given up on *Millennium*, and that the magazine is still immensely important to him. But he will, he says, be on a leave of absence. Erika though, points out that she and Christer will not be able to carry the workload, but Blomkvist counters that he is not really functioning anymore and that he is, in effect, burnt out.

It is difficult not to try to read Blomkvist's comment as a possible reflection on Larsson's own life. It was, after all, by common consent the view that the author's immense workload – combined with his unhealthy lifestyle – contributed to his death, and he was too intelligent a man not to realise the necessity of recharging one's batteries (even if he was not prepared to take that advice himself). Blomkvist tries to persuade his partners that the commission is a way of getting to Wennerström, but Erika continues to argue with him. In this discussion, Larsson reminds the reader how good he is at characterising his female protagonists: Erika is not simply there to advance the plot, but she is a plausible and well-rounded character in her own right, with her own reasons for dissuading her sometime lover from his course of action.

The first section of the book ends with a discussion between Armansky and Salander, after Lisbeth is woken by her boss at one o'clock in the afternoon from a deep sleep. He tells her that their client, the lawyer Frode, has instructed them to drop the investigation of Wennerström. She objects that she has only just begun working on the assignment, but is told that the client is no longer interested. They will be paid, but Salander asks what should be done with the material that she has gathered – which, as she admits, contains nothing significant. She is told that she can either shelve it or destroy it, and that there will be a new job for her shortly. The reader, however, will not be surprised to learn that she is not persuaded by this. She is not the kind of woman to drop an assignment she has begun, and the section ends with her conclusion (in italics) that people always have secrets – secrets that can always be ascertained.

Part Two of *The Girl with the Dragon Tattoo* begins with a forbidding superscription: 'CONSEQUENCE ANALYSES' and a telling statistic (relating to the original Swedish title of the book, changed for non-Swedish readers) that '46% of the women in Sweden have been subjected to violence by a man'. This is, of course, one of the most notable motivating factors in the book, and by encapsulating his rage at this situation within the context of a popular genre novel, Larsson makes his points more effectively than a dozen journalistic pieces.

Blomkvist arrives at Hedestad for the second time to a pastel blue sky and a freezing cold atmosphere. This time there is no heated car to greet him and he is obliged to manhandle his two ungainly suitcases to a taxi stand. Everything is covered in snow, and the non-Scandinavian reader is firmly within the territory that they associate with crime fiction from this part of the world – that's to say, a certain frigidity, both physical and (in the case of many of the characters) emotional.

Vanger greets Blomkvist dressed in a heavy fur coat. The journalist is told that he has to be a little more prepared for the weather in this part of the world, and an interesting tactic is employed by Larsson here: although Blomkvist is the same nationality as those around him, he has become a visitor to this part of society and is now something of a conduit for the reader. He is shown the guesthouse, which is comfortable and well-equipped, although he is warned that it can be very cold. A telephone has been ordered for him, to be installed shortly. It's then pointed out that Blomkvist's neighbour is Gunnar Nilsson, the caretaker (although the latter is more of a superintendent for all the buildings on the island and even some on the nearby islands). Blomkvist is reminded that the explanation for his presence is that he is here to write Vanger's autobiography, and that the actual assignment will remain a secret between Blomkvist, Vanger and Dirch Frode.

Vanger takes him to a nearby crossroads and gestures towards an ancient fishing harbour now used by non-fishing boats. Blomkvist is by now extremely cold, but listens attentively as the various inhabitants are described to him, including the elderly painter Eugen Norman, whom Vanger portrays as a painter of rather kitschy canvases. As the various houses in the village are pointed out, the reader is obliged to pay attention, as so often in the *Millennium Trilogy* – it's clear that information imparted here will become significant later. The house which is closest to the Vanger estate belongs to Henrik's brother Harald, and it initially appears to have no occupants, although footprints in the snow give the lie to that impression. Blomkvist is told that Harald is reclusive and has always been at loggerheads with his brother.

In fact, it appears that the two brothers have hardly spoken to each other for the last six decades – Harald is 92 and the only one of Vanger's four brothers still alive. They find each other abhorrent. The house adjoining Harald's is that of Isabella, the mother of the missing girl, Harriet. Isabella, Blomkvist is told, will be 75 this year but is still strikingly soignée, and as conscious of her looks as ever. The journalist enquires about her relationship with her daughter, and Vanger says that the two women were not close, but were not opposed.

Once again we have the post-modern take on the crime novel (of the kind we are reading) signalled by the fact that Vanger points out that the women are obliged to be included among the suspects. Isabella's neighbour is Cecilia, who is the reclusive Harald's daughter, separated from her husband and given the house by Vanger. She is a teacher, and Vanger's indulgence towards her is underlined by the fact that she only occasionally speaks to her father. She was 20 on the day that Harriet disappeared, and Vanger says that she is the one of his relatives of whom he is most fond. Blomkvist, ever inquisitive, asks if this means that Vanger considers her to be above suspicion, but he is told that Blomkvist must make up his own mind. Finally, Blomkvist is shown the house where Harriet's brother Martin lives. Martin, we are reminded, is the CEO of the Vanger Corporation.

In the final building on the east side of the road resides Gerda Vanger, the widow of Henrik's brother Greger, and her son Alexander. She is described as sickly and suffering from rheumatism. At this point (as often in the sequence of the book) the reader is struggling to take in the host of information that has been imparted, and – no doubt sensing this – Larsson has Blomkvist say that he is prepared to write the autobiography but he wants Vanger to remember that he is not a private detective. The reply is that nothing is expected, but neither the reader, nor Blomkvist, believes this. Vanger is reminded that prison is an option for the disgraced writer, but that Blomkvist will be prepared to work on the book (and his actual assignment) in prison but he points out to Vanger that he is the part owner of *Millennium* which is now in something of a crisis. Vanger demonstrates both sides of his personality by offering to help out on the magazine, but reminding Blomkvist in no uncertain fashion that if he discovers he is not doing the work he is being paid for he will consider it a breach of contract.

Blomkvist returns to the guesthouse, shivering with the cold, having asked for the files about Harriet to be sent over. We are then given an atmospherically written rendering of life on the island for Blomkvist with its cold, its regimented routine, and his reactions to things such as the muted clang of the church bell. He tries unsuccessfully to contact Erika, but goes to sleep and wakes to complete silence – a novel experience for him. He decides to take a bus to Hedestad and obtains a library card before borrowing two mystery books by Elizabeth George. Readers might wonder if this reference to one of the possible inspirations for Larsson is a good idea – is it a nod of the head by the author to crime novels he has enjoyed? (A trick repeated elsewhere in the novel by several references to Val McDermid.) After all, is it likely that such a rigorous investigative journalist would muddy the waters by spending his time reading fictional mysteries? Any such objections might be put to rest by the fact that with such a demanding task ahead of him, it is likely that Blomkvist would seek out some kind of relaxation. And why not that of his creator?

Back on the island he has a visitor, a blonde woman perhaps in her fifties, knocking on the kitchen door. She is Helena Nilsson who has come to introduce herself to her new neighbour. Her husband, Gunnar, and Henrik arrive with some boxes for him in a wheelbarrow. Blomkvist notices that the couple do not appear to be curious about his job there, and when he is alone he begins to investigate the contents of the boxes. The largest amount of space is taken up by 26 binders which are copies of the police investigation, but there are scrapbooks, albums of photographs, maps and much other documentary material including binders with information on members of the Vanger family. He starts reading through them, his efforts disturbed only by the appearance of a cat, which he discovers is to be his companion. He tries to contact Erika again but fails, and at midnight takes a walk across the bridge in the icy cold.

Again Larsson shows his skill by taking us into the inner

life of his investigator. By this point, having been seduced into the investigation (it's a cliché of the genre that the detective figure often has to be persuaded to take on a case – a cliché that Larsson confronts authoritatively in these books), Blomkvist is now feeling depressed and is wondering why he has taken on such an intractable assignment and why he is not in bed with Erika Berger in Stockholm, working out how he is to deal with Wennerström again.

We are given in successive pages the details of life on the island, and it's a measure of the author's skills that these remain as interesting as the investigation itself (which is put on the back burner for several pages). He returns to the documents detailing the police reports, and comes across references to a Detective Inspector Gustaf Morell who arrived at Hedeby by boat and took command of the investigation into Harriet's disappearance, interviewing a variety of people. We hear in more detail some of the information that has already been imparted to us earlier in the book, including details of a search party organised while it is still daylight (it is, as we know, a search that bears no results). Interestingly, even though we are with Blomkvist reading these reports containing information – some of which we already know – they remain interesting, and we struggle to discern significant facts, just as the protagonist does. Blomkvist notes a tone of frustration in the official notes when the search is called off and Vanger's lengthy period of torment has begun.

Chapter 9 begins with Blomkvist getting up late on Epiphany Day. He calls upon Vanger, but is greeted by an overweight man who resembles his employer. It is Martin Vanger who welcomes him to Hedestad and already appears to be acquainted with the cover story (i.e. that Blomkvist is writing the family chronicle). He hurries away and Blomkvist finds his employer chuckling over an item in the paper which comprehensively sticks the knife into *Millennium* magazine ('The editor in chief is a feminist who wears miniskirts and pouts her lips on TV'). There is also a dig at Blomkvist, using the 'Kalle' nickname that he so dislikes. He is still touchy about this issue and is unable to treat the matter as lightly as Vanger, who tells him that it's never a good idea to get into a fight that you are sure to lose.

We now switch to Salander, who is calling on the advocate Nils Bjurman. What follows is, in plot terms, quite as significant as anything involving Blomkvist – but Larsson is careful not to intimate too early quite how crucial the episode (and its incendiary consequences) will be in the context of the novel. We learn that Salander is under social and psychiatric guardianship, and Bjurman is her new contact. In another of Larsson's characteristically sharp pieces of background-filling we are told that Salander has been assigned to this treatment by the court for 12 years, based on the fact that she is clearly emotionally disturbed and has demonstrated violence towards her classmates; she may also be dangerous to herself.

This reference to the latent violence in Salander is something of a heads-up to the reader from the author – a harbinger of spectacularly shocking developments later in the trilogy. We also see her difficulties in relating to any authority figure, particularly in regard to any discussion of her emotional state of being. Her body language is confrontational, with folded arms and a steadfast resistance to any kind of psychological tests. Those who have attempted to deal with her have found her impossible to handle, although at the age of 15 it was concluded that she is not dangerously violent or particularly given to self-harming. But she nevertheless has a history of problems with the police, having been arrested several times when drunk, once with her clothes in disarray with a drunken (and much older) male companion. The last arrest, we are told, involved an assault on a male passenger at a railway station; her defence is that the man made sexual advances to her. There are witnesses to support this, but her troubled background (and psychiatric problems) means that the court has ordered a psychiatric evaluation which, of course, Salander refuses.

The details of the hearing are conveyed with understanding and sympathy by Larsson, and it is made clear to the reader that the author will always be on the side of the misunderstood and alienated members of society, in his fiction as in his life. This, of course, may be said to be a characteristic of crime and thriller writers of the Left (less evident in those of a more right-wing persuasion), but that's not to say that left-wing readers will not occasionally be furious with Salander – despite the sympathy that Larsson extends to her, she is still an infuriating figure and a severe test of left/liberal indulgence in such areas. In fact, it might be argued that the books could be said to reinforce certain right-wing prejudices against those on the fringes of society rather than making a persuasive case for them.

Salander's original counsellor, Palmgren, somehow managed to get past her resistance and succeeded in helping her, but dealing with Bjurman is a different ball game. He is far less sympathetic and considers that Salander has been allowed free rein to behave as she liked. As she is lectured by him, she conducts an inward colloquy with herself, which Larsson describes in italics ('*I've taken care of myself since I was ten, you creep!*'). She is asked about her duties at Milton Security, and lies about the extent of the trust that has been invested in her. Given the immensely complicated filigrees of influence shown by her in dealing with her enemies later in the trilogy, this kind of lying is subsequently to prove a good idea – although the reader does not know it at this point.

Blomkvist, meanwhile, is hitting something of a dead end and becoming aware that the suggestion that he can arrive at a conclusion is actually beyond reasonable common sense. He looks into inheritance laws and the complicated arrangements involving the sale of shares – and at this point Larsson provides us with a breakdown table of the convoluted Vanger family tree.

This is perhaps another point at which faint-hearted readers may fall away. Certainly, some people have responded to this forensically detailed information by saying 'How much of this do we really need to bear in mind?' In fact, the answer is: not very much – but not because we will be reminded of the relevant information later (although we will) but because, as with Raymond Chandler, another narrative as significant as the one we appear to be addressing will assume centre stage.

We are reminded of the importance of the internet in this part of the narrative when Blomkvist opens his e-mail to find nearly 350 messages, the first of which is a series of obscene insults (he files it under 'intelligent criticism'). After putting Erika's mind to rest about his new situation, he continues his forensic examination of the Vanger family. What follows, again, is perhaps more detailed than casual readers may like, but it's undoubtedly true that those who fall under the spell of the Larsson books realise that they will be obliged to deal with a great amount of information (and, in fact, the sifting of that information is part of the pleasure of the books).

At the end of Blomkvist's first month in the country (detailed in Chapter 10) he learns that this was the coldest in recorded memory and is now learning to equip himself with long underwear and woolly socks. The pipes are freezing, but Mikael has some compensations: he is beginning to know the people in Hedeby and spends what turns out to be a pleasant, drink-fuelled evening with Martin who, it would appear, has swallowed the story of Blomkvist's writing the family chronicle. But the journalist has a significant meeting with a blonde woman who introduces herself as Cecilia Vanger. She has been told about the book he is putatively writing. She makes it clear that she is fully aware of the ill feeling in the family and wants to know if she will be obliged to go into exile when the book is published. When Blomkvist replies that people will be able to tell the 'sheep from the goats', she asks where her father is in this equation. 'Your father the famous Nazi?' Blomkvist replies. But she is not to be drawn into anger by this. She acknowledges that her father is insane and she only sees him a few times a year. She tells him that she is headmistress of a preparatory school and asks how much the book will deal with Harriet.

In terms of Larsson's attention to structure and character, it's interesting to note that it is halfway through the book before one of his subjects appears to have caught on to his real agenda – and it's a woman who canny readers may spot as possibly assuming some importance as the narrative moves on. Cecilia makes it clear that she knows Blomkvist is really there to investigate Harriet's disappearance. Larsson has her arrive at this conclusion by simply observing the way he has been behaving – but she points to the fact that the mystery has poisoned the lives of the family for many years and that she considers the disappearance an 'accident'. By now, readers will realise that Larsson is happy to draw parallels with the aspects of popular culture that have inspired him, and likens the meeting with the chilly Isabella Vanger (Harriet's mother) to a meeting with Lauren Bacall. Interestingly, however, this is not the Lauren Bacall of such Humphrey Bogart/Howard Hawks movies as *The Big Sleep*, but the later, more mature actress, as seen in the Paul Newman 1966 film version of Ross MacDonald's *The Moving Target*: the meeting in the book seems to owe something to that memorable scene, with Bacall as a frosty matron.

The unsympathetic Isabella makes no secret of her hostility to Blomkvist's snooping in the family affairs and makes it clear that he is to stay away from her. Of course, one of the 'ticking clocks' in the narrative is the fact that Blomkvist will soon be obliged to spend three months in prison, and he requests that his lawyer find out when this is to happen. He is told that he must present himself at a minimum security prison on 17 March, but is reassured that the sentence may be curtailed. We are told that Blomkvist meets his employer at least once a day for brief conversations in which the journalist posits theories that Vanger then disproves. In his own private time, the Wennerström affair hangs over him like the proverbial Damoclean sword, and he wonders if he is likely to become obsessive.

Blomkvist has a meeting with Erika Berger, but it's an inconclusive one which ends with the couple going to bed. Up to this point in the novel the treatment of sex has been extremely discreet, so those readers perfectly happy with novelists who stop at the bedroom door may have been nonplussed by what is to follow later in the trilogy; certainly discretion is rather waived.

Larsson now takes us back to Lisbeth Salander's third meeting with the unpleasant Advokat Bjurman at which (to continue the notion of sexuality mentioned in the previous paragraph) she is asked about her sex life. She has not the slightest intention of discussing this with him, however, answering such questions as 'Who takes the initiative – you or him' succinctly ('I do,' she replies). As the questions become more invasive, she observes that her counsellor is becoming a potential major problem. At this point in the novel we have not been fully appraised as to what Salander does when dealing with 'major problems', so our apprehension is vague.

Blomkvist and lover/colleague Erika Berger find themselves on the receiving end of Vanger's generosity when he acts on an earlier suggestion and offers to become a partner in their ailing magazine. Meanwhile Blomkvist is making some advances in his investigation: it would appear that, shortly before her disappearance, Harriet Vanger had undergone a change of personality, becoming more withdrawn and uncommunicative. She had been a Christian (without any great enthusiasm) but seemed to turn towards a much more openly pious form of religion. She did not, however, visit Hedeby Island's pastor Otto Falk but attended a more demonstrative Pentecostal church in Hedestad.

Blomkvist notes that Inspector Morell had observed that Harriet's address book contained five names (some of which are initials) and telephone numbers, belonging to a variety of different people, but there is no obvious link between the names.

We are now nearly halfway through the narrative, and readers who had no preliminary idea that Lisbeth Salander was to become a central figure might have been lulled into a sense of her relative lack of importance. Her laptop has been damaged, and she is persuaded that she needs a new machine – one that costs 38,000 kronor. She realises that she needs the approval of a man she actively dislikes – her new guardian Bjurman – to obtain money for this unprecedented expense. She is told to be at his office that evening. It will be a fateful meeting, we are to learn.

But before this encounter we are taken back to the narrative involving Blomkvist, who has called on the intriguing Cecilia Vanger. She proves once again her intense perception by listing virtually everything that has happened to him and why she thinks he is on the island. He finds that he has taken a liking to her, particularly to her humorous response to him telling her that he has the odd sexual encounter with Erika, the editor-in-chief of *Millennium*. Here we see the syndrome which will be firmly established in the course of the novel, which is Blomkvist's consistent (and prodigious) good luck with women. Soon, Cecilia is sitting astride him, kissing him on the mouth as he opens her flannel shirt. And we learn that the sexual encounters in the novels will become more explicit and more frequent.

It is as if the sexual floodgates have opened. Larsson cuts straight from Blomkvist's consensual tryst with Cecilia to a very different sexual encounter: Bjurman is groping Lisbeth as she shows him the statement of her bank account. As so often with the sexual abuse of women in the *Millennium Trilogy*, Larsson could rival such furious feminist writers as Marilyn French in terms of conveying a marked disgust with male sexuality. He is even-handed, but for many readers (both male and female) his position on these issues remains a striking (and multi-faceted) one in the way that it is rendered in his novels.

Salander allows the sexual assault (which mainly consists of Bjurman pressing himself against her) to come to a sordid conclusion, but the alert reader will realise that there is a price to be paid. When she reminds her assailant that she requires money for her computer, he hands her a cheque thinking 'This is better than a whore. She gets paid with her own money.' And we encounter for the first time (but not for the last) a truly unpleasant view of a certain kind of male predatoriness. It's uncomfortable reading, whatever the sex of the reader.

The following chapter (Chapter 12) details Salander's dispassionate examination of the sexual assault that has just happened to her – and the concomitant lack of control she has undergone (albeit knowingly) but she finds that she is now obliged to take seriously, for the first time, her legal status in regard to her guardian – something she did not do when the more benign Palmgren fulfilled that role. Larsson then takes us back to the origins of Lisbeth's violence towards men (as usual, it is a response to attacks on her): having been attacked by a boy at school she lay in wait for her attacker with a rounders bat and hit him over the ear with it. She pays the price but it is an indicator of the fact that she is not to be messed with, something the reader will learn – in no uncertain terms – as the book progresses.

Blomkvist, meanwhile, is learning about Cecilia's jaundiced view of her own family, and we are also reminded of the possible wish-fulfilment element in the novel when Cecilia says to him, 'To be honest, I have been wondering how you would be in bed ever since I first saw you.'

In the next section it becomes clear (to any reader who still thought that Blomkvist was the sole important protagonist in the novel) that Lisbeth is quite as important – if not more so. As she muses on the sexual abuse she has received, we are told that her sexual encounters are usually at her own initiative, and that she has had over 50 partners since her teenage years. For her, sex is an enjoyable pastime – as long as it is on her own terms. And if sex is used as a weapon against her, we learn, she is prepared to take matters into her own hands to solve her problems. The auguries are not good for Herr Advokat Nils Bjurman.

We now begin a relentless parallel investigation, in which Salander acts as her own client with Bjurman as her target. She investigates with tremendous thoroughness (as one might expect) but Bjurman is a difficult nut to crack, inasmuch as his reputation appears to be without blemish. He has regularly acted as a supervisor for youths, but there appears to be no evidence that he has exploited those in his care. Salander knows, as she puts it, that he was a 'creep' and a 'pig', but she can find nothing to prove it.

Meanwhile, Blomkvist's affair with the headmistress Cecilia Vanger is being conducted with great discretion. At the same time, he is professional enough to keep asking her about the family. But the secondary plot of the novel is moving in alarming ways. Salander has decided that Bjurman must die, but in such a way that she cannot be linked to the crime – particularly with her own low standing, as detailed in a variety of reports. She considers using a bomb, and locked in her murderous thoughts, turns down her employer when he has another job for her. She then considers poisons such as prussic acid and even extracting from a carton of cigarettes enough nicotine to act as a lethal substance.

At this point Blomkvist, who is making only tentative progress on the island (possibly because of the sexual distractions at hand), is pursuing a variety of leads but without much success. It's clear that Larsson knows reader attention will have shifted to the more visceral plot involving Salander. She arrives at her assailant's flat, and his cynical assumption is that she requires more money. In a scene that is difficult to read, she makes her way to the bed but provokes him into hitting her. Things are not going well, she realises, as her T-shirt is being torn, and that he is reaching for handcuffs in a drawer near the bed. What follows is an excruciating description of forced anal sex. Even readers who baulked at the fact that Bjurman had to die (however unpleasant the first sexual encounter between the two was) will be persuaded that whatever Salander does – and it is clear that she will do something – will be justified.

To some degree, Larsson is in tune with the feminist writers of an earlier era whose attitude to male sexuality often evoked violence and violation as part of the experience. What is different here, of course, is the fact that the author counterpoints the negative sexual experiences that Salander is forced to suffer with the pleasant, consensual ones between Blomkvist and his new love – in fact, Larsson cuts from Salander's anal rape to the affectionate post-coital conversation between Blomkvist and Cecilia, as if to remind the reader that sex need not be as unpleasant as it has been for Salander.

At the beginning of Chapter 14, Larsson ensures that if we have not acquired sufficient revulsion from the sexual assault in the preceding chapter, we will certainly be provided with it now. Salander spends the week in bed, bleeding from the rectum and with stomach pains and other wounds. As the author puts it, she is now the victim of systematic brutality. She has also been made aware that she may well have died during the night she has just suffered, but the fact that she does not shed a tear gives some indication of the concentration of feeling – and resolve – which is to power her actions. What she does, in fact, is to have another tattoo added to those she already possesses, this time a band on her ankle. It is, she tells the tattooist, a reminder.

One of the things that Larsson is particularly adroit at is the springing of the unexpected on the reader. The speed with which Salander turns up at Bjurman's apartment, and the brevity with which the first stage of her revenge is enacted, both take the reader by surprise. She is leading Bjurman towards the bed – he is under the impression that she is sufficiently cowed – when she suddenly pushes a Taser into his armpit and discharges 75,000 volts. As he loses the use of his legs, she pushes him onto the bed. At that point, Larsson does something which we are to learn is one of his most canny tricks. The reader may want to continue reading in horrified fascination the violent events we have just been party to, but Larsson (audaciously) decides instead to develop the character of Cecilia Vanger a little more, as she drinks a bottle of wine alone and muses on her new lover, and her relationship with her father. We learn that her own marriage had ended with domestic violence: consistent abuse, violent blows to the head and being knocked to the floor. Even concerning what may be seen as a secondary character, the central motif of the novel is implacably played out.

But then Larsson takes us back to Bjurman, lying naked on the bed, handcuffed. Salander has placed an anal plug between his buttocks, and she tells him that she has found his 'toys': a riding whip and other paraphernalia are spread out on the floor. But the most surprising object in the room is the massive TV and DVD player. Using recordings she has made of the sexual assaults on her, Salander tells him that he will be looking at a DVD showing him raping a 'handicapped' 24-year-old girl (herself, of course) for whom he was appointed guardian. She will now, she tells him, be the only one to have access to her bank account. His reports on her welfare should be written as positive and upbeat. And if he ever tries to contact her again, the copies of the DVD will be sent to every newsroom in Stockholm.

She reads a list of other requirements, but the spread-eagled Bjurman is already thinking that some time – some way – he will manage to obtain the incriminating DVD. But then she climbs upon him, grasping a needle. Salander tattoos him with words that cover his stomach from his chest to his genitals: 'I AM A SADISTIC PIG, A PERVERT AND A RAPIST.' It's a measure of the lengths to which Salander will go to avenge herself.

Salander turns up once again at Armansky's office and he remarks on the fact that she has been incommunicado for so long. But the two hear a report on the radio about the fact that the magazine *Millennium* will have a part-owner, Henrik Vanger, and that Blomkvist will once again be publisher after he has finished his prison sentence. 'Well, isn't that something,' says Salander, and the reader realises that after what appears to be a diversion, we are back onto the main plot. In fact, of course, the main plot principally involves the abuse of Salander and at this point, almost halfway through the novel, we may be said to have had its parameters laid out before us. Or have we? At home,

Salander marshals her facts: the lawyer from Hedestad has hired her to investigate Blomkvist, a man given a jail sentence for a libel against the all-powerful Hans-Erik Wennerström. Subsequently, Vanger joins Blomkvist's magazine as a financial partner and talks about a conspiracy to destroy *Millennium*. And – with what we will soon learn is her customary prescience – she has discovered that Wennerström worked in the Vanger corporation in the 1960s. There are multiple skeletons in a host of cupboards which Salander then decides to investigate.

Part Three of *The Girl with the Dragon Tattoo* is called 'Mergers', and once again has a superscription relating to a particular concern of the author's: '13% of the women in Sweden have been subjected to aggravated sexual assault outside of a sexual relationship'. By now, of course, readers will have realised that this is a crucial leitmotif of the novel, and it will feature once again in a significant fashion. This section of the book begins with Blomkvist being released from prison on Friday 16 May, some two months after his incarceration. As had been predicted, a recommendation was made for a reduction of his sentence, and his period in prison had been pleasant enough (a lesser novelist might have made this section harrowing simply to increase the pressure points on the reader, but it is refreshing that Larsson treats this in a realistic fashion). His protagonist returns to the cabin in Hedeby, joined by the cat that adopted him previously. Meeting Vanger again, he asks him how it feels to be involved with the magazine, and his elderly employer tells him that he is actually having fun doing it.

When Blomkvist leaves Vanger, it is dark but he senses that spring is near. We are reminded again of the author's skills at evoking atmosphere, season and locale. Unsurprisingly, Blomkvist makes his way to the door of his new lover Cecilia Vanger's home. But instead of the warm welcome he expects, she seems not particularly pleased to see him and asks him to leave without offering an explanation. He had, before his incarceration, returned the Vanger documentation on Harriet, as he did not wish to leave it in a deserted house. But looking at the remaining reports, he finds that he is reading them again and looking at photographs which had been taken on the day the young girl disappeared. Something strikes him. He is looking at a young Henrik Vanger and a young Harald (he has still not met the latter, reclusive figure) but in the crowd of onlookers he notices a young woman in a light-coloured dress. It is Cecilia.

Some time later, Cecilia herself arrives at his door and says that she has decided to tell him the reason for his unwelcoming reception earlier. She informs him that she has had only had five sexual partners in her life and that the period when he began his imprisonment was a desperately unhappy one for her. She found herself an old maid in her fifties again.

In all the best crime and thriller novels, of course, the personal element has a way of intervening and derailing the probing of the detective/investigative figures. It happens to Blomkvist when Erika Berger turns up and finds Blomkvist in bed with Cecilia Vanger. Needless to say, she doesn't take it well, and despite his attempts to defend his position, he finds himself on the back foot. There is an uncomfortable dinner, at which are present Vanger, Erika, Blomkvist and Cecilia; the conversation stays on the relatively safe territory of *Millennium*'s development and the new subscribers it has managed to attain. Blomkvist decides to tell Cecilia that he has spotted something in a photograph album, but does not elucidate.

Blomkvist continues his investigations, including a search through Gottfried's cabin – and it's here that we get another of the references to the crime fiction that Larsson is so enamoured of. In fact, the reference is to Mickey Spillane's 'thick-ear' novel, *Kiss Me Deadly*, and Larsson mentions the (as he puts it) classic covers by Bertil Hegland, an illustrator not known to British and American readers. Surprisingly, Larsson also references another celebrated mystery series, the *Famous Five* novels by Enid Blyton and, of course, books by Astrid Lindgren, including *Pippi Longstocking* – a book, which as we now know, figures in the background to the trilogy we are reading. He finds Harriet Vanger's confirmation Bible and wonders if this was a place which she tried to imagine (during her period of religious brooding) had the feeling of a convent. He subsequently tells Cecilia that their relationship is becoming a little complicated for him and asks if she would be prepared to leave him in peace for a while.

If the reader is now a little impatient for momentum in the plot, Larsson has been cannily withholding it until Chapter 16, when we are told that the case of Harriet Vanger 'cracked' when Blomkvist managed to piece together new aspects of the mystery. One involves the last photograph taken of Harriet while she had been watching the Children's Day parade. The wide-angle lens has included the front of one of the floats featuring clowns and other figures. Harriet's gaze is settled upon something, which Blomkvist examines with a magnifying glass. He takes the photograph to the building from which it was taken, and finds that it is a shop. He asks the proprietor if he might see the view that she saw on the day. He then discovers what he says is 'new evidence'.

He realises that the chain of events leading to Harriet's disappearance has begun earlier, when she saw something or someone that disturbed her. Larsson again utilises the careful 'parcelling out' of clues to construct an accretion of detail.

Later he asks Vanger whether or not the family still has an interest in the *Hedestad Courier* and requests access to the photographic archives from 1966. What he discovers (after lengthy investigations of the archives) is that Harriet is observing the blurred face of a woman – though it is impossible to make out the features. He works out her height in relation to the window. She was about 5ft 7in. Again, the facts point to the 20-year-old Cecilia Vanger. Blomkvist is now convinced that Harriet has seen something which has shocked her – she attempted to talk to Vanger about what she has seen, but the meeting was not destined to happen. She subsequently vanished, never to be seen again. A classic piece of jigsaw-puzzle plotting.

Harald Vanger accosts him, saying that his 'whore isn't home'. Blomkvist shouts back that this unpleasant man is talking about his own daughter but from this conversation he learns from Vanger that Cecilia has had a striking sexual history: her lovers include a man called Peter Samuelsson, a financial assistant for the Vanger Corporation. This individual is the reason for Harald's splenetic hatred of his daughter, as he has discovered that her lover is Jewish – and we are given another emblem of Harald's unpleasantness (as Larsson would expect readers to perceive it).

Looking once again at the evidence involving Harriet, he finds a series of particularly bloodthirsty quotations in her Bible (including, from Leviticus, 'And the daughter of any priest, if she profanes herself by playing the harlot, profanes her father; she shall be burned with fire.'). Biblical quotations, of course, are always bad news in the lexicon of crime fiction. At this point, as the pace of the revelations begins to increase, the reader is pleasurably thrown into unexpected territory by Larsson. *Millennium*'s new partner (and Blomkvist's employer) Henrik Vanger has had a serious heart attack. Blomkvist visits the lawyer Frode and is told that the old man is alive but not doing well in intensive care. Frode assures him that the terms of his conditions do not change. Blomkvist says that he has found a connection with the murder of Rebecka Jacobsson in 1949, and that the murder of this girl appears to have something to do with Harriet's disappearance – she has written her initials in her date book alongside the references to Old Testament quotations concerning burnt offerings.

Rebecka Jacobsson was burnt to death – and she worked for the Vanger Corporation. Frode asks if there is a connection with Harriet that can be explained, but Blomkvist says that he has not deduced this yet. Blomkvist has decided to follow up the photographic lead and try to find out what it was that Harriet saw, but in order to research all the information he will need an expert research assistant. At this point, nearly 300 pages into the novel, Frode utters the words which will ultimately bring the two protagonists together: 'Actually I believe I know of an expert researcher... She was the one who did the background investigation on you.'

Blomkvist insists on seeing Lisbeth Salander's report and finds it a strange, unsettling experience. As a journalist himself, he notes that Salander is clearly, as he puts it, 'one hell of an investigator' and he realises that she has information that can only have been obtained by entering his computer. He says aloud, 'You're a fucking hacker.'

It has been some time since Larsson has allowed the reader into the company of Lisbeth Salander, but as usual, when he does the results are always fascinating. She has gone to bed with a woman, Mimmi, and this leads her to think about her own sexuality. She has, apparently, never thought of herself as a lesbian or even, for that matter, bisexual – this is all of a part with her rejection of labels of any kind (not a rejection her creator shares). Her problem with men has been finding those who can attend to her sexual needs but not be 'creeps' afterwards – a combination she is finding difficult to accept.

Her doorbell rings, and at the door is a man who greets her cheerfully. It's Blomkvist, who has arrived with filled bagels for her breakfast; he has researched her preferences. She screams at him, saying she doesn't know who he is, but Blomkvist points out that she knows him better than almost anyone else – and what's more, he knows how she does it, he knows her secrets. She tells him that he should talk to her boss, but he points out that he has already had a conversation with Armansky. He then tells her, peremptorily, to have a shower. And finally, the two central characters in the *Millennium Trilogy* have met.

What follows is a fascinating colloquy between the two characters, full of interesting detail, such as the fact that Blomkvist is mildly disgusted by the less-than-hygienic fashion in which Salander lives. The dynamic of the relationship between the two is already intriguing, and while we are clearly looking at Salander through Blomkvist's eyes (inasmuch as he is the more open 'normal' character), it is her response to the conversation that fascinates us – particularly as we know that her responses can, as Americans say, 'turn on a dime'. Blomkvist asks about the job she has been employed to do and he tells her why he needs a skilled researcher for the assignment he has undertaken for Vanger. The initial commission was, she understands, for some historical research. But Blomkvist tells her – in no uncertain terms – that he wants her to help him identify a murderer.

He tells her all the details of the Vanger case and how he has identified the 'RJ' from the list in the date book as Rebecka Jacobsson. She asks if he considers all the other names in the list to be murder victims, and he replies that they may be looking for a killer who was active in the 1950s (and also the 1960s) and who is in some way linked to Harriet Vanger. She agrees to help but tells him that he must sign a contract with her boss, Armansky. On returning to the island Blomkvist finds that his cottage has been ransacked.

Salander is musing on her meeting with him. It is clear that he has to some degree got under her skin and she is reacting to him as she has done to so many males who had the upper hand in her past. But as he said, he was not there to blackmail her, only here to ask her to help. She could say 'yes' or 'no'. But the partnership is now a foregone conclusion – as Larsson knows readers will want it to be.

Blomkvist learns from Martin Vanger that Cecilia is very much against him continuing with his investigations. After he leaves, Blomkvist pours himself a drink and, as Larsson puts it, picks up his copy of a Val McDermid novel (another nod to an important influence on Larsson's work). While Blomkvist tries to identify a car with the AC plates, he finds himself getting closer to the mystery. Salander, too, an expert in methodology, is trying to track down the identity of the individuals who may have been killed by the unknown murderer. She finds that a Magda (one of the names in the list) is a name in a grisly killing in April 1960. She also finds that the subject had been subjected to a grim sexual assault and murdered with a pitchfork – and that one of the animals at the farm on which the killing took place suffered similar stab wounds.

Suspicion had fallen on a neighbour in the village, a young man accused of a homosexual crime, but Salander is bemused as to why a reputed homosexual would take part in a sex killing against a woman. As the duo begin to peel back more layers of the mystery, Blomkvist tells Frode that he is no longer convinced that Cecilia is central to the Harriet mystery, and is now looking at the emotionally cold Isabella. Inevitably, of course, Salander has to travel to Hedeby Island, and we are reminded once again that the novel began with an Agatha Christie-style murder in a cloistered setting. However, that was a springboard for the events that followed in which the rules of the classic English mystery have been shaken up and exploded. Now this highly unorthodox character is travelling to a crucial location. As Blomkvist sautés lamb chops for Salander, he finds himself sneaking glimpses of the tattoos on her back. Further suggestions that the relationship between the two will develop in some way.

She gives him a series of reports on the names on the list, all of which have been identified. After the first girl, Rebecka Jacobsson, there was a prostitute who was tied up and abused, with the cause of death being strangulation – a sanitary towel had been forced down her throat. Blomkvist finds the verse in Leviticus that reads, 'If a man lies with a woman having her sickness, and uncovers her nakedness, he has made naked her fountain, and she has uncovered the fountain of her blood; both of them shall be cut off from among their people.' It's clear to both Blomkvist and Salander that Harriet Vanger, in compiling the list, had made the same biblical connection. Other examples follow in which biblical allusions are found for the various murder victims. With the kind of plotting ingenuity which is characteristic of the trilogy, Larsson allows his characters to make connections between the names of the victims (and to cut a path through some obfuscation). They find a preponderance of traditional Jewish names and, of course, the Vanger family is noted for its passionate anti-Semites. Blomkvist remembers Harald Vanger standing in the road and shouting that his own daughter was a whore.

At this point, Blomkvist tells Salander that he considers the job she was hired for is finished. But, unsurprisingly, she replies, 'I'm not done with this.' She is now as dedicated to the extirpation of evil and the revelation of the mystery as Blomkvist – and we have a classic detective fiction trope: the end of an investigation is not the end of the narrative. But she tells him something significant in the context of both Larsson's preoccupation and the original Swedish title of the book: 'It's not an insane serial killer who read his Bible wrong. It's just a common or garden bastard who hates women.'

In Chapter 21, on the principle that a variety of threats and obstructions should be directed against his protagonists as a dramatic imperative, Larsson has Blomkvist subjected to a scurrilous attack on his journalism, but the journalist is more concerned by the revelation he has arrived at from the photo that he was tracking down: a blurred figure standing behind the spectators. It is a six-foot man with dark blond, long hair. The image is manipulated, but neither Blomkvist nor Salander is any closer to learning his identity. As the investigation progresses we are party to Lisbeth's thoughts, and once again Larsson renders these as more fascinating than those of his male protagonists (there is perhaps an echo of another Swedish arts icon here – Ingmar Bergman, who frequently demonstrated more sympathy with his female characters than his male protagonists). She is totally disconcerted by the fact that her new companion has reached further into the secrets of her personality than anyone she has encountered, and although her responses to him are positive, she is not happy with this.

Salander decides to do something which (although readers may have been coaxed into willing it by now) still slightly smacks of the wish-fulfilment element that many people have identified in the book. Salander makes her way to the room where Blomkvist is reading a novel by Sara Paretsky (one of the umpteen references to the crime fiction novelists who had inspired Larsson). She has a sheet wrapped around her body and stands in the doorway. She proceeds to the bed, takes the book from his hand and kisses him on the mouth. When he does not object, she leans across and bites him on the nipple. He tells her, pushing her away so that he can see her face, that he doesn't consider this move to be a good idea as they are working together. She replies, 'I want to have sex with you. And I won't have any problem working with you, but I will have a hell of a problem with you if you kick me out.' Blomkvist tells her he has no condoms. Her reply is, 'Screw it.'

In the celebrated series of crime and thriller novels (featuring a highly capable male and female duo) by Peter O'Donnell – whose protagonists are alpha female Modesty Blaise and her male sidekick Willy Garvin – O'Donnell was careful never to allow his hero and heroine to sleep together, considering that this would alter the dynamics of the relationship. Readers at this point might be forgiven for thinking the same thing of Larsson, but he knows exactly what he is doing – and this dynamic is to shift again on several occasions. As if to remind us that the novel is not about pleasing sexual encounters but about the coercive ones, soon after their tryst, the couple find the body of a cat which Blomkvist assumes has been left by somebody who knows about the work they are doing – and about the progress that they are making. Salander tells him that she is going into Stockholm to buy some gadgets. She at this point demonstrates that she is more ready to deal with violent attacks – and in a forceful way – than her male journalist companion.

The focus shifts to the pastor of the island, Otto Falk, who was 36 when Harriet Vanger vanished. He is now in his seventies, younger than the seriously ill Henrik Vanger but in a confused mental state and living in a convalescent home. When Blomkvist calls on him, Falk tells him that Harriet must read certain passages of scripture and that she needs guidance. Falk tells Blomkvist that she is looking for a forbidden truth and she is not a good Christian, before drifting off into his own confused state. Religious judgements (as in practically every crime writer, James Lee Burke apart) are, of course, a signifier of negativity and hypocrisy.

Blomkvist and Salander begin to make biblical connections with the Apocrypha, and we are reminded that another key character, Armansky, has a concern for Salander who he sees as a perfect victim – a victim who is tracking down an insane killer in a remote place. In the meantime, Blomkvist is attempting in vain to contact Cecilia Vanger and as further evidence of the fact that the duo are getting closer to the killer, Blomkvist, while crossing a field, is shot at and throws himself to the ground. He stumbles into a bush and takes the long way home where he encounters

Salander, telling her that he looks worse than he is (his face is smeared with congealed blood). Instructing her to stay where she is, Blomkvist makes his way to Cecilia Vanger's house and begins to ask her several questions: Where was she when he was shot? Why did she open the window of Harriet's room on the day she disappeared? She decides that she will give him answers, but tells him that it is not her in the photograph.

By now, Salander has started to install a variety of surveillance objects around the property, as it is clear that their lives are now on the line. She tells Blomkvist that Harriet had realised that there was a serial killer, someone they knew. Of the *dramatis personae* they have talked about here are at least 24 possible suspects but most of them are no longer around (except for Harald Vanger, who is now 93 and unlikely to be the marksman who attacked Blomkvist). Cecilia Vanger is seen in the photographs talking to Pastor Falk, and also with one of the Vanger brothers, Greger. He has a camera in his hand. It is starting to look as if some members of the family are pulling together to conceal a serial killer who may be one of the elder generation. But why the mutilated cat, an obvious reference to the killings? Interestingly, at this point – with the pace of the book accelerating and the reader aware that the last sixth of the text will deliver the revelations – Larsson allows a discussion between Blomkvist and Salander in which the latter reveals her self-loathing, calling herself a freak. It is another example of how the author has cannily realised that the characterisation of his protagonists is quite as important as the exigencies of the plot.

The couple make their way to Frode who is initially concerned by Blomkvist's damaged appearance. They tell him that a possibly insane killer has realised how close they are getting to the truth and they ask about corporation archives. Blomkvist is sent to Alexander Vanger who shows him a box of unsorted photographs. There are connections to the Swedish Nazi Party apparent in the photographs (more evidence of Larsson's own particular interests, but now comes a revelation of the kind outlawed in classical mystery solutions: the double). There is no question that Larsson would not have been aware of this stricture that crime writers placed upon themselves to avoid cheating, but he is clearly enjoying himself, bending the rules. It is not Cecilia Vanger in many of the pictures. There are two girls, and they are now seen in the same frame. It is her sister Anita, two years younger and living in London. They then identify the mysterious young man spotted earlier in the photographs. He is Martin Vanger.

Martin Vanger, an introverted child, had been stranded on the wrong side of the bridge on the fateful afternoon and was received by Vanger himself, among other people. But if he was undoubtedly on the wrong side of the water, how could he be in the significant photographs on the other side? At the same time, Salander has discovered that Gottfried Vanger had been situated where at least five of the eight killings were committed. The problem is that Gottfried had drowned while drunk in the 1960s, before the last murder was committed. It is pitch dark when Blomkvist walks towards Harald Vanger's house.

However, Blomkvist encounters not Harald but Martin Vanger standing in the dark. He says he has questions. Martin replies, 'I understand.' He hands him a key to a door and opens it. It is at this point that one remembers that novelists such as James Patterson ensure their readers keep turning to the next chapter by the choice of a sentence which means the reader cannot put the book down. Larsson at this point comes up with such a sentence: 'Blomkvist has opened the door to hell'. The author here takes us closest to the gruesome territory inhabited by writers such as his admired Val McDermid. It is a territory that when utilised by male writers has occasioned much criticism – and hardly less so when used by female writers such as McDermid (or even male writers with the correct feminist credentials, such as Larsson).

The space into which Blomkvist is ushered is a private torture chamber. On the left-hand side are chains and metal eyelets in the ceiling and the floor, a table on which (the reader presumes) luckless victims are strapped to have the most appalling horrors enacted upon them. And, chillingly, there is an array of video equipment. It is a taping studio. It is perhaps at this point that the reader remembers Lisbeth Salander, and why she is particularly good at dealing with the sinister nemeses she comes up against. Blomkvist is instructed to lie on the floor on his stomach. He refuses. Martin replies, 'Very well... Then I'll shoot you in the kneecap.' Blomkvist finds himself obliged to comply.

He is constantly thinking how he will deal with the nightmare situation he is now in. What begins is a period of intense pain as he is kicked and punched trying to protect his head and take the blows in the softer parts of his body. A half hour of this torment follows before Blomkvist has a chain put around his neck and is fastened to the floor via a metal eyelet. He asks why all the punching and kicking is necessary, but the relentless Martin replies that he should have gone back to *Millennium* magazine. His tormentor asks Blomkvist how he tracked him down ('You and that anorexic spook that you dragged into this'), and Blomkvist shocks his captor by telling him about murders that he knows he has committed, and attempts to bluff him that everything is over, that too many people know. Then Martin drops his bombshell: Lisbeth Salander is not going to rescue him, he knows exactly where she is, and a night watchman will tell him when she leaves.

This abrupt ending of Part Three, of course, ensures that very few readers will be able to put the book down before Part Four, which is called 'Hostile Takeover'. Once again a 'violence against women' superscription adorns the title page: '92% of women in Sweden who have been subjected to sexual assault have not reported the most recent violent incident to the police'. Surprisingly, Part Four picks up exactly where the preceding part ended, with Blomkvist chained to the floor by his tormentor Martin Vanger – tantalisingly Larsson perhaps guessing we'll expect him to defer the resolution of the climax. Blomkvist asks the murderer why he acts as he does – and why he has this chamber of horrors, indicating the torture chamber around him. Martin replies that it's easy – that women who nobody misses, such as immigrants and prostitutes from Russia, vanish all the time. To his horror, Blomkvist realises that this is no series of murders from the past, but one which is happening today – and he has wandered right into it.

Larsson, micro-managing the tension, shifts the scene to Lisbeth Salander, wading through the documentation, making connections. She identifies the man with the long blond hair: Martin Vanger, who is studying in Uppsala. 'Gotcha,' she says in a low voice – and the reader worries, knowing what she does not know. She puts on her motorcycle helmet and uses her mobile to call Blomkvist, but he cannot, of course, be reached. The reader knows why. On arriving at the Vanger house, she looks at the surveillance footage showing Martin Vanger appearing in the camera's viewfinder and experiences a cold fear.

We are now back in the torture chamber with Martin Vanger and Blomkvist, as the former explains his rationale as a serial killer. He is cool and dispassionate, commenting on the choices he has made and how the moral and intellectual aspects of his crimes have no significance. He points out that he has a complete life. Blomkvist mentions Harriet, which brings about a violent rage in his captor – but there is a surprising exclamation from the killer. Vanger shouts, 'What the hell happened to her, bastard?' Blomkvist tells him that his assumption was that he, Martin, had killed her. Then he realises that his captor is innocent of this crime. Vanger admits that he had wanted to despatch her but had not done so, which prompts a feeling in Blomkvist's fevered brain: information overload. Vanger begins to tighten a noose around Blomkvist's neck, leaning forward to kiss him on the lips – when at the same time a voice sounds in the room telling the would-be strangler that the situation has changed.

It is Salander, and Blomkvist hears her voice through a fog. He shouts out, telling her to run, but she is like a beast of prey, moving with lightning speed and striking Martin Vanger in the ribs again and again. As Blomkvist is passing out, he sees the knife on the floor – Vanger is trying to crawl away from Salander, one arm hanging. She uses the knife to cut Blomkvist free just as Vanger is disappearing through the door. She grabs the pistol and vanishes. What follows is tense thriller writing of a rare order as Salander stalks Martin

Vanger, who is trying to drive away. The chase ends in a terrible crash and a conflagration. She returns to Blomkvist and begins to remove all evidence that the couple have been present in the torture chamber – and at the death of the killer. Blomkvist tries weakly to protest, but she tells him that if he goes on nagging she will drag him back to Martin's torture chamber and tie him up again. At that he falls asleep.

Chapter 25 is another measure of Larsson's skills – a recapitulation of what we heard before, but with all the detail satisfyingly filled in. Frode is apprised of the facts, i.e. that Martin has been kidnapping and murdering women, but that the bodies are gone. The latter's death is the top story on the 9 o'clock news. Salander, ever the survivor, persuades Blomkvist that it's best to cover up his involvement in the case as he does not wish to be celebrated as the journalist who was stripped nude by a vicious serial killer. The other members of the Vanger family (such as Gottfried), filled with a kind of poisonous evil, are discussed by Blomkvist and Salander and their religious motivation is talked about along with speculation regarding the building of the house and torture chamber. Blomkvist finds, unsurprisingly, that he is no longer welcome with such Vanger family members as Anita, who slams the door in his face.

As the first novel in the *Millennium Trilogy* winds down, we follow Blomkvist and Salander to London, walking from Covent Garden through Soho and having a coffee on Old Compton Street. They realise, however, that their lives in Sweden are burdened with unfinished business. They have to return. Blomkvist visits a member of the Vanger family who has been important to the novel when she was, apparently, a dead woman. It is Harriet, no less – who has hidden herself from unwanted family attention by feigning death. And Blomkvist discusses with her the reason for her assumed death. She talks about the horrors of her family and how she was tied up and raped by Martin. Blomkvist begins to be ashamed that he has not allowed her to maintain her anonymity and that he has disturbed her peace. But she had realised that the way to escape was to disappear. There is more business involving the tying up of loose ends concerning the Vanger family, and it's to Larsson's credit that this remains interesting, although we are past the point of violence and revelations.

Inevitably, the relationship between Blomkvist and Salander comes up again and he protests that, although she has said she likes having sex with him, he is old enough to be her father. She replies that she doesn't 'give a shit about his age', but he points out that the age difference cannot be ignored. He tells her that all the ramifications of the Vanger murders are being tied up and they begin to discuss his discrediting over the Wennerström business. This affair has now moved back to centre stage and Blomkvist has decided that he will discover the truth about the man who has discredited him. Salander, meanwhile, has returned to Stockholm to do a new job for Armansky. She stays with Blomkvist, and begins to feel relaxed for what might be the first time in her life.

However, the novel has issues to resolve, and it involves Salander travelling to Zurich and equipping herself with a pair of fake breasts made of latex. In this masquerade, she continues her part of the investigation into Wennerström and, needless to say, nails the essential information. All that is left for the novel is an epilogue (subtitled 'Final Audit') which details *Millennium*'s special report on Hans Erik that takes up 46 pages of the magazine and has a seismic effect when published. The by-line of the story is that of Mikael Blomkvist and Erika Berger. The revelations in the story concerning Wennerström's guilt (and, *inter alia*, Blomkvist's innocence) are picked up by other news media, and a typical headline is 'Convicted journalist accuses financier of serious crime'. The affair is so serious that there are even discussions of Sweden's economy heading for a crash.

When Blomkvist appears on TV, it seems that he has been finally exonerated and the truth about Wennerström is discovered. The latter disappears, but is seen, it seems, getting into a car in the capital of Barbados. Finally, Blomkvist's opponent is found dead in a Marbella apartment in Spain where he has been living under the name (playfully chosen by Larsson) of 'Victor Fleming' (the director of the film *The Wizard of Oz* – in which a plucky girl overcomes insuperable odds).

Salander is not surprised by the death and she has already grown tired of the investigation into his affairs. Blomkvist and Salander meet and have Christmas dinner before returning home to light a fire in the wood stove, listen to an Elvis Presley CD and (as Larsson puts it) devote themselves to 'some plain old sex'. But already we are aware of something that has been clear from their very first sexual encounter: despite their feelings for each other, Salander would never be happy with someone who has penetrated her defences, and the relationship really has no future beyond that of an intense friendship and dependence. Blomkvist has a meeting with his employer, Vanger, and the latter tells Blomkvist that he hasn't finished the job he was hired for – he hasn't written the Vanger family chronicle, which was the assignment, but the journalist declares that he does not intend to write it. There is an accommodation between the two men.

The novel ends in a low-key fashion as Salander closes herself off from the rest of the world and even, amazingly, leaves her computer switched off. Despite her mixed feelings towards Blomkvist, she hankers for him to ring the doorbell but – to what end? It is no longer sex that she wants from him, but simply his company. Refreshingly, Larsson does not offer a personality makeover for his heroine. He reminds us that she has no faith in herself while Blomkvist inhabits a world in which people hold down respectable jobs and orderly lives. She decides to knock on his door but en route she glances towards a café and sees Blomkvist emerging with Erika Berger. The couple laugh and show signs of affection. They also make it abundantly clear that they are sexual partners. Salander is torn apart by the pain of what she sees, and is frozen with dismay. She fantasises about violence against Berger but in the end realises that there is nothing she can do. She calls herself a pathetic fool and turns to return to her home. As she passes a rubbish skip she throws away the 1950s metal Elvis Presley advertising sign she had bought to give Blomkvist as a Christmas present. It was advertising 'Heartbreak Hotel'.

The ending is the perfect choice for a novel which has taken the reader on the proverbial rollercoaster ride, not just through shocking revelations and deception on a massive scale but a lacerating personal journey into the psyches of its troubled protagonists. Had there not been successive novels, there would still be a sense of closure at the end of this first book. But, having said that, the reader who will be aware that there are two more books to come, and is likely to remain hungry to spend more time in the company of the tenacious Mikael Blomkvist and the self-destructive, but more than capable, Lisbeth Salander.

CHAPTER 8

THE BOOKS:
The Girl Who Played With Fire

It's interesting to speculate what new heights of publishing success Stieg Larsson might have achieved had he lived, having already created an entirely new kind of heroine for crime fiction. His freelance investigator, ace computer hacker Lisbeth Salander, couldn't be further from the booze-loving coppers (male and female) who populate most of the genre. She is a surly young woman, relying on her Goth appearance, with tattoos and skin piercings, to keep people at bay (except those she decides to sleep with – on her own terms). But underneath the forbidding exterior she has, as already described, a cutting intelligence.

In the second book, *The Girl Who Played with Fire*, Larsson continues to pair her with the crusading journalist Mikael Blomkvist. But as the book opens we learn that Lisbeth has cut herself off from everyone who knows her; she has (despite her contempt for the opinions of others) had breast enlargement surgery, and has taken up with a naive younger lover. After exacting revenge on a corrupt authority figure who has abused her, she is soon the key suspect in three savage murders, and the ex-security analyst is on the run, the object of a nationwide search. But her ally, Blomkvist, who has just published an exposé of the sex trafficking industry in Sweden, is on her side – even though she dumped him as a lover. As with the first book in the *Millennium Trilogy*, this is exuberant stuff: the 600-or-so page novel may be (like its predecessor) in need of pruning, but its rebellious, taboo-breaking heroine is an absolute winner.

Larsson begins in familiar territory. In the disturbing flashback prologue, Lisbeth Salander is half-naked and tied to a bed with leather straps in a darkened room. She has been imprisoned for 43 days. To keep her sanity she fantasises about setting fire to her abductor. He appears: he is tall, has reddish-brown tangled hair, sparse goatee, glasses with black frames, aftershave, speaks with a dark, clear voice, emphasising every word. He wishes her 'Happy Birthday'. By this point Larsson has reader tension ratcheted up to a high degree. The man attempts to rape her, but she retaliates. He tightens the straps, we think he will try again, but he leaves. She again fantasises about dowsing him with petrol. The author, as aware as ever of the value of withholding key information, hits us with the killer punch line – she is only 13.

As Chapter 1 opens, Larsson has moved the action forward again and we find Lisbeth Salander at a hotel on the Caribbean island of Grenada, watching coolly as a woman emerges from the pool. She is slim with shoulder-length brown hair, an oval face, wearing a black bikini and sunglasses; we learn she is 35 and talks with a Southern US accent. Salander is tanned brown, despite trying to keep in the shade, smokes, and is wearing khaki shorts and a black top. Steel drums, we are told, fascinate her.

Salander is keeping an eye on the woman because she suspects her husband is abusing her – she hears noises of 'muted terror' from them in the room next to hers. Once again we have Larsson's protagonist acting as vigilante/avenger, and once again the male sex is painted in unsavoury fashion. The husband is presumably in Grenada on business. The couple argue strenuously every night while Salander tries to concentrate on a book about the mysteries of maths – typical reading, we now know, for her. She almost kicks in their door to put a stop to it. Next day she notices the woman has a bruise on her shoulder and a scrape on her hip.

We also learn that Salander has become fascinated with a, for her, typically esoteric subject – spherical astronomy. She has visited Rome, Miami, Florida Keys – and is now island-hopping through the Caribbean. She came ashore at St George's, the capital of Grenada, in an off-season tropical rainstorm and is staying at the Keys Hotel. She finds the local fruit, guinep, delightful – like sour Swedish gooseberries. Larsson is adept at this kind of physical preference detail applied to his heroine – and it appears just as we had started to think she isn't quite human: such info 'grounds' her for the reader.

Using the device of judicious switch of protagonists that was one of the pleasures of the first book, Larsson now transports us back to Lundagatan, where Mikael Blomkvist calls at Salander's apartment – as he has done every week or so – and wonders where she is. He remembers the affair they conducted (for half a year) during the events of the previous entry in the *Millennium Trilogy*. Salander, of course, had saved his life – and he recollects her photographic memory and phenomenal computer skills – and the fact that she is a world-class hacker, known online as 'Wasp'. They parted two days before Christmas, with Lisbeth wanting nothing more to do with him. This, of course, is a canny strategy on Larsson's part, as it re-establishes the initial dynamic between the couple, compromised by their abortive sexual relationship.

Salander has a shower. She weighs 40kg, stands 1m 52cm, and has doll-like, delicate limbs, small hands and hardly any hips. But, we are surprised to read, she is pleased with her new, full breasts, following surgery in a clinic outside Genoa when she was 25. This is one of Larsson's more controversial choices for his heroine – surely her utter self-reliance (however damaged her psyche) would have precluded such a remoulding of her body along conventional, male-pleasing lines? But it has made her happier and given her more self-confidence – we may decide for ourselves if we agree with her choices. She now enjoys wearing sexy lingerie because of her fuller figure, another surprising detail, given her usual taste for off-putting physical accoutrements.

Salander takes a bus to St George's, a compact and tight-knit town on a U-shaped bay, with houses climbing up steep hills. She withdraws $300, sits on the veranda of the Turtleback restaurant and watches as the man from her next-door room comes out, sits down, and stares out at the sea.

Some readers may wonder why the author talks in depth about Salander's interest in mathematics, especially riddles and puzzles. There's a great deal here about the book she's reading, the 1,200-page *Dimensions in Mathematics*. We discover all about Fermat's Last Theorem, the puzzle set by a French civil servant in 1601 and only solved in 1993. It apparently takes Salander seven weeks to find her own solution. This accruing of information is a crucial element in the heroine's make-up, and conveying it at length to the reader persuades us that it is not mere literary window-dressing.

The hotel barmaid, Ella Carmichael, tells Salander the couple in the room next door are Dr Forbes and his wife. He is discussing plans for a new high school in St George's – '*A good man,*' says Ella. '*Who beats his wife,*' snaps back Lisbeth. Back in her room she e-mails 'plague.xyz_666' to request information on Forbes and his wife, offering a $500 reward.

If readers feel that Larsson is insufficiently critical of his acerbic heroine, there is a clue to the ambiguity of his attitude in the description of a new sexual relationship Lisbeth has initiated. She visits her lover, George Bland, a student of 16 who she befriended the day after she arrived on the island, helping him with his maths homework. She finds his company relaxing. She does not normally make small talk with strangers, and she doesn't like personal discussions. But she seduces the boy on an impulse, and now they see each other every evening. Lisbeth is unquestionably the controlling, dominant force in the relationship with the immature George – and it might be argued that she ruthlessly uses a variety of means (including her newly augmented body) in a fashion that is not ideologically dissimilar to the men who have dominated her – though there is no suggestion of the grim bullying she has received.

For Chapter 2, Larsson switches our attention to a café on Stureplan, and a nemesis of Salander's. Nils Erik Bjurman is thinking about what Salander did to him. It's another example of Larsson's attitude to his own sex that those who undergo sexual humiliation of the kind they practise on women are splenetic forces of malevolence, bent on revenge at all costs. Bjurman, we remember, was a lawyer assigned to be Salander's legal guardian. Salander was considered a promiscuous child and in need of protection. But Bjurman abused his position and raped her – and consequently Salander took her revenge on him by tattooing his crimes on his belly. A broken man, he gave up most of his clients and wrote fictitious, positive monthly reports on Salander – as she had stipulated. He sets about getting skin grafts to remove the tattoo. Salander had visited him in the middle of the night and blackmailed him with a DVD she had made of the rape: she is going away, but Bjurman must continue writing his reports as if she is still under his protection, or she will make public the DVD. From that moment on Bjurman has an overwhelming desire to destroy her – this galvanises him and gives his life a new purpose.

While Bjurman is bitterly remembering what Salander did, Mikael Blomkvist (unaware of the lawyer's existence) passes him to join his editor-in-chief, and erstwhile lover, Erika Berger, at a nearby table. Blomkvist lights up a cigarette. Erika detests smokers – not a reliable indicator of her character, as the chain-smoking author might be expected to disagree with her – and makes a veiled reference to finding a lover who doesn't smoke. She's meeting childhood friend Charlotte 'Charlie' Rosenberg. We learn that Blomkvist is being sexually harassed by a work-experience girl, the daughter of one of Erika's friends, who is only 17 (both Berger and Blomkvist are 45). This is something of a reversal of the serial sexual harassment practised by males in the books – but Blomkvist's experience is more a nuisance than anything else.

His long-term affair with Berger began 20 years ago when she was a young journo. He radiates self-confidence and is entirely non-threatening, hence (as Larsson tells us) his attraction to the opposite sex (readers may argue with this as a rationale for the journalist's extraordinary success with women). He prefers older women – Salander was an aberration. He doesn't want a repeat of this entanglement with the media school graduate who is working at *Millennium*. She is clearly desperate for him (more Larsson wish-fulfilment by proxy?), and he doesn't want to hurt her.

We switch from these minor problems to a major one exercising one of the trilogy's many villains. The despicable Bjurman is contemplating how to get the incriminating DVD back from Salander (he is unaware of her link with Blomkvist). As her guardian, he has access to all her medical records. Over time, he has tracked down all the information he can find about her. The more he reads about her, the more he sees her as a sick, twisted psycho – but still, tellingly, as he sees it, a whore.

According to notes made by her former therapist, Palmgren, something had set off Salander's madness when she was 12 or 13 (cryptically referred to as 'All the Evil'). Since then, her mother had been incapable of looking after her and she had lived in foster homes. But what was 'The Evil'? Readers will remember the events of the prologue and make a connection. Salander has a twin sister, Camilla, and nothing is known of her father. A missing report dated 12 March 1991 could provide the answer to her trauma, but Bjurman is denied access to it. Two months later he has the 47-page report and discovers the identity of someone else (the abductor) who must hate her as much as he does. It is a grim, if improbable, alliance. He is interrupted in his reverie by the appearance of a towering blond bodybuilder who tells him 'We got your letter'...

Chapter 3 moves back to Grenada. Via her cyberspace contact, Plague, Lisbeth receives e-mailed information about Dr Forbes in the form of documents and photos. Rev. Richard Forbes, of the Presbyterian Church of Austin South, is 42. We get a brief biography – born Nevada, farmer, businessman, newspaper correspondent, certified public accountant, Christian rock-band manager (a typical Larsson signifier!), arrested in 1995 for embezzling the band's money. Salander wakes up to strong winds – Hurricane Matilda is approaching (readers may be reminded of another hurricane that plays a key part in crime fiction, in the work of James Lee Burke). The hotel front desk man Freddie McBain (another crime fiction reference) tells Lisbeth she must come down to the lobby. She freshens up, goes down with her most valuable possessions, and helps Ella Carmichael take blankets down to the storm cellar. Larsson handles this build-up of background tension with customary assurance. Dr Forbes is nowhere to be seen. The storm hits Petit Martinique, a few miles away, so McBain tells them to go downstairs to the already-prepared underground shelter.

Salander suddenly fears for the safety of her lover, Bland, and rushes out into the stormy night to rescue him. As she drags him into the hotel, she glimpses by the illumination of a lightning flash, the Forbes couple on the beach, where she had seen the husband before. The marshalling of elements here has Hitchcockian undertows. They are struggling – Salander realises Forbes is going to murder his wife under cover of the storm. She rushes over to them, brandishing a chair leg. She hits the doctor, who is wielding an iron pipe, before he can deliver the death blow to his wife, then Bland helps her to drag the woman, who has a head wound, back to the hotel. A tornado appears out at sea, although Grenada is not in a tornado zone – a rare mystical moment in the decidedly non-mystical Larsson scenarios – and Forbes is pulled into the sea. After this vividly described episode, Salander tells Bland to say they didn't see the husband, as they carry Mrs Forbes down to the cellar. She recovers a few hours later, her wound not serious.

Next day, they emerge from the cellar. Salander is questioned by Constable Ferguson and denies seeing Dr Forbes. Ferguson says they found his body in the airport car park, 600 metres south. Meteorological reports suggest it was a 'pseudo-tornado' that killed Forbes, the only fatality of the night – no one knows what it was, other than an act of God, although divine retribution is not standard Larsson territory. Geraldine can't remember a thing.

Larsson calls Part Two of *The Girl Who Played with Fire* 'From Russia with Love'; by now, readers will be used to the author's affectionate referencing of other crime/thriller fiction. As Chapter 4 opens, Salander lands at Stockholm's Arlanda Airport. Normally frugal, she takes a taxi, as she now has more than 3 billion kronor in her bank account, thanks to an internet coup and fraud. She buys supplies from a 7-11 store and walks to her apartment in Fiskargatan, avoiding the *Millennium* offices. She lives on the top floor, under the name of 'V Kulla' (a reference to Pippi Longstocking's Villekulla Cottage).

After treatment at the Italian clinic, she didn't feel like returning to Sweden to work for the security firm who employed her previously, investigating corporate crooks till she's 50. She also didn't want to see Blomkvist, who she feels has hurt her, although he did behave 'decently'. She blames herself for falling in love with this serial womaniser, but she ignores all his attempts to contact her.

This closing off of emotional contact (which Larsson is so adroit at conveying) led to her making a decision to travel the world; she had rarely been outside Stockholm before. First Tel Aviv, then Bangkok, then travelling on for the rest of the year, including her sojourn on Grenada. She also went to Gibraltar twice. She enters her bathroom, strips naked and takes a long shower (she clearly enjoys being in her own skin) and sleeps in her new apartment for the first time in a year. Next day, she returns to her old flat, checks that her Kawasaki motor bike in the basement is OK, then rifles through her huge pile of mail – there's only a handful of personal letters: one regarding her mother's estate, which has been settled (she and her sister are getting 9,312 kronor each), and a letter from Blomkvist, which she throws away, unread.

She dons a wig and glasses and, as 'Irene Nesser' (a real person who lost her passport three years earlier, 'acquired' by Plague) hires a Nissan Micra to go to IKEA to buy furniture for her flat – cue a *Fight Club*-type moment with a lengthy list of IKEA products. Necessary? Possibly, as it does demonstrate she is a fastidious person who attends to every detail and is not afraid of spending money – over 90,000 kronor in this case. She vaguely wonders about Blomkvist. In her Jacuzzi, she squeezes her nipples hard underwater until she runs out of breath (one of the various erotic S&M moments which contrast so strikingly with the violent, invasive sex that is a keynote of so much of the books).

Next morning, Blomkvist is late for Berger's planning meeting. Freelance writer Dag Svensson is present – they are buying a piece from him for their May issue on sex trafficking.

Svensson was introduced to the subject through his girlfriend Mia Johansson, who is writing a thesis on it. A huge number of under-age girls are lured to Sweden from Eastern Europe by the so-called 'sex mafia' – we are firmly into the sexual exploitation territory that is for Larsson a mainspring of the trilogy. He wants *Millennium* to publish a book on it, and claims various government figures are intimately involved with the sex-trade.

Salander returns to Appelviken, the nursing home where her mother, Agneta Sofia Salander, spent her final years before dying at only 43. She was beautiful, with a lovely figure, like Salander's sister Camilla and completely unlike Salander who is (as she perceives herself) 'anorexic-looking'. Larsson addresses women's attitudes to their own appearance almost as much as Elizabeth Gaskell does in *Cranford*. The sisters were unlike from an early age – Camilla outgoing and academically successful, Lisbeth introverted and doing badly at school. They were sent to separate foster homes when 'All the Evil' happened; one last meeting at 17 ended in a fight. Salander last visited the home 18 months ago with Blomkvist, but her mother hadn't recognised her. She takes the box of possessions back to her flat and goes clothes shopping, but later discards the sexy underwear she bought as looking foolish on her thin, tattooed frame.

Mia Johansson is serving cheesecake to Berger, Blomkvist and Malin Eriksson, editorial assistant, at the culmination of a working dinner at Svensson's flat. Johansson presents her thesis – 'From Russia with Love' – which unlike Dag's polemic book, is a strictly statistical look at the gender-specific nature of the burgeoning sex trade (boys: abusers, girls: abused). The trafficking laws are not being enforced –

almost no one has been charged yet. The girls are treated like slave labour – if they do not have sex with 'dirty old men', they will be tortured by their pimps. They speak no Swedish and their passports are removed. Although all of this, of course, is standard territory for Larsson the journalist, Larsson the novelist incorporates the data in *The Girl Who Played with Fire* without any sense of proselytising – it becomes a plot element.

Salander's (aka 'Irene Nesser's') IKEA furniture is delivered. She starts dressing the flat and finds a dildo given her by her friend Mimmi, whom she left for Blomkvist (a reminder of the amorphous sexuality of the heroine). She hadn't said goodbye to her when she left the country, or to her friends in the rock group Evil Fingers. She also never said goodbye to the youthful George Bland in St Georges – an omission that may have the reader judging Salander to be as ruthless in her relationships as those she criticises. She knows, however, that she keeps squandering her friends. She surfs the net, ensures the blackmailed Bjurman is toeing the line, and checks out her new breasts in the mirror. She now has short, untidily cropped hair. She had to take out a nipple ring for the surgery, and then a lip ring and a labia ring – unscrewing her tongue piercing, all she has left now (apart from her earlobe rings) is an eyebrow ring and a jewel in her navel. She lies awake, musing in her big new bed. At 3.10 am, Lisbeth sneaks into Milton Security and breaks into Armansky's office. She checks his current jobs, then back at her apartment she logs on to the 40 computers she has access to, including those belonging to Bjurman, Blomkvist and Wennerström.

Salander visits her old friend and lover Mimmi in her studio apartment. Mimmi has short, black hair, clear blue eyes, and slightly Asian features. She is 31 and works part-time at a fetish-gear shop, Domino Fashion. They met when Mimmi was dressed as a lemon doing a weird show at the city's Gay Pride Festival a couple of years before – Mimmi had immediately said Salander was 'the one I want' and they'd spent the night having sex. Mimmi knew she was a lesbian at secondary school and lost her virginity at 17. Their relationship is primarily sexual.

Salander is initially embarrassed at admitting she's had a boob job, but Mimmi is clearly still interested in her, and wants to see her new breasts, with a view to further reacquainting herself with her body. 'Welcome back,' she says. Once again, we are reminded of the disorienting balancing act that is Larsson's attitude to women and sexuality – shaded with a complexity that is sufficiently opaque to suggest both an even-handed acceptance of sex in all its protean forms and a certain voyeuristic indulgence.

A mysterious – unnamed – character appears. He is massive and blond, and carries a sports bag. He stops in the tiny village of Svavelsjö, at the motorcycle club for a drug deal with club president, Carl-Magnus 'Magge' Lundin. Lundin is very happy to do business with the man; there are never any problems – he supplies the meth and just demands his 50% of whatever Lundin makes. The giant asks Lundin to abduct Lisbeth Salander and bring her to a warehouse near Yngern – he hands over personal details and a passport photo – so that his employer can 'have a quiet talk' with her. She needs to be brought there alive, but disposed of cleanly afterwards. All of this is handled with the narrative skill that readers who have reached this point in the sequence have come to expect from the author, with the necessary accumulation of detail married to storytelling nous.

Salander is (wisely) slightly paranoid about being attacked going on her travels, so she rings Mimmi and offers her the flat for as long as she wants. It's interesting to study Salander's relationship with one of her female lovers, as detailed here. While feminist authors have occasionally characterised relationships between women as more authentic and less power-driven than those between men and women, Larsson – unquestionably a feminist author – renders Lisbeth as frustratingly 'other' to her female lovers as she is to male companions such as Blomkvist. In this, perhaps, she is a descendant of the all-things-to-all-men-and-women Lulu of Wedekind, Pabst and Berg.

Erika Berger is relaxing in her office after a hard day putting the March issue of *Millennium* to bed. She will be 45 in three months' time and is starting to feel her age. She is largely content with her life – 15 years of happy marriage, and an inexhaustible lover on the side (Blomkvist). She has, we are told, a passion for sex. She and her husband have indulged in group encounters, when she discovered his bisexual side. Sex with him is not boring; it is just that Blomkvist gives her a different experience. Her husband knows about her lover – in fact, she has his full consent. She couldn't live without both men and wouldn't want to choose between them. She likes Blomkvist's complete lack of jealousy and the freedom he allows her. Their 20-year affair is based primarily on friendship. Inevitably, non-Swedish readers will wonder if Larsson is giving us a snapshot of Swedish middle-class sexual mores (at least in the media arena) – and the non-judgemental authorial voice here contrasts sharply with the lacerating tone of the exposure of his country's corrupt politics. Erika goes to Mikael's flat and lies in bed waiting for him. Her fantasy is for a twosome with him and her husband, but Blomkvist is so straight she knows it will never happen.

Larsson, perhaps aware that it is time to reintroduce the element of mystery and menace in his narrative, takes us back to the blond giant arriving at a log cabin in the middle of woods near Mariefred. He is intimidated by the trees and thinks he sees a dwarf or troll lurking in the darkness. But there is, of course, nothing there. Nils Bjurman – his employer – lets him in. Two of the author's most sinister characters are keeping company.

Mimmi and Salander make love on the newly varnished parquet floor. Mimmi ties her up, and just for a moment Salander is reminded of how Bjurman had done the same to her (another reminder by Larsson of the minefield that is sexual behaviour), but with Mimmi it is different. She surrenders to the moment...

In Chapter 8, Lisbeth visits Armansky and asks if he's angry that she left a year ago without saying goodbye (which, is perhaps a misstep on Larsson's part concerning Salander's mindset – is this concern consistent with her character?). But Armansky is just relieved she's alive, though he reflects on how she doesn't care about her friends, having behaved so selfishly as to vanish to travel the world without telling anyone where she was. She learns that her first carer, Palmgren, is still alive, after his stroke. She had left when he was still in a coma and assumed he had died. She feels very guilty about this – perhaps she *is* a shit, as Armansky has said. Lisbeth is tight-lipped when Blomkvist's name comes up – he has been asking about her every month. Armansky has a job for her, but Salander is now financially independent. As a parting shot, she gives him advice about a case she couldn't possibly know about (the poison-pen letters of a client, actress Christine Rutherford, are a publicity stunt), and he rings the technical department to get a CCTV camera installed in his office.

Larsson is now to address the superscription of this section, a reference to fellow thriller novelist Ian Fleming. Mia Johansson picks up Svensson from the Gamla Stan *tunnelbana* station. He is one month from deadline, but has only had nine of 22 planned confrontations. He can't get hold of Björck at the Security Police, who spends time with the prostitutes. Mia's thesis 'From Russia with Love' has been printed – she is to defend it and become a fully-fledged doctor next month. Svensson tells her that a girl she interviewed, Irina P, has been found drowned. Given the pseudonym 'Tamara', she was brought into the country by 'Anton' (real name probably Zala, a Pole or a Yugoslav). Svensson had recently confronted a 'journalist' called Sandström, who uses teen prostitutes to live out rape fantasies, and also runs errands for Sweden's 'sex mafia'. The one name he gave him was Zala, an uncommon name, and one all the girls are terrified of... we are, of course, back in Larsson's domain of grim male sexual violence.

After showing us the possibilities of positive, organic growth between people (even someone as damaged as Salander), Larsson takes us back to the realm of the twisted psyche. Nils Bjurman arrives home from his summer cabin. The blond giant had told him his people were interested in his (Bjurman's) proposal – a sinister one involving Salander – and it would cost him 100,000 kronor. He inspects his post and discovers a statement from Handelsbanken showing Salander's withdrawal of 9,300 kronor – so he knows the woman who has humiliated him is back on the scene. He rings the blond giant and tells him.

Salander's feelings about Blomkvist are confused. She hacks into his computer with downloads of all his e-mails, Svensson's manuscript and Mia Johansson's thesis. She sees Blomkvist is having an affair with Vanger. By 11.30 pm she has read everything – but the last e-mail makes her sit up in a cold sweat. Svensson had mentioned someone called Zala...

In the *Millennium* offices, Svensson is pondering the significance of Zala. Irina P had been found in Södertälje canal with a broken neck; Zala's name had come up four times in Mia's research, always as a shadowy figure. Svensson had pressurised Sandström for information, but he was frightened for his life. There is a rather similar cliff-hanger ending to the previous chapter – another example perhaps of a need for tighter editing, the boon denied to Larsson by his death.

In Chapter 10, Larsson adroitly choreographs a variety of incidents. Salander, in the Café Hedon, sees the man who brutally raped her, Nils Bjurman. She has no feelings for him; she is coldly keeping him alive so he can be useful to her. She seems to recognise the blond giant he is talking to (Larsson uses the word 'click' – her photographic memory taking a picture?), and follows him when he leaves. He takes the tube to Blomberg's Café at Götgatan. The blond meets a fat biker with a ponytail – Lundin, who we encountered in Chapter 7. The blond gives him instructions, then leaves in a white Volvo; Salander notes the registration number. At her flat, she hacks into Bjurman's hard drive but finds nothing odd, apart from the fact that he has not yet started her report this month. Why so late? First Blomkvist, then Zala, and now Bjurman meeting a thug with contacts to a gang of ex-con bikers. She is, unsurprisingly, worried...

Larsson repeatedly has his heroine breaking in to apartments, and that scenario now reappears: at 2.30 the following morning. Salander breaks into Bjurman's flat, armed with only a Taser. She watches him sleep then goes to his office and rifles through his drawers. Although she thinks something is wrong – papers have been removed from her file – she can't find anything concrete to back up her fears. By now, Larsson has readers in something of a dual conditioned response to his heroine. We admire her armoury of defensive – and offensive – weaponary, but still regard her from the outside – she is not a woman it is easy to identify with.

Salander downloads the images of the biker gang, including Lundin and his No. 2, the photogenic Nieminen (a man with multiple convictions), the man Lundin met at McDonald's. Lundin was the man who met the blond giant at Blomberg's Café. She can find no trace of Zala. The next day, after breakfast in the Jacuzzi, she has better luck searching for Svensson and Mia Johansson. Then she hacks *Millennium*'s intranet and downloads e-mails from Berger, Malm and Malin Eriksson. Finally she finds Svensson's computer and a file marked <Zala>. Larsson is skilfully ensuring that things are beginning to accelerate.

Some readers might find the obfuscation practised at this point frustrating rather than tantalising. Who is the unidentified man driving to Jarna? He has just picked up 203,000 kronor from Lundin for the meth he delivered in January. (This is one of the points in the trilogy when readers suffering from information overload may struggle to keep up with the barrage of data being fed to them.) The three gangs

The man who left too soon – a portrait of Stieg Larsson taken in Stockholm in 2004, the year he died.

Above: Larsson and his long-term partner, Eva Gabrielsson, relaxing over a cup of coffee in Strängnäs, Sweden.

Below: At work at TT, the Swedish news agency, in Stockholm in the mid-1990s.

On a visit to Hong Kong, August 1987.

Larsson on the Trans-Siberian Railway, July 1987.

Working as a news graphic illustrator at the TT Feature and Photo desk.

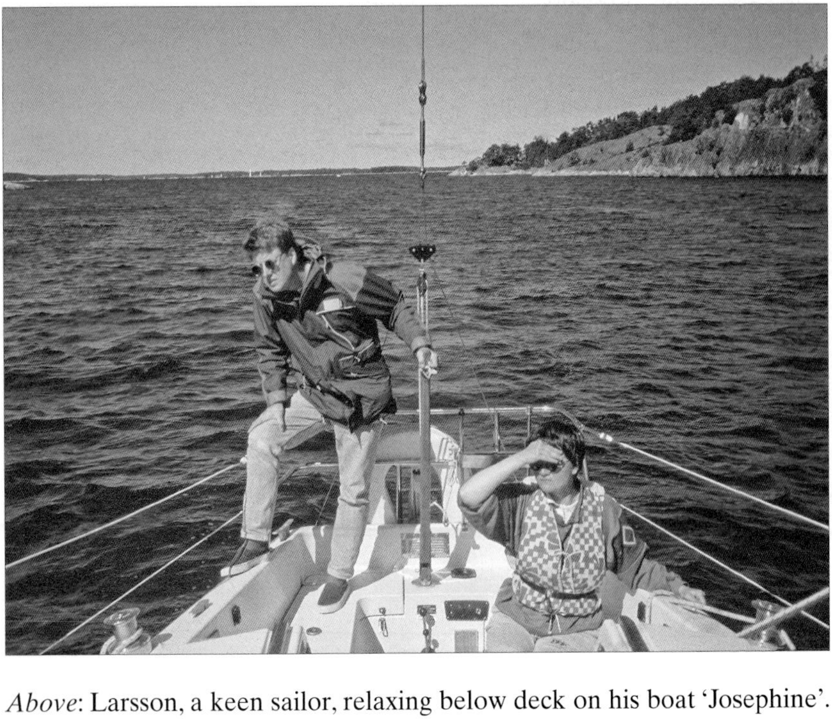

Above: Larsson, a keen sailor, relaxing below deck on his boat 'Josephine'.

Below: Sailing the Stockholm archipelago, with Eva Gabrielsson.

Above: Swedish actress Noomi Rapace, who plays Lisbeth Salander, and Danish director Niels Arden Oplev, at the Paris premiere of *The Girl with the Dragon Tattoo* in May 2009.

Below: Guests wait in line outside the Sergel cinema in Stockholm, 14 September 2009, for the gala premiere of *The Girl Who Played with Fire*, the second film in the *Millennium Trilogy*.

Above left: Eva Gabrielsson, Larsson's partner, pictured holding a copy of the Swedish edition of *Män som hatar kvinnor* ('Men Who Hate Women'), which was published in English as *The Girl with the Dragon Tattoo*.

Above right: Michael Nyqvist as Mikael Blomkvist. © *Alliance Films*

Below: The poster for the last of the three films. © *Alliance Films*

the man supplies bring him roughly 5 million kronor a month. Yet he is in a bad mood because although the demand is almost infinite, he has a problem getting the drugs from Estonia to Sweden. He has already had to punish an inquisitive street vendor, but knows that violence is risky and not good business. Smuggling prostitutes from the Baltics, his other business, gives only small change but he is unlikely to be brought down by the government because 'everybody likes a whore'. Even dead whores don't interest the authorities. But he thinks the business 'sucks'. He doesn't like the women – they're unclean. This is, of course, Larsson shorthand indicating (in incontrovertible fashion) we are in the presence of another woman-hating male scumbag. He also doesn't like the contract in place with Bjurman to kidnap Salander, a contract awarded to Nieminen.

Then Larsson takes us into what looks like Stephen King territory. Suddenly he sees a sinister shape in the darkness, slithering towards him. It looks like a vast stingray with a stinger like a scorpion. A creature not of this world. He runs back to his car and speeds off. The creature tries to strike the car as he passes, shaken. (This is linked with the terror of the blond man in Chapter 7.)

Salander looks at what she's discovered from the *Millennium* files. One source for Svensson's book is Gulbrandsen, a policeman. The <Zala> file is disappointingly slight, only three documents: one about Irina P, one about Sandström, and one about Zala himself. Since the mid 1990s the name had cropped up in nine drug, weapons or prostitution cases. Zala was responsible for Irina P's death. Zala's name first appeared in connection with a botched security van hold-up in 1996. Nieminen, who had supplied the weapons, has links with Nazi organizations, such as the Aryan Brotherhood (we're back to echoes of Larsson's real-life battles with extremist organisations).

Salander sits and smokes for a couple of hours (she has her creator's *laissez-faire* attitude to her own health), knowing she has to find Zala and settle their accounts once and for all.

Blomkvist is returning home from a publisher's party just before 3 am when he passes Salander's old apartment and – in yet another unlikely juxtaposition – sees her step out into the street, only to be accosted by a tall man in a ponytail (it is Lundin). She instinctively turns and slashes him across the face, using her keys like a knuckleduster. She runs away up some steps, followed by Lundin. She throws a sharp stone at him, wounding him still further. She resolves to punish Bjurman for sending a 'diabolical alpha male' to do her harm. All of this is handled with the assurance we expect from Larsson in such moments of action – the prose is economical, but apposite.

'Absurd Equations' is the title Larsson gives to Part Three – and the nomenclature (it has to be said) is appropriate for some of the startling plotting that follows.

Blomkvist is at the *Millennium* offices alone, working through Svensson's manuscript; he has already delivered nine of the promised 12 chapters and Blomkvist is very pleased with his writing. Blomkvist knows the book will explicitly expose the corrupt system and is 'a declaration of war' (of the kind that Larsson, as a journalist, was all too familiar with).

The author is well aware that by this point in the narrative we'll be hungry for another glimpse of his abrasive heroine, and obliges (her appearances are to some extent the allegros to Blomkvist's largos). At nine that evening Svensson and Johansson are visited by Lisbeth Salander. To Svensson she appears to be in her late teens and he notes her cold, raven-black irises. She knows about the book and the thesis, much to the couple's surprise and suspicion. She wants to know why they're asking questions about 'Alexander' Zala. This is the first time Svensson has heard his first name – clearly Salander knows things he doesn't.

Blomkvist tells his lawyer sister Annika about Salander's dramatic reappearance in his life, and asks whether he should be consulting her for legal advice on Svensson's book, as her professional speciality is violence on women. His sister confesses she was hurt when Blomkvist never consulted her over the Wennerström affair, but when he apologises, she says she'd be happy to read through the text.

But it is time for Stieg Larsson to remind the reader about the dangerous world his characters move in. Brother and sister arrive at Svensson's flat, but Blomkvist hears a commotion on the stairwell and senses something is wrong (Annika waits in the car). A group of neighbours are milling outside the open door. Blomkvist goes in to find the writer slumped in a pool of blood: he has been shot in the head. Blomkvist dials 112 for police and ambulance. He finds Mia Johansson in the bedroom, shot in the face with enough force to spatter blood all over the wall three metres away. They are both dead. He is numb with shock. He goes downstairs and sees a Colt .45 on the cellar steps.

Three officers arrive: Magnusson, Ohlsson and superintendent Mårtensson. Blomkvist explains what has happened and says that since only five minutes have passed since the neighbours say they heard shots, the killer may still be in the area. He shows them the cellar door – it is locked. They enter the flat. The couple are clearly beyond help. As Annika comforts her brother, a murder investigation begins.

Blomkvist wonders if the murders are linked to the book, now near publication – has someone Svensson confronted tried to prevent it? Should they publish? Should they tell police exactly what Svensson was working on? The answer is no – because then they'd have to reveal their sources, which they promised not to do. The verisimilitude of these sections is obviously down to the fact that Larsson is dealing (in fictional terms) with a situation he would be all too familiar with from his time at the magazine *Expo* – and would no doubt have come across (or at least heard about) regarding the British sister magazine he also wrote for, *Searchlight*, which has taken on some dangerous opponents.

Critics of Stieg Larsson have taken exception to his 'filling-in' strategies regarding minor characters, where pen portraits are provided for people who will barely figure in the narrative (possibly inspired by Fredrick Forsyth). Such a case might be made against the details given for prosecutor Richard Ekström, who finds he will be leading the murder investigation. He's described as a thin, vital man of 42, with thinning blond hair and a goatee. He is always impeccably dressed, and has spent four years at the Ministry of Justice. The police force, we are told, are divided about his John Birt-style policies of downsizing to increase efficiency, rather than recruiting more police (Birt, one-time Director General of the BBC, used similarly unpopular cost-cutting tactics within his organisation). He rings Criminal Investigator Jan Bublanski (nicknamed 'Officer Bubble'), who is off duty, and asks him to come in and investigate the killings. Bublanski is 52, and has been in charge of 17 murder or manslaughter cases, and has only failed to find the killer in one. Held in high esteem, he is considered a bit odd because of his Jewish background. He is a member of the (fictitious) Söder congregation, but still works on the Sabbath when required.

At 8 am, Bublanski meets with Ekström and they discuss the case. Because of the journalistic angle, they know it will receive huge media attention. Ekström hand-picks Faste, Andersson and Holmberg for Bublanski's team, while Bublanski himself wants Sonja Modig. Sonja is perhaps sculpted by Larsson from similar material to that utilised for Salander – though (unlike the latter) she is part of the establishment. Modig, 39, has had 12 years' experience in the Violent Crimes Division; she is exacting and methodical, but also – very importantly – imaginative. She can make associations that are not necessarily logical, but which can lead to breakthroughs. And – as Larsson likes his idiot cops as antagonists – it's time for another one. Hans Faste, 47, although a veteran in the investigation of violent crimes, has a huge ego and a loud-mouthed humour that winds people up, especially Bublanski; the latter finds it hard to tolerate him. However, Faste is something of a mentor to Andersson and they work well together.

Larsson has conditioned the reader to expect internet thoroughness from Salander, but he now reminds us that Blomkvist is no slouch in this territory. At the *Millennium* offices, the journalist has deleted 134 documents relating to protected sources. We are taken back to the police investigation – and literary proof is provided (if it were needed) that Larsson could handle the exigencies of a straightforward police procedural with quite as much authority as he deals with his two freelancers. Lennart Granlund of the National

Forensics Laboratory rings Bublanski at 10 am – the Colt .45 was made in America in 1981. It *is* the murder weapon, and legally belongs to Nils Erik Bjurman. Fingerprints on the gun identify a second person – Lisbeth Salander, born 30 April 1978, arrested and fingerprinted for an assault in Gamla Stan in 1995.

Larsson maintains his dual narrative. Blomkvist sets to work on Svensson's material, looking for a motive for his murder, while (at the same time) Bublanski and Modig go to Bjurman's flat in Odenplan and his office at St Eriksplan, but he's not in either place. They call on his office neighbour, a lawyer called Håkansson, who tells them Bjurman was seriously ill two years ago, in the spring of 2003, and only returns to his office once every couple of months. Håkansson thinks he had cancer, judging by his suddenly aged appearance. The police repair to a Burger King where Modig has a Whopper and Bublanski a Veggie Burger. It's piquant to notice both Larsson's customary inversion here of masculine/feminine stereotypes (as detailed in his 'mission statement' e-mails) – as well as his referencing of his own taste for junk food.

The crass Faste tells his colleagues what he's discovered about Salander (and it's amusing for the reader to compare this to what we already know of her): she is a psychiatric patient with violent tendencies first demonstrated in primary school, later a prostitute, and 'a real psycho'. But in a reminder of the fact that there are male characters who can act honourably in Larsson's otherwise misogynistic universe (i.e. after inappropriate sexual advances can reign themselves in and behave well), we encounter Armansky again. Bublanski questions him about Salander, but Armansky is poker-faced. He says she was their best 'researcher' (i.e.

private investigator). Bublanski has trouble squaring this with the 'psycho' on their files – one of the author's many examples of his heroine's wrong-footing of those who do not 'read' her correctly.

Holmberg is at the initial crime scene, contemplating the enormous quantity of blood on the floor from the two shootings. He's not interested in the details drawn up by the technicians – he wants to know who the killer is, and what the motivation is. He goes through their flat with a fine-tooth comb and hand-picks four books of interest: *The Mafia's Banker* by Blomkvist (the kind of subject, of course, that Larsson the journalist might enthusiastically tackle), plus three political non-fiction titles and one about terrorism. He finds a great deal of money – so clearly robbery was not the motive.

Bublanski and Faste meet Ekström in his office. They don't know who the 'Miriam Wu' woman is, but judging by the fetish gear she keeps, Faste thinks she is 'a whore'. A social welfare report adjudged Salander guilty of prostitution too, but Bublanski is unconvinced. Ekström thinks that if Johansson's thesis, 'From Russia with Love' was about trafficking and prostitution, she might have made contact with Wu and Salander, which could have provoked them to murder her. Bublanski and Ekström give a televised press conference, explaining they are looking for a 26-year-old woman for three murders: Bjurman is also dead, killed by his ruthless associates. Reluctantly, because he didn't agree with the releasing of her name, Bublanski reads out a description of her. As so often with Larsson, the apparatus of the state is misdirected, targeting the innocent while protecting the guilty – the leitmotif of the author's journalistic ethos.

Sonja Modig is still in Bjurman's apartment at 9 pm when Bublanski arrives. She has unearthed nothing. Although Salander is the obvious culprit, Bublanski still can't balance the 'disabled near-psychopath' of the police paperwork with the 'skilled researcher' so well-regarded by Armansky and Blomkvist. Gunnar Samuelsson from forensics has turned the body over to place on the stretcher, and found the tattoo Salander inscribed: 'I am a sadistic pig, a pervert, and a rapist'. Modig asks if they have found their motive.

Larsson now take us back to Blomkvist at his flat, his mind whirling. He hasn't slept for 36 hours, the horrific images of the double murder ingrained in his mind. He decides that he isn't going to believe the police's conclusion that Salander's the murderer. After all, he owes his life to her – and readers recognise that the authentic characters in the *Millennium Trilogy* never take things at face value.

Blomkvist and Eriksson tape a list of suspects, based on Svensson's book research, on the wall of his apartment. All men, punters or pimps. Of 37 names, 30 are readily identifiable. The trouble is that in order to publish, *Millennium* would have to get independent authentication to prove these individuals were who the authors claimed they were. If Svensson were alive, they could have published everything and allow him to refute objections himself. Again, the exigencies of magazine publication – something Larsson would know all too well from his *Expo* experience – are pressed into service for the narrative. A recurrent paradigm – the discipline of investigative journalism – is more central to this second book in the trilogy than to its companions, and perhaps accounts for the rigour in evidence here (a rigour which is sometimes subsumed in the more verisimilitude-stretching developments of the other books).

Bublanski organises a meeting with Modig, Faste and Dr Peter Teleborian, head physician at St Stefan's psychiatric clinic at Uppsala. There is hostility between Faste and Modig: bad cop and good cop. The boyish Teleborian is short with steel-rimmed glasses and a small goatee. He is one of the best-known psychiatrists in Sweden and is an authority on psychopaths and psychopathic behaviour (the *lingua franca*, in fact, of much of Larsson's fiction). He believes Salander should have been held in an institution. Indeed, she was one of Teleborian's patients in her teens and he had been partly responsible for placing her under guardianship when she turned 18 (a fact that will assume key significance later in the book).

Salander had been turned over to his care just before she was 13. She was, he says, 'psychotic, obsessive and paranoid'. She had behaved violently towards schoolmates, teachers and acquaintances – but never strangers. Which is why Teleborian is convinced she must have known Dag and Mia, if indeed she had killed them. She attacked a stranger in the underground when she was 17, but only because the stranger, a sex offender, had attacked her first – one of the earliest of the many assaults on the spectacularly luckless Salander. When she feels threatened, she attacks with violence – the hallmark of the series. Because of her reluctance to engage with any therapy, doctors haven't properly diagnosed her illness.

Various investigations are now taking place: Bublanski's, who feels he's almost solved it; Armansky's, watching out for Salander's interests; and Blomkvist/*Millennium*'s, actively seeking an alternative suspect to Salander. Modig believes the tattoo on Bjurman's stomach, along with pornographic images on his computer, intimates that Salander was abused by him, and that could be a motive for his death. Faste's theory is that Salander and Wu were involved in some kind of S&M escort service that went wrong, with Bjurman a client, and when Svensson was threatening to expose the sex trade, along with their S&M business, Salander killed him to prevent disclosure.

As often before, Larsson has consolidated a slew of material to set in train against his heroine, upping the ante in narrative terms; it's a speciality that by this point in the second novel he has burnished to perfection.

Blomkvist gets home and checks his iBook, finding Salander has hacked into it, read his letter to her, and replied with a document containing just one word: 'Zala'. He suspects she is close by, somewhere in Södermalm, and feels almost as if she is watching him. He creates another document, asking for more information: 'Who is Zala?' Immediately she replies: 'You're the journalist. Find out.'

Blomkvist receives a cryptic document from Salander about 'Prosecutor E' leaking information to the media, but not 'the old police report'. He doesn't know what she's talking about and asks her to tell him exactly what she knows. She says she will think about it, and this is the first 'rapprochement' Larsson has forged between his protagonists since Lisbeth left Blomkvist – a canny delay, as the author will be well aware that his readers will now feel an impulse towards such a moment – more satisfying if delayed.

It's interesting to speculate on how much Larsson himself may have personally used *Expo* as a weapon, given the tactics he now has his hero employ. When Blomkvist says *Millennium* will expose the sexual abuser, police officer Björck, the man pleads for compassion, but Blomkvist asks him where that quality was when he abused the underage girls. On his way out, Columbo-fashion, he asks him 'one last question' (the TV detective always reserved a final, crucial query): has he heard of a man named Zala? The result, after a moment of disorientation, is dramatic – Björck appears to be in shock: how could Blomkvist know about Zalachenko? (The first time we've heard the man's full name.) The policeman asks him what it's worth. If Björck could lead the journalist to him, will his name be left out of the report? Blomkvist agrees.

With a variety of plot strands in the air, it's clear at this point that Larsson felt the need to concentrate his narrative (and, *inter alia*, the reader's attention), so a compression is effected in terms of incident. Hedström, stopping off at Central Station to have a coffee at George Café, is depressed. He really wanted Salander dead by now, so to have coppers Bublanski and Modig (who he imagines might be an item) suggest she's not even the culprit is very bad news for him. He looks up to Faste for being the only one to speak his mind. Blomkvist has visited a retired judge in Tumba – and we are now presented with another of Larsson's subtle detonations of conventional morality, pointed up by an unexpected reversal of expectations. The judge cheerfully admits seeing prostitutes and supporting their 'honourable profession'. Blomkvist has now crossed off six from his list of suspect names. Eriksson calls him as he is driving back at 10 pm to say the online edition of the *Morgon-Posten* claims that Wu is back. Blomkvist says he will go and see her right away.

In Part Four (which Larsson, in another characteristic popular culture reference, calls 'Terminator Mode'), we are provided with a flashback to Salander's point of view of recent events. She spends the first week of the police hunt in her new apartment in Fiskargatan, mobile off and SIM card removed. She follows the media stories with astonishment, and is irritated by the passport photo used of her, which she thinks makes her look stupid. Supposedly private medical records have been unearthed and are now openly accessible to the public, including her attack on the passenger at Gamla Stan underground station. His name was Karl Evert Norgren, an unemployed man who had tried to sexually assault her on the train.

(At this point, it might be worth considering the fact that Salander in the trilogy is such a persistent victim of violent sexual assaults – does she choose her victimhood, consciously or otherwise? The feminist response to elderly judges' suggestions that women provoke sexual interest by their dress is rightly indignant, but it has to be said that Larsson has the reader wondering why his heroine is such magnet for rapists and brutes. Unless, of course, the answer is in the area of plot exigency: Larsson has to provide a rationale for Lisbeth's crowd-pleasing dispensing of mayhem.)

She had swung on a pole and kicked her attacker in the face with both feet; dressed as a punk she had no hope of escape into the crowd and was apprehended by another passenger. She curses her build and gender – no one would have attacked her were she a man. (Again: is Larsson being disingenuous?)

A high-ranking witness, an MP for the Centre Party, had seen Norgren's attempted rape, and as he already had two sexual offence convictions (and is clearly another of Larsson's army of male dross), the case against Salander was dropped. But she was nevertheless still declared incompetent and put under guardianship.

Depending on which paper you read, Salander was psychotic, schizophrenic or paranoid – but definitely mentally handicapped; and undoubtedly violent and unbalanced. Her friendship with lesbian Miriam Wu had provoked a frenzy. Wu's involvement with provocative S&M shows at gay events (and the publication of topless photos of her) had obviously boosted circulation figures enormously. Since Mia Johansson's thesis was about the sex trade, this could have been a motive for Salander to kill her – because, according to the social welfare agency, she was a prostitute. Then her connection with the band Evil Fingers was revealed and the reactionary press once more had a field day. She was described as a psychotic lesbian who belonged to a cult of Satanists who propagated S&M, hated mankind, especially men, and had international links too (since Salander had ventured abroad).

One article provokes an emotional response: an old maths supply teacher, Birgitta Miass, and a class bully, David Gustavsson, have accused her of threatening to kill them when she was at school, 15 years ago. In fact, the teacher had tried to make her accept a wrong answer, which she had refused to do, leading to violence. The bully, 'a powerful brute with the IQ of a pike' had beaten her up badly, and she had hit him in the ear with a baseball bat the next day as retaliation. She resolves to track them down when she has the time. (Again, Andrea Dworkin and Catharine MacKinnon between them could not have created such a populous gallery of loathsome male grotesques as the male writer Larsson comes up with.)

Salander watches the TV interview with Dr Teleborian who expresses concern for her welfare. But when he had been caring for her, his main treatment had been to strap her down in a bed in an empty room, the idea being that stimuli of any kind might provoke an outburst. In fact, this was plain old sensory deprivation, a common technique in brainwashing and classified by the Geneva Convention as inhumane. She had spent half her time at St Stefan's enduring this 'psychiatric treatment'. Watching him talk turns her heart to ice, and she wonders if he still has her teeth marks on his little finger.

She had thought at first that, after 'All the Evil' had occurred, she would be treated well. But no one in authority would listen to her, and on her thirteenth birthday she was strapped down on the bed for the first time. Teleborian was the worst, most loathsome, sadist she had ever met – worse than Bjurman because the doctor was cloaked in a mantle of respectability. Anything he did could never be criticised. If Teleborian had been in charge of St Stefan's, she would probably still be there to this day. As she watches him being interviewed, she realises there is no one around to question his opinions.

Lisbeth reads with interest the victim profiles in the newspapers. Bjurman (in a typically Larssonian criticism of conventional moral judgements) is described as a saintly do-gooder, a campaigner for the little people, a Greenpeace member, and genuinely committed to his ward. Svensson is just passed off as a sharp reporter, while his partner gets much more space – a sweet, intelligent young woman with a promising career ahead of her. It's not until Easter Sunday that Svensson's link with *Millennium* is established, and there are no details of what he was working on.

When she reads Blomkvist's deliberately misleading quote in *Aftonbladet* about Svensson's research on computer hacking, she realises that he is trying to contact her. She logs into his computer and finds his message to her. Now it is not just her against Sweden ('an elegant and lucid equation') – she has an ally, a 'naïve do-gooder' who she never wanted to see again.

She has not been innocent since the age of ten – 'There are no innocents. There are, however, different degrees of responsibility' is clearly an important concept for her. But 'Kalle' Blomkvist could be useful to her. A stubborn moral crusader, he would need a motive to act on his own, so she gives it to him: 'Zala'.

Larsson now has his female protagonist using her hacking skills – along with her equally honed masquerading talents – to advance the plot (by now, these 'online activity' sections are as skilfully handled and engrossing as any of the kinetic action sequences). She logs in to the police criminal register under the name of Superintendent Douglas Skiöld of the Malmö police, but there is no trace of Alexander Zalachenko. No surprise, as he has never been convicted of a crime. While she's online, she is contacted by 'Plague', the recluse weighing 150 kilograms, who makes Salander look like a positive socialite. He asks her who Zala is and she tells him to fuck off, but then requests that he hack into Ekström's computer. Plague never leaves his apartment in Sundbyberg – Larsson is good on the sociopathic types who boast nonpareil computer skills, elements of whom he incorporates into his heroine.

Salander dons her blonde wig, removes her eyebrow ring, pockets Irene Nesser's Norwegian passport, and packs her

Mace spray and a Taser. It's 11 pm, Friday night, nine days after the murders. She takes a bus to St Eriksplan and walks to Odenplan, where she breaks into Bjurman's apartment.

On finding Bjurman's bloody bed, she is happy he is out of her life (Larsson maintains a ruthlessness in his heroine). But she wants to find what the connection is between Zala and him, and also where her missing case files have gone – part of a brief which summarised her psychological state. She searches his apartment, the attic, and his Mercedes, but finds nothing.

Berger rings Blomkvist at 7.30 on Sunday morning to tell him the boxer Paolo Roberto (a real-life figure who would play himself in the film of the book) will be visiting him – training with him earned Salander the 'Terminator' sobriquet. Roberto arrives and says that he believes his boxing partner to be innocent of the crimes she's accused of.

Larsson is careful to maintain the power plays and bargaining chips his characters utilise against each other – perhaps a metaphor for the subterfuges the author practises on the reader (the misdirection, for instance, that pleasurably interrupts a smooth 'reading' of the text). Björck is worrying about his career in the Security Police if Blomkvist reveals he slept with underage prostitutes. He knows Bjurman was hunting for Zala (Björck had given Bjurman the top secret file about him), and as Svensson had also been hunting him, then Zala is a clue in both murder scenes. On Saturday, Björck had gone to his office and re-read the old documents about Zala, the ones he himself had written. The oldest was 30 years ago, the newest a decade old. 'A slippery fucker', he thinks. Although he doesn't understand how every piece slots together, the connection is crystal clear: to Enskede, Bjurman and Salander. He thinks he knows why Salander killed Mia and Dag and is terrified that if she blabs before she is apprehended and (hopefully) shot dead by the police, she could break 'the whole story' wide open. He knows he will have to confide in Blomkvist so that the journalist keeps quiet about his indiscretions. He has Zalachenko's phone number, and wonders whether he should ring it.

Salander sends Blomkvist a message:

'Keep away from Teleborian ("he's evil"); Wu is innocent; focus on Zala; Björck may be the connection between Bjurman and Zala; why doesn't Ekström know about her damaging 1991 police report?; she didn't kill Dag and Mia, she left them before the murders happened; how did he know about the Wennerström affair?' Blomkvist replies saying how relieved he is to hear her say she's innocent.

It might be noted that Larsson has taken his own sweet time in this book: at last – 400 pages in – there's a link between the two murders. Blomkvist calls Björck and tells him that he will name him at a press conference at 10 am later that day unless he, Björck, gives him information about Zala. The cop knows he has no choice but to agree.

The brutal criminal and rapist Sandström awakes to find himself tied up, lying on the floor in a dimly lit room. Someone slips a thick cotton rope over his neck, and he panics, seeing a block and tackle fastened to the ceiling. He looks up at his assailant, and doesn't immediately recognise the wanted criminal Salander. She has short black hair (a wig), is dressed in black and has a hideous painted face like a mask: white make-up, with a red stripe down her face. 'She looks out of her fucking mind,' he thinks. She hoists him up and sits down in front of him with his own illegal gun, which she loads with bullets. Once again, although Salander has moral right on her side, the reader might question Larsson's use of this repeated tactic of abusing the abuser; while many readers clearly consider such individuals fair game, it's intriguing to speculate if Larsson concurs or is simply following commercial revenge fantasy imperatives.

She holds up a photo she has printed off his computer – of Sandström with 17-year-old Estonian prostitute Ines Hammujärvi – and asks him in a quiet voice why men feel the need to document their perversions. She calls him a 'sadistic pig, a pervert, and a rapist' and says that if he screams, once she has removed the tape from his mouth, she will zap him with 40,000 volts from her Taser, which she had previously used on him outside. This will make his legs go limp and he will hang himself. 'It has probably not escaped your attention that I'm a madwoman who likes killing people. Especially men.' He is crying with fear at this point. But if he answers all her questions, truthfully and without evasion, she will let him live.

The terrified Sandström tells her about Ines. She was presented to him as a favour for smuggling anabolic steroids from Estonia, with a friend called Harry Ranta. Harry's brother, Atho, had offered Ines to him at a party, saying that she needed punishment for not doing what she was told, i.e. not whoring for him. She was living with Harry's girlfriend; Sandström and Atho had driven to her place; Atho had tied her down and Sandström had raped her. He continued to visit her and rape her ('They wanted her to be... to be trained') for a 'good price' (a few thousand) in return for his help with the smuggling. Salander asks who Zala is – he says he doesn't know, other than just somebody Atho knows. Svensson had asked him that too. Sandström had spoken to

Zala on the phone once, when he was asked to drive an amphetamine-loaded car. It was a nightmare: Sandström had refused to do the job and to 'persuade' him, Harry and the brutal Atho put a bag over Sandström's head and drove him to a warehouse in Södertälje. There he found a badly-beaten man (Kenneth Gustafsson, he discovers later) tied up on the floor plus an imposing blond giant and a man with a ponytail, Magge Lundin.

The blond giant broke Gustafsson's neck right in front of him, literally squeezing him to death, to show him what happens to snitches. Then Lundin sawed off Gustafsson's head and hands with a chainsaw (here again, the presiding influence may be said to be Thomas Harris, who upped the ante in terms of blood-bolstered violence in modern crime fiction). The blond then put his hands on Sandström's shoulders, as if to repeat the action, and Atho made a call in Russian to Zala. Zala asked him whether he still wanted out – Sandström, of course, said no. Sandström has never told this story to anyone, including Svensson. But he had told Harry about Svensson's visit. Salander can get nothing further from him and so she lowers him down, washes off her 'mask' make-up and leaves him a knife to cut himself loose. Then she leaves his apartment with his Colt 1911.

As noted in this study, the various popular culture influences on Larsson have been many and varied, and Chapter 25 might be said to reference the modern Jerry Bruckheimer-style action movie rather than more literary sources.

Roberto, Lisbeth's boxer friend, sees Wu approaching her flat after 11 pm – but a dark van pulls up behind her and the blond man jumps out and grabs her from behind. A kick to his head has no effect – with a chop, she is down and he is tossing her into the van. Roberto comes to life and runs to help, but it's too late, the van does a u-turn and disappears in the direction of Högalid Church. He follows in his car. In the van, Wu's nose is bleeding, her lip is split and she probably has a broken nose. She tries kicking her attacker again, but he just smiles. He slaps her face hard, sits on her back and handcuffs her wrists behind her. She feels a paralysing fear.

Blomkvist is passing the Globe Arena on his way home from Tyresö; he has spent the afternoon crossing three more frightened punters off his list of suspects. He rings Berger and Eriksson to see how they've got on but gets no answer. So he tries Roberto and gets a broken-up phone message saying something about a van with Miriam.

At this point, Larsson is comfortably juggling his multiple ticking clocks with the assurance that is his purview by this stage of the trilogy. Roberto's phone has gone dead. He can't even get through to the emergency services. He's in a BMW with a full tank, so he knows he can outrun Wu's abductors, and he pulls back several hundred metres behind to follow them without attracting attention. He's annoyed that he let the 'giant on steroids' beat up a girl in front of his eyes.

Roberto backtracks, looking down each side road until he sees a glint of light in the trees. He gets out and jogs to a warehouse in the middle of a sandy gravel area. In front is a yard full of containers, a front-loader, a white Volvo and the van. The loading bay door opens and Magge Lundin ('Ponytail') appears. There is a half-choked howl from the van – the blond giant carries Wu out under his arm ('as if she were a paper bag') and Ponytail drives the van away. Miriam Wu is dumped on the cement floor of the warehouse; she knows she's going to die here. But she won't die without a fight. She kicks at the giant, to his ribs, his crotch, his hip and his breastbone, but he casually slaps and kicks her, breaking a rib.

We are now squarely into Larsson in action mode – something the author handles with quite as much brio as anything else in his literary arsenal. Roberto follows the sound of her screams and sees the giant setting a chainsaw down in front of her, telling her in an accented high-pitched voice ('as if it had never broken') to answer a simple question: where is Salander? She doesn't know, so the thug picks up the chainsaw. It's at this point that Roberto strides out and punches him extremely hard in the kidneys. But it's like smashing his hand into a concrete wall – the boxer has never experienced anything like it during his 33 professional bouts in the ring. 'Blond' is astonished, but not hurt. Roberto lands heavy blows on him, but Blond is unaffected. He recognises his attacker as the famous boxer he is, then swings a right hook which glances painfully off Roberto's shoulder. Despite being slow, Blond is incredibly strong.

As so often with action sequences, Larsson is on confident ground here. They continue the life-or-death fight. All Roberto's years of training seem geared to this one event, a mere 180 seconds. Every punch he throws has a lifetime's force behind it, but Blond is not affected. At first Roberto thinks he's up against another boxer, but then realises the giant is just pretending. He's slow, telegraphs his punches, can't box effectively – but he has a devastating power in his punch and seems insensitive to pain. They move round the rubbish-strewn warehouse, Blond connecting and breaking one of Roberto's ribs.

Suddenly Roberto has the dreadful, but inevitable, feeling that he's about to lose. He tries to win time, to regain strength, but Blond is just toying with him. Roberto throws a totally unexpected right hook, and at last feels something give way. He avoids the giant's slow, obvious punches and sends in a body blow and a left hook that connects with Blond's nose. Thinking he is now in control, the giant kicks his leg and he drops down. It's all over… until Wu kicks her enemy from behind, landing a blow to his testicles.

Wu had managed to slip her bound hands underneath her and stand up. She had seen Roberto fighting the giant and had done the obvious thing – kicked him in the crutch. But Blond hasn't gone down for long and now he is grabbing her and hits her on the head. As he scrambles to his feet, Roberto swings a plank onto the back of his head. Blond falls forward with a crash.

Roberto, aware of a terrible pain in his right knee where he thinks he's torn a muscle, slings Wu over his shoulder and takes her outside and into the cover of the woods. The giant crashes after them. He picks up a sharp rock, making the sign of the cross – he is ready to kill someone, for the first time in his 'sinful life'. But Blond realises he can't follow them in the dark and returns to the warehouse, picks up a bag and drives away in the Volvo. Roberto sinks back, adrenalin gone, and tells Wu not to be afraid of him, that he has a car not far away. (All of this is handled in customarily pulse-racing fashion by Larsson, as if thinking of the movies that would result from his very cinematic narrative.)

Roberto is driving like a drunk, Wu asleep on the back seat. He gets onto the E20, then the E4 to Stockholm. Every part of his body aches.

Part of the pleasure of crime fiction is, of course, the careful balance of the paying out and withholding of information, and Larsson – despite his all-too-brief career as a practitioner – perfectly judges the apposite moments in this strategy. It's Chapter 26 before we learn the identity of the murderer – neither too soon (to vitiate tension) nor too late (to seem like a conventional 'wrapping up' of the narrative). Bublanski, woken by Blomkvist, meets Modig outside the Söder hospital and they speak to the beaten-up Roberto, who explains what happened the night before, and that Salander used to spar with him at his gym. Blomkvist says that the 'ponytail and beer-belly' guy (Lundin) was the same one who attacked Salander on Lundagatan, that Wu's kidnapping seems to have been done in order to find out where Salander was, that the two thugs hardly seem like members of a lesbian Satanist gang, and that the events have something to do with Zala – the injuries sustained by Roberto and Wu match those inflicted on the severely beaten prostitute Irina Petrova.

Modig arrives at *Millennium* and meets Berger, whom she immediately likes.

Now Larsson reacquaints us with his heroine. Dressed as Irene Nesser (black leather jacket, dark trousers, red sweater and glasses), Salander has taken the bus to Lake Mälaren, where Bjurman's summer cabin is. She searches everywhere but finds nothing. Then she sees a stepladder and realises the cabin has a concealed attic: there she finds two A4 box files containing folders and documents.

Meanwhile, it turns out that the blond giant was worried, but had an enormous respect for Zala's 'almost uncanny strategic gifts'. He drove straight to Dag's apartment in Enskede, parked his white Volvo two streets away, rang their doorbell and shot him dead, along with a woman (Mia Johansson). The only thing he took was a computer. In holding this and fishing for his car keys, he dropped

Bjurman's revolver, which skidded downstairs to the basement. Running out of time, he left it where it was – a mistake which proved fortunate, as the police then concluded Salander, whose fingerprints were on the gun, was the murderer.

So that left Salander as the last remaining link with them – she had known Bjurman and she knew Zala. So she had to be silenced. But everything had gone wrong after they kidnapped Wu. Paolo Roberto, of all people, had turned up and rescued her. After burning down the warehouse in Nykvarn, he had gone to Lundin's house in Svavelsjö, to hide and lick his wounds.

Larsson's narrative strategy often involves his characters tying up loose ends (as he himself conscientiously does as a writer). Thus, the giant suddenly remembers there is another loose end to tie up – Bjurman. The guardian had shown him a file about Salander (when Zala had accepted the job of disposing of her). If this was found, it could lead the police to Zala. He phones Lundin and tells him to get down to Stallarholmen and start another fire...

Jerker Holmberg rings from the gutted warehouse. The sniffer dog has found a man's leg buried in a shallow grave 75 metres away in the woods. And the dog's found another spot 80 metres from the first. Forensics have already been called.

Larsson's parcelling out of information to the reader is at times paralleled by the fashion in which he allows his characters to learn things about themselves. Salander is reading through Bjurman's extensive notes on her, finding things even she didn't know existed. Palmgren's notebook journals are included. He had started writing them when she was 15. She had spent 12 days living with elderly foster parents who expected her to be continually grateful, till she had stolen 100 kronor, escaped and gone to live with a 67-year-old man in Haninge. He had just wanted to look at her naked, not touch her, in return for which she was fed and given a place to live. When someone reported the man's actions, he was accused by social workers of sexual abuse, but Salander denied it, saying that as she was 15 it was legal anyway. (Non-Swedish readers will note the difference in the laws here.) This is when Palmgren took over, writing entries from December 1993. He had put her up in his apartment for Christmas, treated her like an adult and explained that she had a choice – to go back to St Stefan's or live with a foster family.

She discovers the missing police report from 1991, written by Dr Loderman, in which Teleborian features heavily. Then correspondence, dated just after 'All the Evil', between Björck and Teleborian, with the former telling the latter that she should be institutionalised for the rest of her life to stop her from creating problems 'regarding the matter in hand'. She is utterly shaken. Teleborian had known Björck – so when Björck had wanted her buried, he had turned to the doctor. It wasn't coincidence after all – nobody was innocent. She decides to have a talk with Gunnar Björck.

She packs Palmgren's notebooks, the 1991 police report, 1996 medical report and correspondence between Björck and Teleborian, and goes to leave. She hears motorbikes outside, Harley-Davidsons. There's no time to hide – she steps out and confronts whoever it is.

By now, readers will probably no longer consider Lisbeth's outbursts of uninhibited violence surprising from such a physically un-intimidating source – Larsson has by now conditioned his readers to expect it. Interestingly, the novelist Lee Child is keen to avoid his hero, Jack Reacher, being perceived as invulnerable. Readers, Child knows, need to feel that the protagonist is sometimes in real danger and not able to just effortlessly triumph in every confrontation. It's a moot point whether or not Larsson (at this juncture in the sequence) has not fallen into this trap. Lundin and Sonny Nieminen head from Svavelsjö to Stallarholmen, there to meet Salander on the driveway of Bjurman's summer cabin. She gives them a mouthful of invective, and Lundin (still showing the scars from where she injured him with her keys) laughs, thinking, 'How could this skinny kid think she stands a chance with two hard bikers like us?'

Lundin swings at her, but she just steps back. Then she sprays him in the eyes with Mace, kicks him in the groin and then slams her boot in his face as he topples onto his knees. Nieminen unzips his jacket to get out his gun, but Salander kicks him to the ground and fires her Taser into his crotch, using 50,000 volts. Lundin gets up, half blinded, and she coolly shoots him in the foot with his accomplice's gun, a Polish P-83 Wanad. She walks away, and then suddenly turns round and looks at Lundin's bike. 'Sweet,' she says.

Although Larsson is careful to include passages of straightforward, 'normal' sexual activity in the trilogy, he is perhaps most comfortable with misdirection and metaphor in this area – as when Salander rides a motorbike, huge under her tiny frame, all the way back to the fairground at Alvsjö, sensually relishing the sensation of speed and power. She takes a train to Söder, then walks to her flat at Mosebacke and takes a bath.

Björck tells Blomkvist about Alexander Zalachenko, one of the 'most deeply buried secrets' within the Swedish defence system: the extortion, the corruption and everything leading up to his seeking of asylum in Sweden and joining Säpo, the Security Police. Björck and Bjurman were working as junior officers for Säpo in 1976 when Zala made contact, walking straight into Norrmalm police station and seeking asylum. Björck was his mentor, dealing with Bjurman's paranoid behaviour and binge drinking. Björck still refuses to give Blomkvist Zala's assumed name, so the journalist decides to visit Palmgren.

It's not until Chapter 28 that Larsson reveals Zala's true identity. Blomkvist has persuaded Dr Sivarnandan that he must see Palmgren. The elderly doctor accepts that he wants to help Salander and so reveals to him the shocking information that the brutal Zala is... Lisbeth's father.

Her mother was Agneta Sofia Sjölander, who never married Zala but in 1979 changed her name to '*Sala*nder' to be more like 'Zala'. But Zala – absent much of the time – became abusive to her whenever he returned home; Agneta was forced to go to hospital dozens of times. An archetype of Larsson's 'Man Who Hate Women' scenario.

Then 'All the Evil' happened. Zala had returned when Salander was 12, and violently abused her mother. But Lisa interrupted the beating and stabbed Zala five times in the shoulder with a kitchen knife. He was hospitalised, but there was no police report – the result of Björck's intervention. Zala returned, leaving Agneta unconscious, and Salander threw a carton of petrol at him in his car, which she lit with a match. Hence his foot was amputated due to the horrendous burns. Then Salander ended up at St Stefan's.

Larsson's plotting here is as rigorous as one could wish – all of the elements that motivated his narratives perfectly dovetailed. Salander re-lives the time she was taken away by the police for trying to kill her father. Palmgren, meanwhile, tells Blomkvist he's sad he never took up Salander's case properly. Lisbeth herself watches the TV news in astonishment – she had no idea about Wu's kidnap or Roberto's involvement. At least three burial pits have been found by the warehouse.

She hacks into Milton Security, gets a surveillance car hired out in an employee's name, and (in a plot element that stretches the reader's credulity, even given Salander's vaunted expertise) doctors the CCTV cameras and packs her Taser, Mace spray and Nieminen's gun. She uploads her PowerBook contents online, scrambles its hard drive and takes her PDA with her. She picks up her car, a Toyota Corolla, from Milton's garage, having got in unseen, and drives off as the sun is rising.

Blomkvist suddenly (and it has to be said, rather too conveniently, at this stage in the plot) finds Salander's door keys that have fallen out of the bag he picked up from her. One has a PO Box number on it – and almost immediately he is at the Hornsgatan Post Office rifling through her post. Salander goes into the Auto-Expert car hire firm in Eskilstuna and – threatening the mechanic with her gun – finds out who the owner of the hired white Volvo is. It is Ronald Niedermann, 35, a German from Hamburg – the murderous blond giant. She gets his PO Box number and heads to Göteborg. Also in the know (and armed with Salander's Colt), Blomkvist takes the train to Göteborg.

Having cannily engineered the key elements for a confrontation, Larsson now begins to move the tempo to *accelerando*. Salander is now staking out Gosseberga Farm, having followed the man's black Renault into the forests near Lake Anten. She watches as Niedermann comes out, along with a thin older man with a crutch. This is Zalachenko. Her father. She checks the bullets in her gun and puts the safety catch on.

She opens the door to the farmhouse; it is unlocked. She feels uneasy, and her instincts are correct. A trap has been laid – she is jumped from behind by the giant who throws her down onto a sofa. She Tasers him but he doesn't react (Larsson has given him the Bond villain characteristic of an inability to feel pain). Zala enters – the figure Larsson has painted as a monstrous nemesis is now an old, emaciated man, bald, his face a patchwork of scar tissue, with a prosthetic foot and two missing fingers. He regards her without emotion and explains that the farm is surrounded by motion detectors and cameras and they've been monitoring her ever since she arrived. We are reminded just how adroit the author is at creating this kind of fraught scenario – and of maintaining the tension. Niedermann leaves, and Larsson gives the reader a crash refresher course in the unspeakableness of one of his chief villains, Zala, as pungently unpleasant a creature in the author's grotesque pantheon as Larsson created in his brief novel-writing career.

Zala calls her a whore, and her mother a whore who made sure she got pregnant and tried to get him to marry her. He tells her that Bjurman wanted him to get the DVD from her, by having Niedermann saw one of her feet off – appropriate compensation for his own handicap. But when Bjurman panicked after taking Svensson's telephone call, Niedermann, who was in his apartment, made the decision to shoot him there and then.

He calls her a dyke, says Niedermann should have sex with her, that she is filth. Salander tries to rile him, to make him drop his guard, but he refuses to rise to the bait. He asks after his other daughter Camilla, 'the one with brains'.

It was Niedermann – currently out performing 'an errand' – who shot Bjurman. And who is this blond giant? Larsson has reserved another shocking surprise for us: it is none other than Salander's half-brother, from a brief affair when Zala had an assignment in Germany in 1970. Zala tells her she has at least four more brothers and three sisters in various countries, all the products of similar liaisons. In such films as *Psycho* and *Notorious*, Alfred Hitchcock famously created off-kilter, monstrous versions of the family and parental relations; relatively radical in their day. But by Larsson's era, the author is able to forge an even more astringent (and unholy) version of the family: Salander's damaged psyche is, we learn, a result of an anti-family, a perfect perversion.

Salander tells Zala that *Millennium*, Dragan Armansky and Bublanski are all after him, but he is adamant that there is not a shred of incriminating evidence in his home. Niedermann comes back, attaches a silencer to his gun and they all troop out into the woods (needless to say, few readers will at this point be turning the pages in leisurely fashion). There Lisbeth is roughly pushed into a freshly dug pit, but before she is shot by the giant, she holds up her palmtop, claiming everything they've said has been broadcast on internet radio. Zala sees she's lying, and as Niedermann examines her hand she strikes out at the giant with a spade, breaking his nose (again). They fight. But Zala has a gun too and fires three times at Salander… killing her? It appears so. A bullet lodges in her brain, causing massive trauma and... it seems... death.

Zala is shaking, amazed that she almost got away. They

dump her body in the hole and bury her. Zala is relieved that she is dead at last. They go back to his house and he gently tends Niedermann's wounds. Like one of the writers he admires, Ian Fleming, Stieg Larsson has apparently killed off his protagonist at the end of a book (although readers' knowledge that this is Part Two of a trilogy may be an indicator of the surprises to come).

After a long train delay, Blomkvist arrives in Göteborg, takes a cab to a car he's hired and drives out of the city at 10.30 pm.

Salander awakes to find herself buried alive. She starts digging her way upwards through the soil. (An incidental *locus classicus* here might be Tarantino's *Kill Bill Vol. 2.*) Eventually she has surfaced and, in great pain, wanders off through the woods to Zala's farmhouse. She thinks about looking for a petrol can and a match and goes into the woodshed. Zala hears her and goes out to investigate. Salander swings an axe at his face, cleaving into it, then wedges it in his knee. She doesn't have the power to kill him cleanly. He is incapacitated, and she takes out the gun he shot her with – it's only a Browning .22 ('a bloody boy-scout pistol') which accounts for her still being alive.

Having already ratcheted up the mayhem to a near-delirious level, Larsson shows he still has aces up his sleeve. Niedermann wakes up from a nap when he hears Zala's screams. He enters the woodshed and sees Salander, but knowing she is dead he thinks it's a demon. He fantasises that she has a lizard-like skin, a whipping tail, glowing eyes, spiked teeth and spouts flames from her mouth. She shoots at him but narrowly misses. He runs away in abject fear.

She doesn't shoot Zala, choosing to keep her last bullet for Niedermann, and goes back to the farmhouse where she is shocked by her corpse-like appearance – no wonder the giant was terrified. She arms herself with his gun, a P-83 Wanad. She realises how badly she is injured. In another improbable suspension of disbelief, Larsson has us accept that she can feel her brain through the hole in the back of her head.

Niedermann is ashamed of running off, but doesn't think there's any point returning to help Zala – it's a lost cause now. All he needs is a car to take him away to Göteborg, and then he sees one racing towards him. Blomkvist's, presumably.

Salander puts the gun to her head... she is so badly injured that she just wants to end it all.

Blomkvist stops as Niedermann waves him down. Realising who he is, the journalist points his Colt 1911 Government gun at him, gets him to lie down and ties him securely to a road sign, and sets off for the farm. He finds the wounded, moaning Zala in the woodshed. Then he goes to the farmhouse and finds Salander. She has the gun in her hand, but clearly hasn't had the energy to fire it. Her eyes are unfocused. She whispers, 'Kalle Bastard Blomkvist.'

He dials the emergency services.

The ending of the remarkable second book in the trilogy has a markedly different feel to that of its predecessor. Whereas *The Girl with the Dragon Tattoo* functioned as a self-contained entity, Book Two feels very much like the consciously conceived second part of a sequence, with a masterly orchestration of effects leading inexorably to the final book of the *Millennium Trilogy*. And as the trilogy has clearly been conceived as an entity, there is no sense of the famous (and dreaded) 'second book syndrome' – whereby the debut book of a new novelist is followed by a marking-time, lower-key entry. In fact, Larsson didn't have time for such niceties; everything had to be as near-fully-realised in its achievement as he could make it. Did he have a sense of his own pending mortality?

CHAPTER 9

THE BOOKS:
The Girl Who Kicked the Hornets' Nest

A tattooed young woman lies in intensive care, a bullet in her brain. A few rooms away is the man who has tried to kill her – her father. His body bears multiple axe injuries (inflicted by the young woman). If she recovers, she will face trial for three murders – but not if the man down the hall is able to kill her first.

There's no arguing that *The Girl Who Kicked the Hornets' Nest* hits the ground running, and the pace rarely lets up for an arm-straining 600 pages. It's an exhilarating, if exhausting, read. But the book is also something very special, and unique, in the world of crime thrillers.

Once again, Stieg Larsson grabs our attention with his two protagonists: Lisbeth Salander and the journalist Mikael Blomkvist, who fights to clear her name – even though she dumped him as her lover. Salander's numerous enemies here include some very nasty types, from her hideous father to equally murderous secret organisations and self-serving politicians. And these various nemeses all want her discredited

– or dead. Larsson is unsparing in the area of grisly violence (one more characteristic – along with a vulnerable heroine – he shares with another bestselling author, Thomas Harris). But this is a strong and satisfying conclusion to a massively ambitious, richly detailed trilogy, and readers will regret that this is our last opportunity to share the invigorating company of Lisbeth Salander – until we watch the various films of the books.

The minute and detailed analysis of plot incident with which the first two books have been addressed seems not quite as appropriate here; not because there is less plot (in many ways the narrative is as densely packed as before), but because there is a trajectory in which individual incident is perhaps not as important than the rounding off of certain themes and notions about the central characters. Part One is entitled 'Intermezzo in a Corridor', and this musical allusion is certainly on the ironic side. The musical form employed throughout this book is largely *accelerando* with none of the languor of an intermezzo.

The chapter begins with a superscription concerning the hundreds of women who served during the American civil war disguised as men, and Larsson makes points about historians having difficulty dealing with gender distinctions. (His remark about women taking part in Swedish moose hunts has a certain unintended irony from a left-wing writer such as Larsson, when most readers' image of a moose-hunting woman will be the extremely right-wing presidential hopeful Sarah Palin.) He goes on to discuss Amazons and warrior women, mentioning Boudicca, honoured with a statue in London on the Thames near Big Ben, and suggests that the reader 'say hello to her if they pass by'. One might argue that his own warrior woman, Salander, is somebody one would be ill-advised to say a casual hello to. Particularly if you are a male who has been engaged in any inappropriate sexual activity.

The doctor, Jonasson, who is reporting on Salander, is tired after a variety of life-saving operations, and is described as a goal-keeper standing between the patient and the funeral service, with his decisions ineluctably life-and-death ones – ironically, of course, life-and-death decisions are those repeatedly taken by the two protagonists throughout the length of the story. Jonasson is told that the girl lying injured in the hospital room is Lisbeth Salander – the girl who has been hunted for weeks for a triple murder in Stockholm. This does not particularly interest him, as he perceives his job to be that of saving a patient's life. We are given a vivid picture of the barely controlled chaos of an A&E department, and a brief character sketch of the doctor, which some readers might see as irrelevant, but will now recognise this as a part of Larsson's strategy to flesh out the bones of his narrative. We are given a report on the woman in her mid-20s who is lying, barely alive, with a weak pulse and various bullets in her body. The fact that she is still alive after having a bullet lodged so near her brain is considered something of a miracle.

After this arresting opening, Larsson cuts to Blomkvist, looking at a clock and discovering that it is after three o'clock in the morning. He is handcuffed, exhausted and sitting at a kitchen table in a farmhouse near Nossebro. Blomkvist is remonstrating with a man who is keeping him prisoner, calling him an imbecile: 'I warned you he was dangerous, for Christ's sake... I told you that you would have to handle him like a live grenade.' Blomkvist is in a state of some depression, having found Salander after midnight, wounded in what might be a mortal fashion. He had sent for the rescue service and the police. The medics had also taken care of Alexander Zalachenko. We are reminded that this man was both Salander's father and her worst enemy – he had tried to kill her and had earned an axe wound in his face and considerable damage to one of his legs for the attempt.

Calling Erika Berger on his mobile, Blomkvist fills her in on the situation, pointing out that Salander is the one who is in considerable danger. The policeman with whom Blomkvist is so infuriated is Paulsson, who is presented by Larsson as the most thick-headed kind of copper. Blomkvist tries to explain that the man who had actually committed the murders in Stockholm was not Lisbeth but Ronald Niedermann, an incredibly powerful man who had been left sitting tied to a traffic sign in a ditch. The attempt to arrest him by Paulsson's men has, of course, resulted in bloody violence and the escape of a highly dangerous man. Blomkvist insists that a call is made to Inspector Bublanski – a policeman that the journalist knows he can trust.

We then cut to another sympathetic copper, Inspector Modig. She has awoken at four o'clock to learn from Bublanski that everything 'has gone to hell down in Trollhättan'. She is told that Blomkvist found Salander, Niedermann and Zalachenko, and her colleague gives her a rough idea of the state of things. These two intelligent police officers realise that the situation has degenerated into something like chaos. A further police discussion ties up plot elements with which the reader is now familiar – such as the fact that the ruthless Zalachenko is Lisbeth's father and was a hitman for Russian military intelligence, who defected in the 1970s and has been running his own criminal network since that date. All of this is conveyed by Blomkvist, who now looks utterly exhausted. Inspector Erlander, listening to the summing up (including the fact that Salander is innocent of the murders she is accused of) finds himself willing to listen, particularly as he does not give much credence to the deductions of the inefficient Paulsson. However, the story is so outrageous that he finds his credulity being stretched.

Larsson takes us back to the hospital room where Doctor Jonasson is pulling off his bloodstained gloves after the operation. We don't yet know the result. Blomkvist, meanwhile, has persuaded Erlander that Salander was shot and buried at the farmhouse, but has somehow managed to survive and dig herself free. The police continue to search for the escaped monster who had cut a swathe through their ranks – a missing patrol car is discovered, and it is supposed that the escaped criminal has switched vehicles. Blomkvist asks if there is any information concerning Salander's condition and is told that she has been operated on during the night, with a bullet being removed from her head. He asks about Zalachenko and the police at that point are not aware who he is talking about. However, Blomkvist learns that Lisbeth's father was also operated on last night for a deep gash across his face and another below the kneecap. His injuries are severe but not life-threatening. Blomkvist is talking to Modig who, broadly speaking, he trusts. He points out that he knows Salander's secret hideout, but as she has spent considerable time creating the bolt hole for herself he has no intention of revealing it to them. Modig reminds him that this is a murder investigation, to which Blomkvist snaps, 'You still haven't got it, have you?' Lisbeth is in fact innocent and the police have violated her and destroyed her reputation in ways that beggar belief.

This is, of course, part of the strategy that has been necessary throughout the three books and is not a million miles away from the tactics utilised by Hitchcock in such films as *North By Northwest* and *The Thirty-Nine Steps*: make it absolutely imperative that the central protagonist cannot call on the police for help, so that they are always at the extreme reaches of danger from both the heavies and the forces of the establishment. Of course, things are ratcheted up to the nth degree in the *Millennium Trilogy*, but the process remains a sound one in terms of engaging the reader's sympathy. Blomkvist, of course, is more like most readers in being the person who is able to talk to the police and, to some degree, help to clarify the strands of the tangled narrative.

By now, more and more police are involved, several of whom are convinced that Salander was guilty of murder, and there is perhaps a danger that the author has introduced too many police officers, both sympathetic and otherwise, into the narrative – it is undoubtedly true that even the most well-disposed of readers sometimes have to struggle to remember which particular copper is being talked about at any moment (perhaps another reminder that a few profitable pruning sessions with an editor would have been an asset for Larsson). Later, Blomkvist remembers that his rental car was still at the farm, but he was too exhausted to call for it. Erlander arranges for the car to be picked up. It is at this point that the journalist makes a significant call, to someone he can trust – his sister Advokat Annika Giannini, a woman who will figure importantly in the narrative. When he has explained Salander's extreme situation, Annika asks if Lisbeth might require her services as a lawyer. Her brother replies that the accused woman isn't the type to ask anyone for help, but it is clear that from this point on – whether she wants it or not – Salander is to have someone else on her side. It might be noted that Larsson both admires Lisbeth's self-sufficiency and simultaneously regards it as, finally, inadequate – she needs help, just as she herself offers it to a chosen few. She is, we are reminded, an incomplete personality.

The police search for the grotesque Niedermann continues, without much success (Larsson is aware that a man of such a distinctive appearance should be easy to track down, and does have his characters acknowledge this). The police talk about an inventory of the woodshed in which Zalachenko was found and there is another one of the author's famous trouncings of an unsympathetic character (in this case, not – as is usual – a violent one). The wrong-headed Paulsson is disbelieved by all of his colleagues and has collapsed from exhaustion. There is general dissatisfaction about the fact that the incompetent policeman arrested Blomkvist. Finally, the ludicrous idea of a lesbian Satanist gang in Stockholm is trashed, and the police realise that Säpo, the security services, are involved and that perhaps – as Blomkvist claimed – there has been some kind of cover-up. The reader, of course, is aware that Zalachenko is being protected after his defection, and the attempted framing of Salander is all part of this fairly despicable attempt at concealment. The police finally realise that the next logical step is to interrogate Zalachenko with a view to finding out what he has to say about the murders in Stockholm – as well as learning Niedermann's role in Zalachenko's business (it is accepted that Zalachenko may be able to point them in the direction of the violent missing man).

As often happens in the trilogy, we are taken back to the offices of the magazine *Millennium*, and it is interesting to note how well these sections always function within the context of the novel – possibly because while much authorial invention is required for the more outlandish developments in the plot, in the sections involving the magazine, Larsson is able to draw upon his own experience in such environments to create a total verisimilitude. Erika Berger is talking to Blomkvist's sister Annika, and the editor tells the lawyer that she is planning to resign from the magazine but hasn't yet been able to tell her colleague and lover as he is so involved in the chaos surrounding Salander. Erika is, in fact, leaving to be the editor-in-chief of another prestigious journal – basically, an offer she cannot refuse. For the rest of the chapter, we are filled in on the dynamics of *Millennium* itself – not least the fact that its survival is now possibly in some doubt.

Chapter 3 begins in the company of the deeply unpleasant Zalachenko, who has been awake for several hours when inspectors Modig and Erlander arrive in his room. He has undergone an extensive operation in which a large section of his jaw has been realigned and set with titanium screws. The axe blow has apparently crushed his cheekbone and taken off a section of the flesh on the right side of his face. He is now, appropriately, physically the kind of monster that he has long been morally. Zalachenko's approach with the two policemen is to pretend that he is now a broken man, old and lacking in physical resources. He points out that he had felt threatened by Niedermann, and when he is asked why his daughter threw a Molotov cocktail into his car in the early 1990s, he replies in a hostile tone that Salander is mentally ill.

Provocatively (playing good cop, bad cop), Modig decides

to go in for the kill, by asking if his daughter's actions had anything to do with the fact that he, Zalachenko, had beaten Lisbeth's mother so badly that she suffered long-term brain damage. Zalachenko's reply is characteristic: 'That is all bullshit. Her mother was a whore. It was probably one of her punters who beat her up. I just happened to be passing by.' Zalachenko points out that he wishes to press charges against his daughter for trying to kill him. Modig decides to dispense with any attempt at politeness and points out to Zalachenko that she now understands why his daughter would try to drive an axe into his head.

At this point in the novel, of course, its most charismatic and iconic character has been notable for her absence for some time – Larsson appreciates that he needs to ration out the appearances of his characters for them to retain their mystique. Salander awakes, aware of the smell of almonds and ethanol, and voices around her note that she is finally coming around. She can barely speak as Doctor Jonasson tells her that he has operated on her after an injury. Lisbeth has only vague memories of the appalling violence and conflict she has been through – and in which she has taken a considerable part herself.

Having established his heroine again, swimming back to a kind of consciousness and coherence, Larsson returns the narrative to Blomkvist, who has booked himself into a hotel room and is starting to feel human once again. Blomkvist is stunned to learn that Erika has decided to take a job on another magazine and rather hurt to find that he is the last to find out. As often before, Larsson now reintroduces us into the company of his deeply unpleasant heavies, notably the violent Nieminen, still smarting (both physically and otherwise) over the punishment he has undergone at the hands of the slight (but devastating) Salander. Nieminen and his equally unpleasant colleague Waltari find the murdered bodies of two of their associates: the woman's neck has been broken and her head turned through 180 degrees, while the man has had his larynx rammed deep into his throat. The criminals are conscious of the fact that Niedermann was on the run and needed cash – the man he has murdered is the one who handles the money. The duo realise that they must track down Niedermann, which will require every contact they have in the clubs all over Scandinavia (one of them says: 'I want that bastard's head on a platter').

Salander, in the hospital room, is slowly recuperating and talking to another doctor. At the same time, Zalachenko, still in extreme pain, is being visited by the police (including 'that bloody Modig woman') but he is not offering any suggestions as to how to track down Niedermann – now pursued by both the police and the heavies. Zalachenko begins to calculate how he is going to come out at the other end of this situation, and consults his colleagues in the security services as to how he can effect damage control. While Larsson presents the spooks as unsympathetic, they are mere beginners compared to the man they are helping, who says – about his own daughter – that she has to disappear. Her testimony must be declared invalid, and she will have to be committed to a mental institution for the rest of her life.

We are, of course, once again in the kind of situation that Larsson has frequently created for his beleaguered heroine, and it is a mark of his skill that he is still able to persuade the reader that such things could still happen, given the number of people who now know how Salander has been framed.

However, it is perhaps easy to see from this that the perfect number of books to feature Salander was three – after a trilogy, it would be extremely unconvincing if the author were obliged to keep putting his heroine back into this particular situation *ad infinitum*.

Of the various scenarios that Larsson created to turn the screws on his protagonists, perhaps the most striking is the fact that Salander is recuperating in a hospital room just a few doors away from her murderous father. Blomkvist visits the other sympathetic male 'protector' of Lisbeth – her sometime employer Armansky – and asks the latter whether he can trust him or not. Armansky replies 'I'm her friend. Although, as you know, that's not necessarily the same thing as saying she's my friend.' But while Armansky is not prepared to engage in any sort of criminal activity, he is happy to listen to any strategy that Blomkvist might suggest in order to help Lisbeth. This, of course, involves Blomkvist's sister Annika representing her legally. At this point, Larsson introduces another new character, an ex-Senior Administrative Officer at the Security Police, the elderly Gullberg who, although he has retired, still maintains a professional alertness.

We are then given one of the extensive Larsson character fill-ins that either help illuminate (if you are a sympathetic reader) or infuriate (if you are not), but which undoubtedly have the effect of bringing to life characters who become involved in the narrative. Gullberg had been involved in the Wennerström debacle, which caused major problems in the Security Police. Gullberg and his colleagues were financed through a special fund, but outwardly did not appear to exist within the structure of the security policy. Gullberg is at this point unaccountable to anyone. It is here that the author once again brings in real events by having Gullberg remember Election Day, 1976, and his own thoughts on the suitability as prime minister of real-life politician Olof Palme (who was, of course, assassinated). But in connection with Zala's defection, Gullberg remembers a young man who would be prepared to bend the rules in the service of his boss: Gunnar Björck, who has, of course, figured throughout the narrative. Björck had dealt with Zalachenko when the latter requested asylum, and the two men were involved when a massive structure of secrecy was built around the prize defector.

Also involved in the reception for Zalachenko was the lawyer Nils Erik Bjurman who, of course, was one of the many sexual abusers of Salander and the man who has had particular cause to regret what he had done to her. Larsson has now provided us with another spectacularly nasty set of individuals, with Lisbeth's murderous father at the centre. Gullberg makes it clear that even the very name 'Lisbeth Salander' instilled in him a deep displeasure, but he has also grown to loathe his charge Zalachenko. He is well aware that the latter is a 'sick bastard', but considers that making moral judgements is not his particular problem. In another lengthy exposition, Larsson tells us that Björck came up with a solution to the Zalachenko problem – after the latter's attack, everyone involved in the case was to be quietly filed away with Salander committed to an institution for the insane. Björck's boss Gullberg thoroughly approved the operation. After this filling in of the back story – actually fascinatingly handled (though there is no doubt that Larsson could occasionally be pedestrian in this kind of passage) – we are taken back to Salander in her hospital bed removing her neck brace and hunting for a weapon. We are reminded that whatever has been done to her, she remains the ultimate survivor.

Critics of the *Millennium Trilogy* have pointed out that Salander's implausible capacity for survival in this final book is worthy of a super-heroine, but while the author has always maintained a level of verisimilitude, he has also tacitly requested a certain suspension of disbelief where the abilities of his heroine are concerned. And most readers who have got this far would be more than prepared to extend that suspension.

Zalachenko is moving around the room on crutches and training himself to be able to move again. Salander opens her eyes when she hears a scraping sound in the corridor and a grim thought occurs to her: 'Zalachenko is out there somewhere'. She is still in a neck brace and finds it difficult to move. Gullberg is informed that Björck is on sick leave – and the Zala affair is still very much on Gullberg's mind. In the department there is a discussion of Salander and her fractious relationship with her sister Camilla, who was informed that Lisbeth was violent and mentally ill. They talked about their spectacular fight. It's known that she has attacked a paedophile and that Bjurman was Salander's guardian. They also discuss the fact that Inspector Bublanski considers that Bjurman raped Salander – news that astonishes Gullberg. He is told that Bjurman had a tattoo across his belly which read: 'I am a sadistic pig, a pervert and a rapist'. Gullberg shows at this point an unusual streak of black humour: 'Zalachenko's daughter... You know what? I think you ought to recruit her for the section.'

Ironically, these enemies of Salander are prepared to accept the truth of this incident – a fairly unusual happening given the reluctance on the part of any establishment figures to believe that Salander is anything but the violent sociopath she is portrayed as. Gullberg and his associates discuss the fact that Bjurman made a contract with Zalachenko, hoping to get rid of the man's daughter. The Russian, of course, had good reason to hate Lisbeth, and he gave the contract to the hulking Niedermann.

At this point, Larsson takes us back to a situation which is both threatening and fraught with a certain black humour. Salander is now fully *compos mentis* and is discussing her condition with the doctors. She learns that her father ('the old bastard') is down the hall – and realises that the scraping sound she heard was that of his crutches. Zalachenko has made it perfectly clear to Gullberg that unless the whole situation involving his hated daughter is resolved, he will crack the section wide open by talking to the media. They realise that he will have to be offered something.

Interestingly, Gullberg and his colleague Sandberg now consider the real problem is Zalachenko, not Salander (who they feel they can handle). They begin to examine the other people involved in the case, including the prosecutor Ekström and the policeman Bublanski. They note the fact that the policewoman in the investigation, Sonja Modig, is something of a special case, as is the 'tough customer' Anderson, who was sent by Bublanski to arrest Björck. Realising that the stage management of the affair is now getting ever more complex, Gullberg finally discusses with his colleagues the troublesome journalist Blomkvist, the man who submitted Björck's report to the police. They are aware that Salander is somehow the link between everyone, but come to no conclusions.

Larsson now details for the reader the complex strategy used by Gullberg and his associates to deal with a convoluted situation. Dissenters from the view that Larsson justifies the immense amount of attention that has been paid to him have pointed to this section of the book as needlessly complicated. But aficionados know that nothing here is overcomplicated for its own sake – all of these elements have to be put into place so that the various resolutions will have sufficient dramatic weight. One element of the plan is to bug everyone connected with *Millennium*: Berger (even though Erika has left the magazine), Blomkvist and his lawyer sister Giannini.

Meanwhile, the doctors have decided that Salander's condition is stable enough for her to receive visitors. These include police inspectors, who spend 15 minutes with her – one of them is Erlander and the other Modig. Lisbeth has reluctantly agreed to be represented by Blomkvist's sister Giannini and she is told that the police are looking for a German citizen whose name is Niedermann, wanted for the murder of a policeman. She tells them that she thinks Niedermann will go abroad. When asked why, she replies that while Niedermann was digging a grave for her, Zalachenko mentioned that things were getting too hot and that it had already been decided that Niedermann should get out of the country.

Then (just in case the reader is thinking that things are finally going well for the beleaguered Salander) she is told that her father has made a formal accusation of murder against her, and that the case is now at the prosecutor's office. She is, in fact, already under arrest for having attacked Zalachenko with an axe. Modig leans forward to tell her that the police put no faith in the Russian's story. This unexpected move from the police surprises Salander: her standard response to them is one of loathing, and her initial impulse to think that perhaps she has finally encountered some human beings on the force is quickly dispensed with ('there will be some ulterior motive' is her cynical summing up of the situation).

In Chapter 7 there is a meeting between Blomkvist and Salander's old employer, Armansky. Those who could recollect the beginning of the very first book in the sequence will remember that it wasn't immediately established that Salander was really the central character of the sequence (despite the fact that she is the eponymous subject of all three books – at least in the English translations of the titles). But it's perfectly clear by this stage of the final book that everyone – including the characters – know that they are all satellites revolving around the short-tempered shooting star that is Lisbeth Salander. Blomkvist says to Armansky, 'When this is all over I'm going to found an association called "The Knights of the Idiotic Table" and its purpose will be to arrange an annual dinner where we tell stories about Lisbeth Salander.'

The object of this attention wakes up with a start in her hospital bedroom, aware that she is being watched. She sees a silhouette with crutches in the doorway. It is Zalachenko. She thinks about stretching out her arm to break off the rim of a glass – it would take half a second to push the broken glass into her hated father's throat if he came close to her. But he quietly retreats into the corridor. Salander has a meeting with her new attorney, Blomkvist's sister. (Blomkvist, in the meantime, is reading all he can about the secret services.) Giannini conveys a message from her brother concerning a DVD – Salander is to decide whether or not she should tell her advocate about it (it is, of course, the film of Bjurman raping Salander). Salander is instructed that she is not to say anything to anyone except her lawyer – needless to say, this is something that Lisbeth is happy to accept without question.

Some readers may be led to speculate exactly what Stieg Larsson's view of humanity was. Certainly, the central characters of his books, including the two principal protagonists, and several of those with whom they interact, are individuals with whom the reader can, to some extent, identify – although the terrifyingly violent Salander behaves in a way that is (it has to be said) off the scale for most readers. But these relatively sympathetic individuals are far outnumbered by the unspeakable miscellany of criminals, rapists and lowlifes with which the duo are obliged to deal. Certainly, life is cheap for most of the other characters in the sequence, notably such establishment figures as Gullberg.

It is in Chapter 7 that the real ruthlessness of this character is demonstrated, in a fashion that is reminiscent of a similarly abrupt murder in James Elroy's *LA Confidential*. Gullberg visits Lisbeth's father Zalachenko and asks him if he really planned to betray them after all they had done for them. The Russian replies that he is a survivor, and does what he has to do to survive. To his surprise, Gullberg snaps back that he considers him to be evil and rotten, and that he is not going to lift a finger to help him this time. Gullberg unzips the outer pocket of his case and pulls out a nine-millimetre Smith & Wesson revolver. 'What are you going to do with that, shoot me?' laughs Zalachenko. And at that point Gullberg squeezes the trigger and places a bullet in the centre of the Russian's forehead. He follows this up by placing the muzzle against the Russian's temple and pulling the trigger twice (reasoning that 'he wanted to be sure this time that the bastard really was dead').

Down the corridor, Salander hears the shot, but doesn't realise that a job she had tried to do has been finished for her by someone else. Gullberg leaves the building, making no attempt to force his way into Lisbeth's locked room. But Larsson's surprises for the reader in this chapter are not over. Gullberg raises the gun a final time, presses it to his own head and pulls the trigger. In fact, he does not kill himself and lies somewhere between life and death.

Blomkvist is at a coffee bar when he hears of the death of Zalachenko, and leaving his coffee untouched snatches up his laptop and rushes to the editorial offices of *Millennium*. He asks immediately who the killer is, but nobody as yet knows (inevitably, he will be drawing the wrong conclusion). Erlander discusses with Malmberg the identity of the murderer – a 78-year-old man called Evert Gullberg who they say is a retired tax lawyer and who has a habit of sending threatening letters to people in government (including the minister of justice). But a discussion between Gullberg's associates has Clinton delivering some significant information about Gullberg – he points out that he has been carrying the gun around for six months. He had cancer in the stomach, colon and bladder, and his violent act was one last favour for the section. His assignment was to make sure that Zalachenko never got a chance to talk.

When Gunnar Björck hears about the shooting in the hospital, he experiences a deep panic, and realises that he is now vulnerable and exposed. He goes back to the cabin and is astonished to see that the ceiling lamp has been removed and that in its place hangs a rope from a hook above a stool. He turns round, his knees buckling beneath him and sees two men of southern European appearance. They carry him to the stool, and calmly lift him up, gripping him under his arms.

Larsson provides an interesting paragraph for the policeman Erlander, investigating the elderly man who has killed Zalachenko. He wonders if he is one of the pathologically obsessed individuals that the world appears to be full of, such as those who stalk celebrities and look for love, and when the love is not returned – as inevitably it isn't – it turns to violent hatred. Larsson then provides a similarly dispiriting list of the stalkers and psychopaths who populate the modern world, including conspiracy theorists and those who have the gift to 'read messages' hidden from the world that most of us inhabit. The passage is one that has a certain strength, as one feels that these are the people who concerned the author himself, as much as the right-wing extremists who were his target when working for *Expo* and suchlike. It was not a comfortable world, the one inhabited by Stieg Larsson – and perhaps his creation of two characters who can (to some degree) bring order out of chaos was an attempt at some kind of amelioration of the real world in fictional terms.

Continuing the physical personal threat that is one of the hallmarks of the final book in the trilogy, there is an assault on a character who has already been threatened with a gun – Blomkvist's sister. She arrives with a black eye and a gash above her eyebrow to tell him that her briefcase has been stolen, and it contained the Zalachenko report that he gave her. Although he says it doesn't matter and that it's possible to make another copy, he realises with horror that she is now a target.

Part Two of *The Girl Who Kicked the Hornets' Nest* is entitled 'Hacker Republic', and begins (as is customary with Larsson) with a feminist superscription, this time from an Irish law of the year 697 which forbade women to be soldiers – suggesting (as the author points out) – that women had been soldiers previously. Again we have a reference to the Amazons, almost as if Larsson thinks the reader may have forgotten this particular metaphor being conspicuously drawn for his combative heroine. It's interesting that Larsson also speculates on the fact that the traditional image of the Amazon with the right breast removed in order to facilitate the drawing of a bow (the word literally means 'without breast') is not verified by any drawing, amulet or statue of a woman in a museum.

After a section in which we see Erika Berger attempting to fit in to her new magazine post, Larsson shows us Blomkvist under observation from Malm. The latter notes that Blomkvist is, in fact, clearly being tailed. In a conversation with Armansky, the journalist identifies the men who have been following him as representatives of Säpo. In the middle of the discussion between Blomkvist and Armansky there is a section in which the author's own views are (one feels) made clear. It's suggested that the Security Police invariably made fools of themselves – the natural order of things – and Larsson adduces for his argument examples from all over the world, such as the French Secret Police sending frogmen to New Zealand to blow up the Greenpeace ship *Rainbow Warrior*. Blomkvist learns something useful from Armansky – the latter has a contact within Säpo who is to be trusted, and in the battle ahead, this contact will be worth his weight in gold.

If Larsson at times invites the reader to be irritated at the actions of his characters, that is nothing compared to the irritation they cause in those they interact with in the narrative. Giannini is tired and frustrated after her dealings with Salander – she knows she is hiding something, as is Annika's brother. Giannini tries to convince her client that her constant withholding of information will mean that she will be convicted, but Salander doesn't seem to care.

We are then given another passage in which Larsson demonstrates his mastery of the psychology of the book's protagonist: Lisbeth examines in her own mind the effect she has on many of the people around her. It isn't the case that she simply doesn't care how she is received; things are more complex than that. But the element of self-loathing and self-destructiveness that was evident in the first book is still a motivator for her actions, often as powerful as her hatred of those who have set themselves against her.

Salander's doctor, Jonasson, is visited by a man who is (he informs him) Peter Teleborian, the head physician at a psychiatric clinic in Uppsala. He was, he tells Jonasson, Salander's psychiatrist when she was institutionalised, and the two men disagree on a diagnosis – the more sympathetic Jonasson suggests Asperger's syndrome, but the reply is that Asperger patients do not generally set fire to their parents. The visiting psychiatrist believes her to be a clearly defined sociopath. Teleborian, however, is unable to persuade Jonasson that a visit with Salander is in order and leaves abruptly.

Blomkvist, meanwhile, is convinced that Salander is, as before, being set up for a fall and the articles he is writing for *Millennium* present a problem – he is not sure how to portray her in these pieces. The journalist has arranged a meeting with Idris Ghidi, a man he feels can be useful to him.

The latter's brothers were murdered by Saddam in the 1980s, along with his uncles a decade later. Blomkvist tells him that he has a job for him which is not illegal, but unusual. He tells him that he knows that one of his jobs is at the Sahlgrenska Hospital, cleaning a corridor in the intensive care unit six days a week. Ghidi nods assent to this, and Blomkvist tells him what it is that he wants him to do.

Of course, Larsson is fully aware that elements of conspiracy are *de rigueur* in any novel in this trilogy, and the ante is upped when Ekström continues to orchestrate a campaign against Blomkvist, based on the fact that he may reveal information about Zalachenko. He persuades others that they must do as he says in this regard, as Sweden is now in a particularly exposed position and that the fate of the country is in the hands of those who will help him silence the journalist. Even the KGB is invoked as part of the destabilising campaign supposedly orchestrated by Blomkvist and the dangerous Salander (she is considered, in colloquial terms, 'stark raving mad').

Bublanski learns to his dismay that the continuing investigation of Salander will be conducted by the highly inappropriate Hans Faste, and that both he and the equally untrustworthy Ekström will be handed all the information concerning her, along with the story about Björck and Säpo. Modig is as disturbed as her colleague to hear this, but they realise that their hands are tied – and that their principal job is still to find the killer.

The psychotic Niedermann has, to all accounts and purposes, vanished from the face of the earth. For some time, Larsson has been conducting his plot on the level of conversational moves and counter moves – all fascinating, but lacking the suspense generated by physical detail. This is to come – forcefully – when Ghidi, hired by Blomkvist, is to perform a series of actions outside Salander's room, including unscrewing the screws in the cover of a vent. This is of course as an aid to communicating with Lisbeth, and to this end, Blomkvist contacts her doctor Jonasson and asks the reluctant surgeon to hear him out – he tells him that he is an investigative journalist and knows the truth about what happened to her. (He also points out that Annika, his sister, is her lawyer.)

He reminds the doctor that she has been described as a psychotic and a mentally ill lesbian mass murderer which is (as he says) nonsense. He also mentions the German Niedermann, a man without a shred of conscience who is being sought in connection with the murders. Finally, he tells the astonished doctor that the reason Salander was put into a children's psychiatric clinic was because she had stirred up a 'secret' that Säpo was trying to keep a lid on – that Zalachenko, her father (who was murdered at the hospital) was a Soviet defector and a spy. He also points out that the police officer Hans Faste – who works for the prosecutor Ekström – is corrupt. In order to help her, Blomkvist needs to give her a hand-held computer and battery charger – the key weapon in her arsenal – but Jonasson is still not convinced. Then the journalist takes a folder from his briefcase and tells him some sobering facts about Dr Peter Teleborian.

Chapter 12 continues the balancing act that Larsson is able to pull off so effectively in terms of advancing his plot while making cogent political points which are clearly dear to his own heart. We meet Superintendent Torsten Edklinth who is a director of constitutional protection at the Security Police. He has known Salander's employer Armansky for 12 years, ever since a woman MP had received death threats. Edklinth's association with the sympathetic Armansky is, of course, something that ensures that the reader will be well disposed towards him. However, he is not prepared for Armansky 'lobbing a bomb with a sizzling fuse' into his lap. When the latter tells him that the Security Police are involved with straightforward criminal activity, Armansky qualifies it by saying that *some* people within the Security Police are involved in such activity. This leads to a section in which Edklinth has a stream of consciousness which at times seems to directly reflect its author's opinions: 'Swedish democracy is based on a single premise: the Right to Free Speech (RFS); this guarantees the inalienable right to say aloud, think and believe anything whatsoever'. As Larsson notes, this would also include crazy neo-Nazis – his own *bêtes noires*.

As a sort of 'catch-up', Larsson allows Edklinth a few paragraphs in which he assesses what he has been told: Security Police officers had ignored the fact that a series of brutal attacks took place against a Swedish woman (Salander's mother), then her daughter was incarcerated in a mental institution on the basis of a fraudulent diagnosis, and finally, *carte blanche* was granted to an ex-service intelligence officer to commit criminal offences which involved sex trafficking and weapons. Needless to say, Edklinth is not enthusiastic about the idea of getting involved in this. He is however obliged to submit a report on the situation to a prosecutor. The woman he contacts is Inspector Monika Figuerola and she similarly regards the whole affair with horror and dismay.

Erika Berger is suffering something similar to the kind of misogynistic attacks that Salander has been the brunt of, although the attacks are in the nature of abusive e-mails. Meanwhile, Salander's physical condition is being assessed by her doctor and he asks what she thinks of Teleborian – she replies that he is a beast. Lisbeth is soon in computer contact once again with Blomkvist, and Larsson renders their exchanges in an uncharacteristically humorous fashion (particularly at this point when the trilogy is at its darkest). There is, *inter alia*, a discussion of the difference between dedicated computer hackers and those who create viruses ('hackers [are] implacable adversaries of those idiots who created viruses whose sole purpose is to sabotage the net and crash computers') – perhaps an example of Larsson's own credo here. The Hacker Republic who are now in touch with Salander are unknown to her, but become a useful source of information. Blomkvist tells her that the police haven't found her apartment and do not yet have access to the DVD of Bjurman's rape. Blomkvist doesn't want to turn it over to Annika without her approval.

One of Larsson's particular skills in the trilogy is the creation (one might almost say along assembly lines) of noxious villains, and another one is discovered by Blomkvist – Erika Berger's boss is a crook, a man who exploits child labour in Vietnam. If any reader were in doubt about those whom the author regards as the lowest of the low by this point in the book, they haven't been paying attention. Berger is informed of the situation by Blomkvist – she is, of course, shocked, and has to take seriously his suggestion that she must resign from *Millennium*'s board before the article is published exposing her boss, or resign from the new job ('you can't wear both hats').

Salander meanwhile has enlisted the aid of her computer

associate Plague (he greets her, as usual, as 'Wasp'). She tells him she needs access to the computer of Göran Mårtensson. By the end of Part Two of the final book, Larsson has created what is undoubtedly his most labyrinthine series of plots with a rather unwieldy *dramatis personae*. Even the most faithful reader may feel a little tasked, but Larsson aficionados will know that he will be able to draw all the strands together.

Part Three is called 'Disk Crash'. Once again we have a superscription, this time involving the Amazonian reign (described as a 'gynaecocracy'), and Larsson reminds us that these women rejected marriage as subjugation, and that only a woman who had killed a man in battle was allowed to give up her virginity. The motif sounded in all the other superscriptions is, in fact, maintained here.

Erika Berger, meanwhile, continues to be the subject of a vicious assault conducted through jpeg images and Photoshop. She is sent a pornographic image of a naked woman wearing a dog collar, down on all fours, being mounted from the rear. There is a single word at the bottom of the picture: 'whore'. This is the ninth message she has received containing this word, sent by someone at a well-known media outlet in Sweden. She is being cyber-stalked.

Intriguingly, as Larsson propels his protagonists through an increasingly baffling investigation, one of the tactics he allows his characters to employ is the analysis of faces in photos – a throwback, in fact, to the tactics used by Blomkvist in the first book in the sequence. Blomkvist is taking his investigation to the highest levels – including the Prime Minister – while Salander is finally writing a detailed journal of the abuses she has suffered at the hands of her many and varied enemies. It is a scarifying document, and something of a précis of the three novels we have been reading. Berger is now experiencing considerable apprehension, convinced that her cyber assailant is someone working for her new organisation, SMP, and enlists the aid of a bodyguard from no less than Armansky, Salander's former employer.

Continuing the wistful theme of the attractions of mature male journalists, Blomkvist, the eternal middle-aged Lothario, has attracted yet another woman – Monika, the Säpo investigator who is working with him. She knows that he had a relationship with Salander – she points out that the young woman is Zalachenko's daughter – but the couple agree to keep things on a friendly level despite the sexual attraction. Berger's house, which has been equipped with surveillance along the lines suggested by her new minder, does not give her reassurance – particularly when she finds that her drawers have been rifled through and the familiar five-letter word, 'whore', has been spray-painted inside. Ironically, Berger finds herself with an unlikely ally – the combative Salander, who contacts her over the internet (needless to say, the psychological violence Berger is undergoing is very familiar territory for her).

There is a fascinating discussion between the two women of the nature of stalkers – Salander considers that the person tormenting Berger is like a parody of real stalkers (she, of course, knows what she is taking about). We are nearly 400 pages into the final book of the trilogy, and Larsson is still pulling off the trick of allowing Lisbeth to direct events (to a large extent) from a hospital bed. She tells both Berger and Blomkvist that the sinister Teleborian is meeting Jonas at Central Station – they only have a few minutes to get there.

Jonas is, of course, an undercover agent. Blomkvist monitors the meeting. Also involved is the canny Modig, who is able to observe Teleborian having a rendezvous with a grey-haired man she has never seen before, along with Ekström. Are the men meeting to finalise the procedure for nailing Salander at her trial? Lisbeth, herself, meanwhile is still logging in to Berger's e-mail and notices something about the company she works for – all the heads of department are men. Is one of them her stalker?

At times throughout the trilogy Larsson has played in a post-modern way with the concept that the reader is aware they are reading a fiction; he brings up the notion again in an electronic discussion between Blomkvist and Salander. She tells him that she is being moved to prison tomorrow and that Plague is helping out on the net. 'So,' he says, 'all that's left is the finale.' The finale is, of course, the last 200 pages or so of the novel and it is undoubtedly true that, as before, Larsson is able to accelerate the tension at a steady and controlled rate. Plague tells Salander he has discovered that a man called Fredriksson, a colleague, is almost certainly the stalker – he accessed his work computer from home and Plague has found that he has pictures of Berger scanned onto the hard drive. Salander sends a succinct e-mail to Blomkvist, using his first name: 'Mikael. Important. Call Berger right away and tell her Fredriksson is Poison Pen.'

The unpleasant Inspector Faste who was also involved in the meeting that was being monitored earlier, encounters Salander for the first time on Sunday morning when a woman police officer brings her into Göteborg's headquarters. He has already decided that she is 'fucking retarded'; she, meanwhile, is not even prepared to acknowledge his existence. Berger, during this time, has informed security guard Susanne Linder that Poison Pen is her stalker – Linder realises that the information could only have come from the enigmatic Salander. Unsurprisingly, Linder is later involved in a violent confrontation with Fredriksson, utilising the same uncompromising tactics that we have seen Salander use against sexual predators. She handcuffs him after knocking him to the ground.

In Fredriksson's apartment, Linder finds incontrovertible proof on the former's computer (while Fredriksson looks on, cursing splenetically that he is Berger's stalker). Later, Berger is given the news and experiences a rush of relief, and she makes the decision to give Susanne Linder an expensive Christmas present. In her prison cell, Salander receives a very unwelcome visitor who greets her with a friendly 'Hello, Lisbeth'. It is the unlikeable Teleborian. Readers who begin Part Four of *The Girl Who Kicked the Hornets' Nest* (called 'Rebooting System') may experience a certain twinge of regret that this will be their final encounter with the characters they have come to know so well. Once again there is a superscription involving Amazon warriors but it appears that Larsson has – largely speaking – run out of interesting things to say about them, as there is nothing that appears to illuminate the narrative we have been reading.

Chapter 23 begins two weeks before the trial of Lisbeth Salander. The case against her is closely argued and documented. The section begins with Blomkvist talking to the attractive Figuerola, telling her about his relationships with both Salander and Berger. He even admits that he is now in love with her. As we are moving towards the end of Blomkvist's multiple conquests during the course of the trilogy, readers, both male and female, may be prepared to extend a little indulgence to him in these concluding pages. Blomkvist makes a call to another woman – one of the few who it appears is not prepared to fall at his feet – promising her an exclusive on an 'absolutely massive story' that he is about to break. The reader, of course, is fully aware what this is. Now begins a truly impressive task of marshalling a diverse *dramatis personae* to get the beleaguered Salander off the hook. All of the remaining nemeses of the diminutive computer hacker slowly become aware that a phalanx of evidence is being directed towards them, with Blomkvist as the progenitor. The battle is turning in Salander's favour.

Desperate last-minute tactics are utilised by the Säpo heavies, including attempts to frame Blomkvist, but the momentum has shifted against them. And because such a resolution of the plot might seem a little sedate after the extreme violence of what has happened earlier in the sequence, Larsson allows violence to explode in time-honoured fashion as a burst of fire from a sub-machine gun is directed against Blomkvist. A massive struggle ensues, in the assailant is knocked unconscious.

Salander's trial begins. Blomkvist notices a tactic that his sister Giannini has utilised – that is to dress Salander in her customary confrontational leather gear rather than trying to present her in some kind of sanitised version that the jury will be suspicious of. But there is still a considerable mass of evidence levelled against her. All of Salander's nemeses are paraded in the court, including Zala and Bjurman, with attempts by the prosecution to whitewash the latter. And, unsurprisingly, the most damning case is made against her by the manipulative Teleborian, who calls the autobiography she has lodged with the court 'a total fiction'. But then

Giannini begins her expert demolition of Teleborian, pointing out that he began strapping down her client when she was 12 years old – at a time when she did not possess a single tattoo. All of the antisocial traits that he has criticised her for manifesting are torn away, and he begins to look both ridiculous and unprofessional. Then, the clincher: the involvement with Säpo is made clear, and the report damning Salander in the interests of protecting Zalachenko. By now, the momentum with which Teleborian's position is being demolished is unstoppable. Giannini is even able to bring in Teleborian's attacks on Salander's sexuality and sexual behaviour, dispensing with those just as efficiently as she had made his earlier attacks seem less than objective. And Teleborian's claim that Salander's account of her rape by Advokat Bjurman is a fantasy is torpedoed when Giannini shows the judge the 90-minute film that Salander herself had made of the rape. She need only show a few short extracts – the judge instructs that the film be turned off. But the point is made. Satisfyingly, Teleborian himself is arrested – specifically for the possession of 8,000 pornographic pictures of children found on his computer. As he is led away, Salander's 'blazing eyes' follow him inexorably.

At this point, Giannini suggests to the judge that her client be acquitted on all counts and released immediately – and that, further, she should be adequately compensated for violations of her rights that have taken place. Salander, as uncompromising as ever, has to be persuaded to testify after her release about the Zalachenko affair. She reluctantly agrees. Larsson now begins a satisfyingly valedictory 50 pages, in which we are given some indication of how his characters will live the rest of their lives. Giannini warns

Salander that her brother is not someone to make any emotional investment in, as he has a capacity to hurt women who regard sex with him as anything more than a casual affair. Salander replies, 'I don't want to discuss Mikael with you.' However, Lisbeth grudgingly acknowledges that she has at least been able to form a relationship with her solicitor, Annika, which in the younger woman's terms is a major admission.

It's time for Salander to begin a new life, which she does by travelling to Gibraltar, her third visit to the 'strange rock'. She spots a big male ape climbing on a wall and says to it 'Hello, friend... I'm back.' The metaphor for a meeting between two creatures capable of savagery (Lisbeth knows better than to try to pet one of the apes) is apposite. Soon, she is allowing herself to get so drunk that she is falling off her stool, and approaching middle-age men, telling them that she has 'an irresistible urge to have sex with somebody' before giving out her room number. Naked in her room but for a bath towel, there is a knock on the door, and soon a classic Salander example of what the writer Erica Jong called the 'zipless fuck' is taking place. However, despite giving in to her too-long suppressed libido, Salander is also ensuring that her finances are in order. With her low boredom threshold she is soon in Paris and calling up Miriam Wu. Revealingly, she admits that she wants Mimmi as her friend.

The epilogue of Stieg Larsson's final book is called 'Inventory of Estate' and begins with Giannini meeting Salander in the Södra Theatre. True to form, Lisbeth proposes a no-strings-attached sexual encounter to Annika; the latter says that she is not in the least interested – but thanks her for the offer. Salander abruptly and firmly declines to benefit from her father's estate – she wants nothing whatsoever to do with it ('I don't want a single öre from that pig'). She is happy for a settlement to be made upon her sister. Larsson, however, is not quite finished with the grisly shocks that have been such a constituent element of his books.

Salander, working for Armansky again, investigates a building associated with Zalachenko and notices a nauseating stench in a workroom. She pushes a rod into a pool of stagnant water and a decomposing corpse rises to the surface. She lets the body sink back and discovers something that might have been another corpse. Then she hears a noise. 'Hello little sister,' says a cheerful voice. It is the monstrous Niedermann, with a large knife in his hand. He casually informs his horrified listener of all the diversionary tactics he has used since his disappearance – and he, needless to say, is responsible for the brutal murders. ('All women were whores. It was that simple.')

Larsson has, of course, been saving up his most powerful violent confrontation for the end of the book, and what follows is a spectacularly exciting orgy of violence in which Niedermann begins to feel that Salander is a supernatural force and a monster. With his feet nailed to the floor by his smaller opponent, he finds himself with a nail gun held to his spine, just below the nape of his neck. The suspense is rigidly maintained, as Lisbeth quickly reviews in her mind all the things that this grotesque psychopath has done. But she lowers the weapon. She tells the police where he is, and one wonders if, all along, Larsson had planned for this radical change in the modus operandi of his, usually implacable, heroine. Does this represent a humanising of her? If so, the reader might be forgiven for thinking that we have been invited to enjoy the unfettered blood-letting unleashed by his protagonist against thoroughly deserving monsters, so it is perhaps a little rich to think that we can accept her new change of heart. Nevertheless, it is a highly satisfying, almost-final glimpse of the character.

Salander is at home in the bath when the doorbell rings; she is annoyed but finds that it is Blomkvist. 'Hello' he says. She does not answer. He tells her that he thought she would like to know that Ronald Niedermann is dead, murdered by a gang. He had been tortured and slit open with a knife. 'Jesus,' replies Salander. The mob was arrested but put up quite a fight. And the biker surrendered at 6 o'clock. He asks what she was doing. 'I was in the bath,' she replies. He has bought bagels and some espresso coffee. What he is offering is just company. He is a good friend who is visiting a good friend – 'If I'm welcome, that is.' She realises that this man who has been so much a part of her life for several years is someone she knows all the secrets of – just as he knows all of hers. She also realises that she has no feelings for him – at least not 'those kind of feelings'. And it no longer hurts her to see him.

Larsson then gives us the final line of the trilogy (as it currently exists): 'She opened the door wide and let him into her life again.' It is, in fact, a highly satisfying ending to the novel in every conceivable way. The reader needs this emotional release after the nigh-operatic outbursts of violence and labyrinthine plotting, counter-plotting, betrayal and deception. But it is not the kinetic diversions of the narrative that one is finally left with but the relationship between the two brilliantly realised central characters. It is a measure of Larsson's considerable achievement that it is this emotional connection rather than all the crowd-pleasing action that is the backbone of the *Millennium Trilogy*.

CHAPTER 10

THE FILMS

It was, of course, only a matter of time before filmmakers took advantage of the immensely cinematic properties of Larsson's work, and it is perhaps appropriate that a Swedish company was the first to take the plunge – and enjoyed considerable success by doing so. Yellow Bird is the production company that first optioned *The Girl with the Dragon Tattoo* – and carried the project through to a critically acclaimed, and commercially successful, result. The company's main offices are in Stockholm, but the partners launched a subsidiary, Yellow Bird Pictures, in Munich. The company was originally founded by the Swedish crime novelist Henning Mankell and producers Ole Søndberg and Lars Björkman in order to create films inspired by Mankell's highly thought-of Kurt Wallander novels. It was subsequently bought by Zodiac Entertainment (located in Denmark) in 2007, and was cannily involved in a co-production deal with the company responsible for the British *Wallander* series starring Kenneth Branagh.

Thankfully, the company was not content with simply filming the crime novels of one Swedish master and began to look further afield to swell its portfolio. Its 2009 film of Stieg Larsson's *The Girl with the Dragon Tattoo* – now prefixed by the word *Millennium* – proved to be a highly creditable stab at the late author's work. Needless to say, a considerable amount of filleting was necessary for a novel so crammed with incidental detail – along with a certain compression of character. But this surgery was performed by director Niels Arden Oplev and screenwriters Nikolai Arcel and Rasmus Heisterberg with great intelligence and a keen understanding of Larsson's literary strategies.

A commendable decision was made in keeping the steady, accumulative pace of Larsson's writing rather than injecting synthetic excitement and incident. The result is that when passages of violence occur in the film they have considerably greater impact: a good example is the sexual assault by the corrupt Bjurman on Salander – forcing her to fellate him – and her subsequent violent revenge with dildo and tattoo needle. While the violence and sexual encounters (consensual and otherwise) are powerful, they are relatively discreet by contemporary standards, and one wonders if Larsson might have preferred something totally uncompromising along the lines of Lars von Trier's *Antichrist*. However, the matching of actor to character is exemplary, with both Noomi Rapace and Michael Nyqvist strongly cast as Salander and Blomkvist. Interestingly, there has been a certain negative reaction to the physical attractiveness (or otherwise) of the leading actors: Noomi Rapace is almost always deliberately alienating in her appearance as Lisbeth (although the actress is appropriately striking as the new-look blonde Lisbeth after performing her 'feminising' makeover at the end of the film).

But it is possible to speculate that the mental image readers might maintain of Larsson's heroine – rebarbative behaviour, tattoos and facial jewellery but compelling and fascinating in her sexual omnivorousness – is really more feasible on the page than in the more reductive arena of the cinema.

Regarding Michael Nyqvist's Blomkvist, it might be argued that a man so sexually attractive to women – even though the film cuts down on the number of his sexual conquests – might have been represented by a more charismatic actor with, it has to be said, less markedly pitted skin. But that is not to criticise Nyqvist's trenchant and subtle performance, always intelligent and truthful.

While utterly modern in its trappings, there are some pleasing reminders in the film of Sweden's great cinematic past: one of Ingmar Bergman's most considerable actresses, Gunnel Lindblom, makes a brief appearance as a frosty matron of the Vanger family, while Sven-Bertil Taube (of Jonas Cornell's *Hugs and Kisses*) beautifully – and movingly – renders the more sympathetic Henrik Vanger.

I spoke to leading British film critic Kim Newman, who was one of those impressed by the film, describing it as 'an extremely satisfying mix of mystery, detection, psychosis and social criticism with fully engaging lead performances'. He went on: 'It's no wonder these characters and situations have been so resonant and successful throughout Europe. It takes its time with the separate stories of the protagonists – Mikael is a long-time social campaigner working for a radical magazine, who is forced to cut loose from his circle (*Millennium* is the magazine he works for) so as not to drag them down, while Lisbeth has to cope with a sexually abusive social worker (played by Björn Granath) and her own simmering rage as she is intrigued against her will by the fact that she sees through a part of the puzzle that has resisted solution for decades. In typical Swedish fashion, it's no big deal that the unlikely partners in detection start having sex, but a huge thing when they finally hold hands. The eventual revelation of who the culprits are in the crimes isn't that surprising, but does lead to an unusual moment in which the hero is in jeopardy in the killer's torture room and the girl not only comes to his rescue but gives chase when the baddie tries to get away.'

Newman continued: 'Lisbeth Salander – the girl with the dragon tattoo – has become a major literary heroine, and the unusual-looking, intense Rapace is liable to become an international star off the back of this role (which she's reprised in the two follow-ups). She's the most important Euro action heroine to emerge since Anne Parillaud's Nikita, and an interesting mix of credibly screwed-up victim (her parricidal back story emerges in fragments) and resourceful super-heroine (after her probation officer rapes her, she exacts fitting revenge with a camcorder, a stun-gun, a dildo and a tattoo needle).

'The Swedish title (*Men Who Hate Women*) hints at the sin which binds together the major and minor villains, and there's certainly a feeling for the pattern of misogyny and abuse that has wrought the long-lasting evils. But it's also good on procedural stuff, with clues tracked down in old photographs and newspaper archives and an exhilarating on-the-trail strand as Mikael and Lisbeth uncover a 1950s serial killer in the family history, but also pick up on traces left behind by the elusive, presumed-dead-but-perhaps-not girl whose disappearance has kicked off the plot.'

Newman added: 'It occurred to me that the Blomkvist–Salander team is an effective update of the Steed–Mrs Peel dynamic in *The Avengers*, with the mature man representing decent values and traditions and the younger woman aggressively modern and independent. It's just that now our idea of decent values are those of a 1960s liberal leftie rather than an old Etonian fighter pilot.'

Using members of the same creative team, Books 2 and 3 were also adapted by Yellow Bird in 2009. *The Girl Who Played with Fire* takes an interesting approach in forging the second film in a pre-sold sequence, maintaining a respect for the books but adopting a markedly different, cooler tone to that of the first movie. The original cast is satisfyingly in place, though the director this time is Daniel Alfredson. As befits the novel's passionate concern for women's rights, that theme is foregrounded here, though the orchestration of tension in the various set pieces is less sure-footed. The palpable hit that the film of *The Girl with the Dragon Tattoo* became (it is now comfortably the most successful Swedish-language film of all time) pointed up the problem of how to adapt its successor, *The Girl Who Played with Fire.* The narrative structure of the film is more straightforward and less nuanced than its predecessor, with the parameters for the novel's central conspiracy against Lisbeth, falsely accused of three murders, nicely delineated, along with massive explosions of bloody violence – but with a temperature-dropping sense that, to some extent, the narrative is 'marking time' before the resolution of the final film. Like the novel, the film assumes that the audience will be aware of the bond already established between Salander and Blomkvist – a bond doggedly resisted by her and fought for by him – which essentially means that viewers who have not seen the first film will not understand the essence of the relationship; the protagonists do not meet until the climax, when Salander is lying on the ground, bruised and bleeding (the deferring of this moment, needless to say, gives it considerable emotional force). There is a counterpoint to the shocking scene of sexual abuse in the first film with a graphic lesbian encounter between Lisbeth and her sometime-lover Miriam Wu (shocking to those disturbed by such things, that is; this is a consensual encounter). The casting of the principal villains is hit or miss: Micke Spreitz is perfect as the hulking, impervious-to-pain blonde giant Niedermann, although the Bond villain characteristics are perhaps too obvious on screen, but Georgi Staykov is notably too young as the monstrous Russian paterfamilias, with burn make-up that recalls a low-rent horror film.

The final film – the adaptation of *The Girl Who Kicked the Hornets' Nest*, by the same director as the second movie – is perhaps a disappointment after its predecessors. The first two films accommodated Larsson's somewhat prolix plotting by utilising brisk cutting and condensing the narrative strands, but here Daniel Alfredson seems to feel that the tortuous plot, and much of the dialogue, needs to be given its head – and that is not to the film's advantage in terms of pacing. The tautness of the first film is undoubtedly dissipated. Nevertheless, it's a solid adaptation that does justice to the resolution of Lisbeth's story – even if the knitting together of elements in the finale seems a touch abrupt. In some ways, the last of the *Millennium Trilogy* adaptations is reminiscent of another of the successes of the production company responsible, Sweden's Yellow Bird: the original Henning Mankell *Wallander* television series. There is the same low-key, reined-in playing by the cast, resolutely non-tourist venue location shooting, and the steady accretion of facts and information through which the narrative unfolds (in contrast to the more straightforward, in-your-face style of most American television series and movies). Of course, this aspect of the film most clearly reveals its origins as a Swedish television series, but it is none the worse for that; the reverse, in fact, as it is a refreshing antidote to the hyper-dramatic, unsubtle style of most contemporary thrillers.

As in the previous films in the sequence, the necessary telescoping of events and characters to whittle things down to an acceptable screen running length is done with intelligence and skill, and even has the effect (as in the adroit adaptation of the first book) of lending the plot – almost by accident – a greater level of plausibility. And in the same way in which Mikael Blomkvist's unlikely list of sexual conquests is reduced to a more persuasive number in the first movie, another credibility-challenging element is finessed at the beginning of the film of *The Girl Who Kicked the Hornets' Nest*: although the severely injured, groggy Lisbeth, lying bandaged in her hospital bed after the removal of a bullet from her head, is made aware that her murderous father is in the same hospital, the nocturnal prowlings by Zalachenko are removed. Although, of course, readers of the books will be surprised by this change – one among many – however intelligent the motivation behind it. Similarly, the business of the poison pen e-mails received by a worried Erika Berger has been altered – the immense complexity of the original plot may have been profitably simplified here once again, but it is to the credit of the filmmakers that they have been bold enough to take this initiative.

The film of *The Girl Who Kicked the Hornets' Nest*, of course, boasts two James Bond-style villains, who are more reminiscent of their literary, and cinematic, antecedents when portrayed on the screen by actors than they are on the printed page. Lisbeth's grotesquely mutilated father, for instance, given to sinister Blofeldian laughter in order to convey his malign nature, and the implacable, superhuman giant Niedermann, whose body count in this final entry virtually goes off the scale. We see – briefly – several of Niedermann's luckless, often bound victims as he is en route to his objective, his half-sister – and the fact that we are not shown their subsequent murders is chillingly effective. But – as those who know the novel are aware – Zalachenko is speedily (and bloodily) dispatched when he becomes a thorn in the side of the rogue secret service agents in Swedish intelligence who have been protecting him. And while the hulking Niedermann once again presents problems of plausibility, he is a useful element in a narrative that proceeds at a much more stop-and-start pace than its two predecessors. After the court case in which Lisbeth is finally exonerated (a lengthy sequence handled, incidentally, with real skill), her hulking half-brother is still around for a satisfyingly violent confrontation, a characteristically pulse-raising sequence that audiences perhaps need after the statelier pace of the courtroom drama. Director Daniel Alfredson resists the temptation to show us Niedermann's death – at the hands of vengeful bikers rather than Lisbeth, although his feet have been nail-gunned to the floor by his half-sister – keeping it as information we merely hear reported briefly. If this isn't particularly cathartic for the viewer, it's still dramatically effective.

Even more than in the previous films in the trilogy, the talented Noomi Rapace (who moved on to the second Guy Ritchie/Robert Downey Jr Sherlock Holmes movie after this, playing the part of a gypsy) is obliged to convey acres of meaning while constantly maintaining an inexpressive, masklike face – and the fact that she does so with such understated force is characteristic of the actress's skill. A particular pleasure is watching her struggle with the natural, human impulse to thank people who deserve her thanks – especially Blomkvist and his sister, Annika Giannini, who handles Lisbeth's defence with little help from her client – this is clearly torture for the undemonstrative Salander. And Lisbeth's striding into the courtroom in full-on Goth gear, with gelled hair, outrageous make-up and chains, rather than a more courtroom-friendly suit, is a lovely Boudicca-into-battle moment. (Even with her future freedom on the line, Lisbeth remains ineluctably more fuck-you than conciliatory.)

If the final encounter between Lisbeth and Blomkvist after the case has been won lacks the touching quality of its original literary template, and has no real valedictory feel, unlike the moving end of the third book, it is nevertheless handled with understanding and nuance. Perhaps audiences expecting a more dramatic or affecting conclusion to the film trilogy will have reservations, but once again the adaptation – largely speaking and with some important caveats – does justice to the original.

It's hardly surprising that even in France and Sweden (the initial marketplaces for the three *Millennium* films), the Hollywood dream casting game has been played by cinemagoers. For the inevitable forthcoming Hollywood remake, a slew of names were initially evoked: Natalie Portman, Kristen Stewart and Ellen Page for Lisbeth, and (for Blomkvist) George Clooney and Brad Pitt – although both actors invariably figure in such speculative casting. In fact,

Daniel Craig, on sabbatical from James Bond after the financial woes of the MGM studio put the franchise on hold, looks set to be the first English-speaking Blomkvist in David Fincher's adaptation, with the hitherto little-known Rooney Mara taking on the role of Lisbeth.

Hollywood remakes of European films are usually ill-advised, stripping out and siphoning off all the crucial elements that made the properties so successful in the first place. It's to be hoped that Hollywood breaks this trend when it finally gets round to the novels of Stieg Larsson.

THE GIRL WHO IS LISBETH: NOOMI RAPACE

When Noomi Rapace landed the much sought-after part of Lisbeth Salander, she had everything to lose. The Swedish actress was well aware of the astonishing success of the books in her own country when she auditioned – and was equally aware of the fact that many readers had a strong mental image of Larsson's difficult, uncommunicative heroine. She knew that you had to be at the top of your game to meet these very high audience expectations – and not just for a local Scandinavian audience, but for the worldwide market that these films (originally made for television) would almost certainly reach. But the youthful actress had another problem: how to play what is essentially an impossible character? In the books, Lisbeth is a bizarre conglomeration of disparate, unrealistic elements, and her creator's mastery lay in his ability to make the reader believe in this unlikely elfin figure who is nevertheless capable of extreme violence. That Noomi Rapace has also made her a believable character – and has done so with such consummate success – has not only consolidated the appeal of the trilogy of Swedish films, but has offered her the possibility of a stellar career abroad. Her first post-Lisbeth, English-language undertaking was a signing for the sequel to the first Guy Ritchie/Robert Downey Jr Sherlock Holmes film – and a more striking contrast of milieu to the *Millennium* films couldn't be imagined.

Director Niels Arden Oplev, to whom was granted the task of bringing the Larsson trilogy to the screen, knew full well that the casting of the principal female character was absolutely central to the enterprise, and became quickly convinced that in Rapace he had hired the right person. But the director initially had to be persuaded, so fraught was the casting process when it came to Lisbeth. Oplev was seeking an actress who would have the deepest possible relationship with the character, someone who worked along the lines of total identification espoused (initially) by the master Russian acting coach Stanislavsky and later by the 'method' school of acting, as popularised by Lee Strasberg's Actors' Studio in New York. This complete immersion in the character – both physically and psychologically – was something that Rapace took on board with dedication (it was her own chosen approach to the acting process) – and the result in all three films is some of the most strikingly authentic acting in modern cinema.

Oplev first interviewed Noomi Rapace in 2007. She had acquired a considerable reputation in several serious Swedish films as well as making a mark in a variety of theatre productions, but the director was not persuaded by this impressive track record at the start, and thought that Rapace looked too feminine and attractive – hardly the appropriate appearance for the in-your-face, tattooed, black leather-wearing Salander. But the actress was aware that the part was one to be fought for (and, if necessary, suffered for) – not only offering a challenge for an ambitious performer such as herself, but also presenting a career-making opportunity that would be second to none. She made it clear to the director that she was prepared to make all the physical and psychological changes necessary to be persuasive in this difficult part, and began a rigorous diet, cutting out virtually everything but protein – and, as she realised, possibly creating health problems for herself in the future. The parallels with the reckless Salander, whose lifestyle is hardly a healthy one, were obvious. At the same time, Rapace adopted a regime of extreme physical exercise, attempting to give her body a lean, boyish appearance with the merest suggestion of subcutaneous fat – and in this transformation, as the films' occasional nude scenes demonstrate, she succeeded all too well. Punishing martial arts were also part of the actress's training, notably kickboxing and Thai boxing. Her natural aptitude in this area gave her the confidence to tell the director that she did not want him to rely on stunt doubles, and that she was keen to tackle the sheer physicality of the role. Other physical necessities for the part included the ability to ride a motorbike – a skill that is crucial to the action sequences in the films – so Rapace also worked on obtaining her licence.

Her physical commitments, however, extended beyond making her body shape more androgynous. She had her hair cut short and undertook genuine piercings, eschewing the cosmetic simulacra of such things that were offered to her initially.

All this physical immersion in the role paid off handsomely in terms of creating a startling look for Salander, but of far greater importance was the inner life that the actress was to bring to her character. Rapace has stated that she perfectly understood the rebellious, anti-establishment stance of Larsson's heroine, which has echoes in the actress's own turbulent teenage years. But it is the edgy, distrustful core of Salander that Rapace portrays with such absolute understanding. And the actress realises that the humanity and vulnerability of the character – elements that Lisbeth does her best to repress – must be displayed to the audience, but with subtlety. We may at times look at Lisbeth with the same dismay as the sympathetic characters around her, but we must always be able to locate the human, caring part of her psyche – the part that only a few of the characters (Blomkvist, his lawyer sister Annika, Salander's sometime-lover Miriam Wu) are able to access. It is a measure of the actress's success that she is able to synthesise all these elements in a totally persuasive fashion – largely deprived, what is more, of one of the key elements in an actor's armoury: dialogue. Unlike in the books, where frequently we are party to Lisbeth's thoughts, it is left to an often silent Rapace to convey the inner conflicts of her character. We find ourselves studying the most minute flicker of facial expression to 'read' her feelings – and Rapace is particularly adept at the moments where common human feeling dictates that she thank someone who has helped her – but she cannot break through the sociopathic barriers she has built around herself. For Noomi Rapace, Lisbeth Salander is a hard act to follow.

MILLENNIUM MUSIC: JACOB GROTH

A key element in the Larsson films is the music – the edgy, nervous scores. Jacob Groth is an admirer of Bernard Herrmann, the composer who provided the perfect marriage of music and image in the films of Alfred Hitchcock. So, in suspense terms, the Danish composer had a true master to emulate when scoring *The Girl with the Dragon Tattoo, The Girl Who Played with Fire* and *The Girl Who Kicked the Hornets' Nest.* But Groth is no stranger to challenges when it comes to scoring films. Five times an Emmy Award-winner, and a nominee on a further occasion, he has established himself as a film composer of great authority. His music communicates a subtle atmosphere, mostly downplaying orchestral bravura and maximising an effective Nordic restraint. Like Tim Burton's house composer Danny Elfman, Groth has a background in rock music. Originally a guitarist, he began some 25 years ago to fine-tune his talents as a composer on Danish movies, and in the 1990s he made his debut as a composer for television. His big break came with *Taxa*, a long-running success on Scandinavian TV, but his chef d'oeuvre – and the calling card for his international reputation – was his score for *The Girl with the Dragon Tattoo*, which was nominated in the 'best score' category by the European Film Academy in 2009.

It would be hard to overestimate the added value provided by Jacob Groth's music for the three Swedish films of the *Millennium Trilogy*. Listeners – and film buffs – are still divided over the vexed question as to whether or not a film score should call attention to itself or work subliminally to complement the action on screen. Groth is very much of the latter school. He has enjoyed a particularly close professional relationship with Niels Arden Oplev, the director of *The Girl with the Dragon Tattoo*, a relationship honed over several years of working together. I heard about this over prodigious Blomkvist-style quantities of coffee during a fascinating couple of hours when Groth was in London in 2010. I met the composer in a penthouse flat high above the noise and bustle of Soho as he worked on a console, creating the score for a new film. It was an instructive experience. Groth, amiable and articulate, is a professional musician who takes a completely businesslike approach to his job. However, he says wryly, it is an approach that took a battering when he was working on the *Millennium* films.

'I became totally involved emotionally when scoring the Larsson movies,' he revealed, 'and kept having to remind myself that my job was to ensure that every dramatic element in the film was given its proper value – and that way, justice would be done to Stieg Larsson's memory. Which it had to be. Niels and I – everyone connected with the film, in fact – had that objective very much in mind. But it was often disturbing to work on the films – and to enter that dark world again and again. In fact, much more so for me when working on the films as opposed to reading the books; I found it impossible not to feel a hot flush of shame – shame for my own sex. It has to be said that Larsson is under no illusions about the depth to which men – some men – will sink. I suppose that's an attitude which is reflected in the Swedish title of the first book and film, *Men Who Hate Women*. But I tried to force myself to be objective when scoring the films – I knew I had to keep a certain distance – and it wasn't all dealing with negative energy. To some degree, I could maximise the musical elements connected to the more sympathetic men in the films – obviously Blomkvist is the principal example.'

But was the job made more difficult, I asked, by the very detailed performances of Noomi Rapace and Michael Nyqvist? Was there a fine balance between enhancing their performances and detracting from them? 'Do you mean in the sense that their performances were so complete it was up to me as a composer not to get in the way? The answer to that is obviously yes – where the actors are doing very subtle work (which clearly is most of the time with performers as skilled as Noomi and Michael), a composer such as myself must adopt the lightest of touches. But when the director wants to accentuate the drama and menace of a scene – and there are plenty of edgy, dangerous scenes in the trilogy which fit that description – I am able to employ all my resources, which in the case of these films included a large orchestra... a larger orchestra, in fact, than I'm usually able to use. And – as to whether or not a composer's work should be noticed – well, if people didn't notice my work, I'm not offended. I consider that means I'm doing my job – the music is hopefully working on a subliminal level to bring out things that perhaps the director and actors have not found. I was, in a way, a handmaiden – or facilitator – to a particular vision of Stieg Larsson's world. I hope – had he lived – he would have been happy with what I did.'

CHAPTER 11

THE MILLENNIUM TOUR:

In Larsson's Footsteps

It was hardly surprising, given the worldwide success of the Lisbeth Salander books, that the canny tourist operators of Stockholm would come up with a 'Millennium Tour'.

There are, of course, many such literary tours worldwide built around celebrated characters and series of books, and those taking such tours range from the intellectual literati to those of a frankly fannish persuasion. And many people who have taken part in such walking tours are familiar with those for whom the dividing line between fantasy and reality is a touch blurred. There are those, for instance, who send letters – in the 21st century – to 221b Baker Street asking for help from Sherlock Holmes, presupposing that the Great Detective is not the fictitious creation of Sir Arthur Conan Doyle, or that Holmes is the oldest surviving Victorian.

Those who attend the Stieg Larsson walking tour in Stockholm represent a particularly interesting mix, both in age and social background. But there is one unifying factor: a voracious appetite for any information concerning Stieg

Larsson and his three remarkable novels. The walk includes a 7-11 shop, which, of course, features in the trilogy, and the staff is familiar with groups of up to 24 people pausing on the wide shopping street of Götgatan on the island of Södermalm, looking attentively through the windows as if they were gazing at a religious shrine.

Thriller writer Robert Ryan (author of such novels as *Signal Red*) also pens a series of pithy travel pieces for *The Times*, and he has noted that the guide on the tour he attended said of this store, 'You will see packets of Billy's Deep Pan Pizza, a snack that figures prominently in all three novels.' And apparently, at least one of the party can always be counted on to go in and buy a packet of this appetising souvenir. As Ryan notes, the *Millennium Trilogy*, as reflected in this walking tour, is 'no gourmet guide to Stockholm: the hero and heroine exist on a diet of cheap microwaved pizzas, Whoppers, coffee and cigarettes, with vodka and lime or aquavit thrown in'. The guide points out that this was the way Larsson himself lived: 'Working too hard, eating junk food, smoking too much. It's probably what killed him.' In fact, this macabre observation is perfectly appropriate in the context of the tour celebrating a series of books which take readers into the furthest excesses of human behaviour. Despite this, Stockholm's pride in the city's dark chronicler is unbounded, and any tourist carrying copies of the books can count on locals taking a personal interest, and asking if the book they're reading is living up to expectations (the canny tourist will diplomatically always answer in the affirmative).

It is inevitable, given the topography of the books, that the majority of the locations included in the tour are on Södermalm Island – where most of the principal protagonists reside – which has the upwardly mobile, and distinctly trendy, elements of certain parts of London.

The ever-increasing number of visitors travel from all parts of Europe, and the tours are accordingly conducted in Swedish, English, Italian and French. Needless to say, most of the questions thrown at the footsore guides relate to Lisbeth Salander and Mikael Blomkvist. The guides, who work for the City Museum, are used to this, and have ready answers for the oft-repeated questions.

The initial meeting point is Bellmansgatan, which is the location of the attic apartment of the novels' investigative journalist, Blomkvist. The apartment overlooks the water, and is a striking location. Robert Ryan has suggested that it is worth following the tourist example and starting from here, following the prescribed route to get a feel for Södermalm.

The district was once working class but has since transmogrified into a key area for the arts and media community, with a markedly bohemian feel. A snapshot of the kind of locals residing here may be discerned from the portraits in Café Rival at 3 Mariatorget, which include actors such as Stellan Skärsgård, the director of the much-acclaimed film *Let the Right One In*, Tomas Alfredson, the pop singer Robyn, and the actors who appear in the *Millennium* movies. The entire complex, with its talented residents is, in fact, co-owned by Benny Andersson of the erstwhile band Abba.

The route along which walkers on the Millennium Tours are led encompasses steep but attractive examples of the best of eighteenth-century Sweden's cobbled streets, and these are, of course, the location for a variety of clandestine sexual encounters in the books. Visitors are taken past ancient churches which have been cursed by witches and an anonymous-looking synagogue, before coming to a significant location.

This is the HQ of Greenpeace, an organisation celebrated for its crusading work exposing the iniquities of all-powerful (and often bullying) multinational corporations – so where better for Stieg Larsson to locate the fictitious offices of Mikael Blomkvist's similarly crusading magazine *Millennium*? Shortly after passing this building, visitors are then able to see some beautiful views of the city's atmospheric waterfronts and canals.

One of the most striking vistas may be glimpsed from Montelisvägen, a wooden walkway which offers a view of Kungsholmen, with its remarkable city hall, police headquarters and courthouse – all of which, of course, figure in the novels.

To the west of this are the offices of *Expo*, and the magazine on which Larsson worked is one of the more sombre locations on the tour. For many years, Larsson held down a job with a truly prodigious workload, and burned a phenomenal amount of energy fighting for the many causes which were dear to his heart. This is the building where Larsson was taken ill at his desk before dying in hospital (that hospital also features in the *Millennium Trilogy*).

During the two hours of this fascinating trawl through the locations of Larsson's novels, the interest level of most groups remains high. Robert Ryan reports that on the trip he took, a Canadian in the group announced that he was planning to read all the books again (apparently this remark is *de rigueur* for many visitors, according to the tour organisers), and half a dozen of Ryan's group headed for the Grand Hotel. One of Stockholm's most iconic buildings, the hotel overlooks the ferries which leave for Sandhamn, a beautiful island in the outer archipelago, where, in the novels, Blomkvist owns a cottage – and where he sleeps with Lisbeth Salander during their brief and unsatisfactory affair. The location has great natural beauty, with (beyond the yachting centre) summer cabins located on exquisite untouched beaches.

As a tourist destination Sandhamn is a test of the seriousness of the Stieg Larsson fan – only the most dedicated Salander/Blomkvist followers need apply, as the island is to be reached after a three-hour boat trip, and, as Eva Gabrielsson has pointed out, the exact location of the journalist's cottage is not specified in the novels.

Details of the tour may be obtained from The City Museum (Ryssgården, Slussen 00 46 8 508 31 659), at www.stadsmuseum.stockholm.se, and tickets are available at the museum or tourist offices. It is also possible to buy a Millennium map for a self-guided tour.

APPENDIX A –
Stieg's Rivals: Scandinavian Crime Fiction

Sales of crime fiction in translation from Scandinavian countries have been forging ahead in recent years, and it's perhaps not hard to see why. This striking vein of new writing offers something that is often more quirky and atmospheric than UK/US fare. But why has the field of crime in translation generally – for so long a backwater – become such a hot ticket? There are several reasons. The astonishing success of Peter Høeg's *Miss Smilla's Feeling for Snow* was a wake-up call: here was crime with all the textural richness of literary fiction, opening up to readers a fascinating new location – Denmark. But *Smilla* was the tip of the iceberg: the Scandinavian countries offered a sweeping panoply. Henning Mankell's Sweden was also the haunt of Liza Marklund, with her tenacious investigative journalist heroine. And we had Mari Jungstedt, taking us to the windswept and atmospheric island of Gotland, where violence lurks. Then we could visit Åke Edwardson's menacing Göteborg, or the Reykjavik of Arnaldur Indridason, and Karin Fossum's Norway.

By now, a legion of Scandinavian crime aficionados were spoilt for choice. Who next for a shot of Nordic criminality? Pernille Rygg? Johan Theorin? But better to have an embarrassment of riches than a drought. No danger of the latter though, as new names appear daily – such as the woman who is already a massive success in the Nordic countries: Camilla Läckberg. Interestingly, Läckberg is known to be inspired by British crime writers – showing that crime horizons now stretch from Oxford to Oslo – and back.

STIEG'S RIVALS: HENNING MANKELL

Over the years, non-English-speaking crime fiction practitioners such as Georges Simenon have garnered classic status, but if there's one modern writer who is the Trojan horse for foreign crime in translation, it's Sweden's Henning Mankell. His laconic detective Kurt Wallander (something of an alter ego for the similarly laconic Mankell) is one of the great creations of modern crime fiction: overweight, diabetes-ridden and with all the problems of modern society leaving scars on his soul. Wallander is as rounded a character as any in more literary fiction. In such books as *Sidetracked* and *Firewall,* British readers were taken into pungently realised Scandinavian settings that were subtly similar to the UK, but also fascinatingly different. Wallander's Sweden is not a good advertisement for the success of the welfare state – the cracks in the consensus of Scandinavian society widening, Swedish family life riven by deep psychological traumas.

But like the director Ingmar Bergman (to whose daughter Mankell is married) the writer frequently confounds all stereotypical expectations of Nordic gloom and produces books crammed with humanity and optimism, plus the bloodshed and murder that are prerequisites of the crime genre. The keen social conscience that illuminates Mankell's books chimes with his own commitment to make disadvantaged people's lives better: he has done a great deal of theatre work in Africa, and his reach as a writer extends beyond the crime genre, with such books as the ambitious *Kennedy's Brain*, *Depths* and *Eye of the Leopard*.

STIEG'S RIVALS: YRSA SIGURDARDÓTTIR

It's to be hoped that the children who so avidly consume Yrsa Sigurdardóttir's juvenile novels don't accidentally pick up *Last Rituals*, as the author's first adult book was a very different kettle of fish from her first work. ('I had five books worth of bad thoughts I needed to vent – *Last Rituals* was a sort of release for my darker side,' she noted.) In fact, new careers are a speciality for Sigurdardóttir; this is (at least) her third, as she's also a highly successful civil engineer in Reykjavik, with prestigious hydro-construction projects under her belt. The latter clearly wasn't slaking her creative instincts – good news for lovers of quality crime in translation, as Sigurdardóttir arrived, fully formed it seems, as something of a unique talent in the field. She needs to be – the once rarefied field of Icelandic crime thrillers is now becoming somewhat overcrowded.

In *Last Rituals*, the body of a young history student is discovered in Reykjavik, his eyes gouged out. He has been researching witchcraft and torture, and his moneyed German parents won't accept the police theory that he was killed by his drug dealer. What makes Sigurdardóttir's writing such an exhilarating experience is the fashion in which she takes familiar, perhaps even over familiar ingredients – for example ill-matched, combative detective duo, murder victims with their eyes removed – and throws off a series of dizzying and innovative riffs on these concepts. Sigurdardóttir clearly realises that women writers are obliged to be every inch as gruesome as their male counterparts these days, and matches such writers as Tess Gerritsen and Kathy Reichs in the blood-chilling stakes. But like all the best Scandinavian writers, it's her acute sense of place that gives such individual character to her work, and readers may feel a keen desire to visit Reykjavik after reading her books.

STIEG'S RIVALS: HÅKAN NESSER

When I asked Håkan Nesser why non-Swedish readers should pick up one of his crime novels rather than those by his more celebrated countryman Henning Mankell, he replied, 'Well, I'm eight inches taller than him...' But if this isn't a persuasive enough reason for you to read Nesser, just a few pages of *Borkmann's Point*, *The Return* or *The Inspector and Silence* will undoubtedly do the trick. This is splendid stuff: Scandinavian crime writing that is so rivetingly written it makes most contemporary crime fare – Scandinavian or otherwise – seem rather thin gruel. Nesser's tenacious copper, Chief Inspector van Veeteren, is one of the most distinctive protagonists in the field (lauded by no less an authority than Colin Dexter: '... destined for a place among the great European detectives'), and the handling of the baffling, labyrinthine cases he tackles has a rigour and logic all too rarely encountered.

But Håkan Nesser's is no overnight success story. Being born and raised in Kumla – the most prestigious prison town in Sweden – may have helped put the author on the right criminal path (at least, the kind of criminal path where you're paid rather than arrested), but it was via his clandestine scribbling away at novels in the classroom for 20 years, when he should have been polishing young Swedish minds, that allowed Nesser to develop into the master he is today. *Borkmann's Point*, dealing with two savage axe murders in a sedate coastal town, marked the UK debut of Nesser's chess-loving copper and instantly established a following. *The Return* consolidated the success of the earlier book, with van Veeteren investigating a corpse rolled up in a carpet in an otherwise sylvan beauty spot, while a double murderer prowls the area.

Nesser already has a slew of Scandinavian crime awards under his belt for his novels, which have received enthusiastic welcomes in nine countries. And as his reputation gathers momentum, it is only a matter of time before British fans will be learning how to pronounce his name (a good approximation is 'Hawk Ann Nessair').

STIEG'S RIVALS: MAJ SJÖWALL & PER WAHLÖÖ

Sjöwall and Wahlöö are the pinnacle of Nordic crime writing – truly *sui generis*. Now that English readers can sample all the novels of this highly influential husband-and-wife team of crime writers in solid translations, their true achievement – which is considerable – can be fully appreciated. For many years the lamentable fact was that these taut and socially committed novels never seemed to be available all at the same time in the UK and US (they slipped out of print all too quickly). These days, the reputation of

Maj Sjöwall and Per Wahlöö is rock solid, with fellow crime authors routinely describing them as the very finest practitioners of the police procedural.

In Sweden, the Martin Beck series has long had the highest possible standing (the proselytising left-leaning agenda of the books clearly not alienating readers, whatever their individual political stamp). Beck is, of course, one of the great literary detectives, and continues to influence writers long after his creators have laid down their metaphorical pens. Stieg Larsson was, naturally, an admirer of the Beck books – as he was of the British writer Val McDermid's Tony Hill and Carol Jordan series – the influence of which is also clearly discernible in his books. Jens Lapidus, with his remarkable *Stockholm Noir* trilogy, is in some ways a spiritual heir of the duo.

STIEG'S RIVALS: ARNALDUR INDRIDASON

After Indridason won the CWA Gold Dagger, many felt that he would be one of the foreign language crime writers who would break the stranglehold that Henning Mankell maintained on this particular branch of the genre. The signs are that this remarkably talented writer has yet to do that... so far. British and American readers may have problems pronouncing his name, but are fully aware of the highly distinctive talents of these Reykjavik-set thrillers. The remarkable success of *Silence of the Grave* was followed in 2006 by *Voices*, another taut and beguiling thriller. Indridason's detective, Erlendur, comes across echoes of his difficult past when the doorman at his own hotel is savagely stabbed to death. The manager attempts to keep the murder quiet (it is the festive season) but Erlendur is, of course, obliged to find out what happened. As he works his way through the very bizarre fellow guests who share the hotel with him, he encounters a nest of corruption that gives even this jaundiced detective pause for thought.

The particular pleasure of these books is the combination of the familiar and unfamiliar – while the detective is cut from the familiar cloth, the locales and atmosphere are fresh and surprising for the non-Scandinavian reader. In *Jar City* (2003), the body of an old man is found in his apartment in Reykjavik; DI Erlendur has only an enigmatic note found on the body to go on. The murdered man's computer contains pornography, and it transpires that he has been accused of rape in the past. A photograph of the grave of a young woman leads Erlendur towards a solution quite unlike anything he has encountered in his career. It was inevitable that this Scandinavian crime novel would be compared with previous successes by Henning Mankell, and that DI Erlendur would be racked up against the former's Kurt Wallander. Both readers and critics did not find Indridason or Erlendur wanting in the comparisons. The cop here is much given to philosophical speculations, and has a very dark view of human nature. Science (and not just forensics) is a crucial part of the plot, and as with Mankell, the scene-setting has a freshness and novelty that are very striking to the non-Scandinavian reader. As a debut novel for yet another saturnine copper, this pushes all the right buttons.

STIEG'S RIVALS: KARIN FOSSUM

At one time, the crime novels of Karin Fossum were something of a well-kept secret, known to a growing band of aficionados but not to the larger crime readership. Not any more. In fact, Fossum's highly atmospheric and involving books are among the best being produced in the genre today, and her work certainly deserves the widest possible audience. *Don't Look Back* was a psychological thriller that was both economical and forceful, and *He Who Fears the Wolf* (2003) is an even more persuasive piece of writing. In an isolated village, a horribly mutilated body has been found, and the suspect (spotted in the woods nearby) has recently been committed to a psychiatric institution. Then a violent bank robbery occurs, with the thief grabbing a hostage and escaping. As the gunman becomes more and more desperate, paradoxically a strange calm seems to descend on his hostage. And as the hunt continues for the murderer, only the young suspect's doctor maintains his innocence.

Like the best of Ruth Rendell, this is a dark and unsettling novel about the reasons people commit crime and the devastating effect it has on the protagonists' lives. All the characters here are exuberantly drawn, notably the resourceful police inspector Sejer and the under-suspicion misfit Errki. But for the English reader, it's the evocation of Nordic society (not a million miles away from our own) that is so effective here. Fossum's novels featuring Konrad Sejer have been published in 16 languages, and so it's only a matter of time before mainstream English readers take these books to their collective bosom.

STIEG'S RIVALS: CAMILLA LÄCKBERG

As readers in Britain and America eagerly seek out other Nordic writers, the discovery of Camilla Läckberg was something of a no-brainer. Already celebrated in her native Sweden with much accomplished work to her credit, she has been introduced to the UK with *The Ice Princess* and has earned the sobriquet of Sweden's new Agatha Christie, which isn't quite the whole story. True, in this book there is a Christie-style small village (Läckberg's birthplace, Fjällbacka) and a slew of candidates for a grisly killing. Also in the style of The Queen of Crime is the effortless plotting – but Läckberg takes on social issues assiduously, serving up a vision of Swedish society that is acute and trenchant. Erica Falck is a writer who has travelled to her home town after the death of her parents, but discovers a divided community. A friend, Alex, has been found with her wrists cut, frozen solid in a bath that has turned to ice. Erica opts to pen a book about the secretive Alex, dealing with her own writer's block as well as the puzzle of Alex's death. As with her other equally accomplished novels (such as *The Stonecutter*), Läckberg shows here that she is another star in the Nordic pantheon.

STIEG'S RIVALS: ÅKE EDWARDSON

The British – as opposed to many non-Russian nations – felt an instant connection with the work of Anton Chekhov, recognising a common cause with the Russians of his plays. These morose, stoic types in their inhospitable climate dreamt of bettering their lives, and lacked the unrealistic optimism of, say, the Americans. Long after Chekhov's death, in the now popular genre of crime in translation, residents of Albion have latched on to Scandinavian essays in murder and detection – the bleaker, unvarnished view of life in these novels has a surprisingly British air, as does the uncritical acceptance of eccentricity. But while the ex-journalist and novelist Åke Edwardson hasn't yet enjoyed the success of his better-known colleagues, the auguries are good, with the youthful Inspector Winter (and his older, more saturnine colleague Ringmar) bidding fair to make a breakthrough in the fashion of Mankell's copper Kurt Wallander.

In, for instance, *Frozen Tracks*, the narrative has a Mankell-like grip: autumn in Göteborg, and two unpleasant series of events are to cause headaches for DCI Erik Winter. Two children have been lured into a car by a man proffering sweets. Reports are filed, but as different day nurseries and different police stations are involved, the reports are not correlated (Edwardson implies that a lack of joined-up thinking is just as endemic to Swedish policing as it is to British). As in such books as *Never End*, Edwardson shows his skill in both his succinctly characterised coppers and a nicely labyrinthine plot. The queasy glimpses into the psyche of a dangerous paedophile are intelligently and responsibly handled, and the narrative has all the fastidious skill of the best crime writing.

STIEG'S RIVALS: ÅSA LARSSON

Are readers ready for another Scandinavian crime writer called Larsson? As the popularity of crime in translation grows apace, such novels as Åsa Larsson's *The Savage Altar* are devoured by aficionados searching for something innovative in the field. Åsa Larsson takes us to different locales (here, a vividly rendered Sweden unlike that of the subject of this book) and plotting of more heft and character than may be discerned in many UK or US crime novels.

Åsa Larsson's gritty novel boasts a pithily realised heroine who is to feature in future works: corporate lawyer Rebecka Martinsson, arm-twisted by her friend Sanna, who is under suspicion regarding the grisly murder of a celebrated writer of religious books, Viktor Strandgård, who has been mutilated – both hands and eyes removed in a church in Northern Sweden. Also caught up in the subsequent investigation is canny police inspector Anna-Maria Mella, dragooned into the case by a colleague, despite being incapacitated by her advanced state of pregnancy. Like Lynda la Plante's Jane Tennison, these are women who are struggling in a world of unsympathetic men and Larsson – like her male namesake – peoples her cast with some extremely nasty males. But Åsa Larsson's writing is more ambitious than her British colleague, with a level of plotting that excels in both ambition and achievement. It will be interesting to see what the author cooks up for her beleaguered heroine in future books.

APPENDIX B –
Writers on Stieg Larsson

WRITERS ON STIEG LARSSON: JOAN SMITH

Larsson's connection with ordinary readers has been astonishing in its range and passion – but equally remarkable is the response he has engendered in his fellow crime fiction practitioners and critics. Several were happy to talk to me about their Larsson enthusiasms for this book – while others grimaced and said 'Can I tell you what I *really* think about him?'

Joan Smith is celebrated as a crime novelist (for such impressive books as *A Masculine Ending*), but it is perhaps as a journalist and commentator that her work most coincides with that of Stieg Larsson, with a particular concern for male violence against women and the repression of women in Islamic societies – two issues which much exercised the late Swedish writer.

'I was an early supporter,' she says. 'It is Stieg Larsson who most describes an incredibly detailed vision of modern

Sweden. He presented it as a modern European country – there isn't that small-town, gossipy feel we'd had before, the notion that time is passing, but things don't really change very much. This wasn't what Stieg Larsson presented in his creation of a city of the modern era, an incredibly recognisable modern world.

'The other element that intrigued me about the first book was, of course, something that is summed up in the original Swedish title of the novel, *Men Who Hate Women*. Even if I had not known at the beginning, I would have realised that Larsson was as fascinating and horrified as I am by the whole phenomenon of misogyny and the deep-seated hostility some men have towards women. It's unusual to find a man who makes that absolutely the central theme of his novels – obviously, a lot of men are aware of it, but to tackle the subject as directly as Larsson does, for a male novelist is unusual.'

In this, of course, he had a parallel with the writer Joan Smith – who as well as being a novelist addressing these themes, was (as a journalist) arguing for the rights of women in repressive religious regimes. 'Well,' says Smith, 'Stieg did have the right credentials! Years ago I worked for the *Sunday Times* Insight team doing investigative journalism in the days when newspapers believed in it – and could afford it. And I wonder if the same thing happened to him as happened to me – you come to realise that you have insights into the extraordinary things that go on around the world, and being a journalist of this kind is something of a privileged occupation. I was flying around the world, investigating things like where the Shah of Iran had stashed his money, and writing a book about the Iranian embassy siege. You begin to say to yourself "I know how all this works, but I don't want to be constrained by the facts anymore". You want to write about the underlying truths which can be revealed in fiction, and I can't help wondering if this was part of his motivation as well.'

Does Smith think that Larsson could have sustained the energy and focus had he written the ten-novel sequence he had apparently planned?

'I really think he couldn't have sustained what he achieved in those first three novels; it's noticeable that the last of the three is elegiac in tone, and there's the new personal trajectory he creates for Blomkvist – giving him a new girlfriend, and so forth. The ebb and flow of the relationship between him and Salander had been very convincingly detailed, and I really didn't believe that she would so readily accept the new relationship without any of the animosity of the second novel. It seemed to me a way of tying up loose ends in a not entirely convincing way. Nevertheless, it felt like a trilogy to me.

'The other problem is about continuing the dynamic of the relationship between Blomkvist and Salander. To some degree, having established that she is dysfunctional, part of the achievement is the way in which she is "reached" by Blomkvist. And that feat is achieved – several times – but it encapsulates another way in which it is difficult to see the series continuing. At the end of the third book – with so much resolved, with so many of her problems solved, many of the injustices righted – Salander is a free woman. So what does she do now? Does she find herself a boyfriend, or a girlfriend, and settle down? Does she start her own computer company?'

Of course, the *Millennium Trilogy* crucially addresses gender issues, which is very much the territory that Joan

Smith writes about. But despite his impeccable sympathy for women, has Larsson transcended gender in his writings?

'Oh, he remains very much a male writer, and there is, possibly, a certain male wish-fulfilment element in Blomkvist; he is a shambling figure, but it seems that every woman he meets wants to go to bed with him – and the ones who can't have him look wistfully at him. But you can forgive Larsson this, as you can forgive him so much else. Apart from anything else, when you read the first book, you know that the author is already dead – these three books are all you will get. And there is no sense of an author developing – you are denied this particular pleasure, something that can usually be counted upon when you discover a new writer. Perhaps he might have grown out of that element of wish-fulfilment in the Blomkvist character, and he never had the chance of a series of consultations with an editor – the usual refining process.'

But what about Lisbeth Salander? Smith has spoken highly of her in her various reviews of the books, but did she have reservations?

'Well, I feel she is like a character from a computer game,' she says. 'That's not necessarily a huge weakness, and it's certainly true that a lot of young women identify with her. What I respond to is how intelligent she is, and how ingenious she is – at least, how ingenious Larsson makes her. But my problems, if I have any, are not really with the characters. I'm not entirely happy with the violence of the third book, which is very gruesome indeed. I think that Larsson is feeling that because she was victimised, we are supposed to stand back when this violence is unleashed and not pass judgement on her – and I don't think I'm quite prepared to do that.

'As for women readers sympathising with her – well, personally, I know that I never for a moment identified with her. I read her as someone who was completely outside my experience, and the fact that she is so horribly abused – an abuse that can happen to anyone, whether a boy or a girl – such things can have a devastating effect on the personality. But that's outside my range of experience.

As a journalist, of course, Smith dealt with a lot of the same issues that Larsson tackled. Surely this rendered her a ready-made reader for the *Millennium Trilogy*?

'I thought that from the moment I started reading the very first book,' she replies. 'The details of falling into a libel trap – and then when Blomkvist goes off to lick his wounds, well because of the kind of journalism I did years ago, I found that very easy to empathise with.

'I do have this personal response to Stieg, and I wonder if he'd agree that when one is writing journalism, to some degree it is "here today, gone tomorrow", whereas when you are writing a novel you can address important issues in the guise of entertainment – the issues involved will have more relevance than if they had simply been considered in a journalistic article.'

WRITERS ON STIEG LARSSON: KARIN ALVTEGEN

Karin Alvtegen is comfortably one of the most acclaimed of Nordic crime writers – and is impressed by Stieg's strong heroine: 'Perhaps Salander is not an entirely credible character, but together with so many others readers, I find it enjoyable and comforting to read about an underdog who refuses to be a victim and instead takes command. I'm convinced that one of the explanations of the great success is

Stieg's portrayals of strong women. He turns the traditional gender roles upside down. Lisbeth is the "hero" who has to save Mikael Blomkvist. Since the books are equally popular with both men and women, perhaps all of us feel refreshed by Stieg's obvious crusade against social injustice, xenophobia and preconceived ideas regarding gender roles.

'The sad thing about this unique success is the dispute about the inheritance it resulted in. Perhaps we all can use it as a reminder that we never know what waits ahead – and that we should be more careful when it comes to writing our last will and testament.'

WRITERS ON STIEG LARSSON: ANN CLEEVES

One of the most enthusiastic proselytisers for Scandinavian crime fiction is the UK's Ann Cleeves, author of such atmospheric mysteries as *Blue Lightning* – books which have a rather Nordic attitude to landscape and locale. She has an ambiguous attitude to Larsson: 'I love Scandinavian crime novels,' she says. 'It's something about the bleakness of landscape, the fact that the writers dare to tackle serious social and domestic issues. I read books in translation for the flavour of the place, the petty preoccupations of the people, the smells, the food. Larsson is an unashamedly political writer and his themes are broader and less personal. A caveat: the island featured in the first book isn't a real island. I have no sense of what it would be like to live there, as I do, for example, when I read of Johan Theorin's Oland. Larsson's is a metaphor and a playful gesture towards Golden Age enclosed community mysteries. As a reader I revel in the intimate and the specific and I need to get lost in the story.

WRITERS ON STIEG LARSSON: DAN FESPERMAN

The American writer Dan Fesperman produces very different fiction from Larsson, but is intrigued by the Swedish writer: 'I was introduced to Larsson's work by my American editor, Sonny Mehta, who gave me a galley of *Dragon Tattoo* back when Knopf was still trying to decide what cover to put on the US edition. I think he mentioned that it was already something of a sensation in Britain, and he seemed to think I'd like it. That night I cracked it open on the train ride back from New York (a perfect place to start reading that kind of a novel, I might add – the nightscapes of cities and marshes rolling past outside, the sway and clack of the train car, the intimate pool of light from the overhead beam). By the time we reached Baltimore a few hours later I knew I'd be reading all three.

'It's not easy to pin down Larsson's appeal. It's not his style or the cadence of his language – it seldom is when you're talking about a work in translation. It's more a question of the strange mood he creates – both welcoming and forbidding, comfortable and uneasy. Opening one of his books is sort of like inviting an engaging but mildly unsettling guest to dinner. The company and conversation are stimulating, charming even. But there is also a sense of shared menace in the interplay, which of course draws you closer to the table. With every word you realise this is someone who has been places, who knows things, and who may eventually let you in on some secrets, no matter how dark and unsavoury. Halfway through the main course you've decided to extend the evening as long as possible, so you break out the espresso, the cigars, the port – whatever it takes to make it last, well past the hour when the streets have gone quiet and the neighbours' noisy party downstairs has packed it in. These books are a state of mind.'

WRITERS ON STIEG LARSSON: MARCEL BERLINS

Marcel Berlins is as adroit at characterising the virtues, or otherwise, of a crime novel for *The Times* as he is at unpacking the complexities of Britain's legal system for the *Guardian*. As a crime critic, he has pointed out that he has a limited amount of space, and sometimes reviews novels by omission – and he is careful not to be destructive when it comes to first-time novelists. But when Berlins shows approbation for a crime novel, attention is paid. Stieg Larsson has long been the recipient of the Berlins seal of approval – but with reservations.

'I've been thinking about my reaction to Stieg Larsson,' he said, 'and it's probably a truism to remark that – had he not died – an editor would have said to him, "Come on, let's get it into manageable shape." I was using this argument whenever I was asked about him, but apparently it's not quite the case – the first book was subjected to a correct editing process, but to me it is still in need of tightening up, whatever its virtues – and they are many.

'But it's intriguing to speculate on such matters as: who is reading these books? What is it that makes him so successful? I found myself asking around – speaking to people who were not just crime fiction aficionados, but lovers of really popular novels such as the trilogy has become.

'The plots are convoluted, but one sticks with them, and Blomkvist is of course a sympathetic character; Lisbeth doesn't really come fully into her own until the second and third books. But what really struck me about *The Girl with the Dragon Tattoo* was the fact that the book is rather English in aspect! The unravelling of a mystery which took place 40 years ago is a kind of tip of the hat to the classic English mystery, with a central character a journalist/detective. He's out of work, under a cloud – actually, rather an English figure in terms of the genre. This was all of a part with my speculating as to why the English have responded so much to the books (I didn't get round to the Americans and Europeans in my considerations). I think it's true that – as Henning Mankell and others have proved – Sweden as a country is close in atmosphere and feeling to England (and, indeed, Scotland). It struck me forcibly when reading the early Henning Mankells – and it's a feeling that persisted with Stieg Larsson – that one is really reading about a version of Norfolk; the slate-grey skies, and the attitude of the people. Scandinavian crime fiction is both similar and dissimilar to English crime fiction. This might explain why the hot-blooded Mediterranean writers – Andrea Camilleri, for instance – are less popular; the English are not temperamentally suited to those books in the way that they are to writers from the Nordic countries. I've enthused endlessly to people about how good the Italians are, but the response is often less than enthusiastic – and publishers such as Bitter Lemon who specialise in (among other things) Italian crime in translation have to make something of an effort to sell their books to English readers.

'Blomkvist one can see appealing to the English reader,' continues Berlins, 'But Salander is a very different kettle of fish, and my search within myself as to the reason for her popularity produced some interesting results. For a start, she is very different from anything that English readers are accustomed to. As a rule of thumb, it might be said that English crime readers – at least the readers of such novelists as P D James and Ruth Rendell – are conservative in their tastes (that is, of course, conservative with a small 'c').

'With writers such as James and Rendell, the books are

essentially about the status quo – or, at least, about re-establishing the status quo. Bitter endings are not particularly popular with English readers. So it is possible to say that it is the old-fashioned style which still sells best – so why have English readers taken to Lisbeth with such enthusiasm? She's not what we're used to...

'But as to listing the demerits of Stieg Larsson – well, what about the villains? They are, largely speaking, one-dimensional – look at the Russian heavies. In fact, this leads to what I consider to be the real reason for the success: the books have a certain comic strip element – Lisbeth, for instance, is not a real figure if you look at her objectively – but it is this energy which is obviously immensely appealing to readers. It's a clever move by Larsson to make Blomkvist a believable figure by contrast, which he certainly does – that has the effect of anchoring the narrative in a kind of reality, so that readers are prepared to take on board the more outlandish elements. So my feeling was that English readers, rather than wanting to be convinced of the reality of the character – or, for that matter, pacified by her or the narrative, as much crime fiction does – were happy to embrace Lisbeth on this non-naturalistic, larger-than-life stage.

'Having said that, most of the women I have spoken to about Salander don't actually like her, but perhaps, to some degree she acts out female readers' fantasies on some level.

'In the final analysis, whatever flaws critics like myself might identify in a writer, it's really an academic exercise, when readers decide to vote with their wallets and embrace books the way they have done with Larsson. English readers were not, for instance, put off by the socialist hero at the heart of the *Millennium Trilogy.*

'Larsson is, of course, critic-proof – rather like Dan Brown.

I'm not saying that Brown is the same kind of writer as Larsson – the latter is, of course, infinitely better. But the general disapproval of Dan Brown in critical circles hasn't dented his sales one iota. Larsson, for a complicated series of almost unexplainable reasons, has touched a nerve with crime fiction readers. That is why he has broken (and is continuing to break) sales records in the genre.'

WRITERS ON STIEG LARSSON: MARTIN EDWARDS

The English Lake District is the stamping ground for Martin Edwards, who wrote such Ullswater-set mysteries as *The Serpent Pool*, and he told me that he regarded the first Larsson book as 'an extraordinary achievement by any standards – all the more impressive because it was Larsson's first published novel'. 'As with any debut, there are flaws,' he went on, 'but there is an abundance of riches to compensate. And one of the pleasures of the books that await detective story fans is Larsson's occasional appreciative nods to the genre. He draws on its variety in composing his story line, and setting the tone of the narrative.

'The first book boasts a family tree of the Vangers, and I agree with Larsson's translator, Reg Keeland, that it's a pity that maps of Hedeby Island which make it easier to follow details of the plot were not included. Family trees and maps were a staple of Golden Age detective fiction between the wars, and it's fascinating to see a thoroughly modern writer such as Larsson using traditional devices to add texture to his story. More than that, the central mystery of the disappearance of Harriet Vanger is presented as an example of a classic form of detective puzzle:

"I assume that something happened to Harriet here on

the island," Blomkvist said, "and that the list of suspects consists of the finite number of people trapped here. A sort of locked-room mystery in island format?" Vanger smiled ironically."

'In fact, the setup of the story is really that of a "closed circle" mystery, rather than a type of "locked-room" or "impossible crime"; John Dickson Carr was a notable exponent of the latter form. But this is a quibble; what is so intriguing is that a ground-breaking book so consciously draws upon past fictions, whilst portraying the failings of modern society with unflinching realism.

'The ironic exchange between Blomkvist and Vanger is playful, but subtler than, say, the passage in Carr's classic mystery *The Hollow Man*, in which Dr Gideon Fell remarks in The Locked-Room Lecture: "We're in a detective story, and we don't fool the reader by pretending we're not. Let's not invent elaborate excuses to drag in a discussion of detective stories. Let's candidly glory in the noblest pursuits possible to characters in a book."

'As the story of Harriet Vanger's fate darkens, so do the fictional references. At risk of going "stir-crazy" in Hedeby, Blomkvist borrows two whodunits by Elizabeth George from the library. Looking around in Gottfried's cabin, he finds more murder mysteries, some by Mickey Spillane. Later, on Midsummer Eve, he tries to unwind by embarking on Val McDermid's *The Mermaids Singing*. When, a few days later, he reaches the denouement, we are told: *"It was grisly."*

'So, economically, the mood is set. Larsson's reference to McDermid's story of serial murder is not pointless padding. The shocking crimes that he is about to uncover are very grisly indeed.'

WRITERS ON STIEG LARSSON: RUSSELL JAMES

After ten crime novels, Russell James wrote *Great British Fictional Detectives* and its companion *Great British Fictional Villains*. He takes a characteristically dispassionate view of Larsson: 'After an author shoots to fame it can be that people talk more about who the author is and why they are famous than about the books they wrote. So far it hasn't been that way with Larsson – perhaps because he wrote just three books, and we can get a handle on three books; there isn't a lifetime of writing for us to plough through.

'Larsson's dead, of course, so critics and fellow writers can treat him generously, since there's nothing to fear from him. There are no more blockbusters in the pipeline to be dreaded, as any intelligent reader will dread the next Dan Brown. It seems that there is only this finite, completed trilogy – and what a perfect legacy that is. A trilogy is the perfect product, a publisher's dream, for when a writer writes a mere three books, any one of us can go out and buy the complete oeuvre; any one of us can become an expert on the collected works.

'The man himself, it can't be denied, is a phenomenon: four years after he died he became the second highest selling author in the world. And yet, back in 2004, who would have guessed that he and his creation, a modernised Modesty Blaise, would achieve such heights? Not the modest and hard-working journalist, Stieg Larsson. Certainly not Mikael Blomkvist nor the far-from-modest Lisbeth Salander. Internationally famous as she is, she follows in a long but thinly populated line of sparky heroines of crime fiction. Before her came Modesty Blaise, as I say, and we remember the tough-girl heroines of McDermid, Reichs, Sharp, Duffy and Paretsky, but I suggest that these particular women, created by women, don't carry the same sexual charge as those created by men. [Modesty was created by Peter O'Donnell.]

'In one of the earliest forays into crime fiction, *The Woman in White*, Wilkie Collins gave us a tough, unbeautiful, un-retiring investigator, Marian Halcombe, to tackle the dastardly Count Fosco. Later, in the turbulent turn-of-the-century years, crime writers introduced us to the "new woman" – who rode bicycles, smoked, and talked back at men! But in the Golden Age these women retreated: Miss Marple and Lord Peter's girlfriends were a lesser breed, and it wasn't until Modesty that she lived again. Modesty was tough, her toughness learnt, like Ms Salander's, in an abusive past and, like Ms Salander again, she wasn't afraid to flaunt her sexuality or to ignore gender and tackle her target, man to man. What a frisson that was for *Evening Standard* readers – the same frisson that today's readers find in Lisbeth Salander. And it really is a frisson, a wonderfully liberating thrill for avid readers of either gender, to come across a panther-like woman who prowls onstage to snarl and tense before she springs. Many of us found her, of course, too late, after Stieg was dead. But we did find her. We'll read the trilogy, we'll watch Lisbeth and Mikael on screen – knowing that we only have to stay with them through the trilogy. That's just enough. They won't stick around so long that we grow tired, nor are they here for such a short time that we don't get hooked. They're a duo and a trilogy. They're perfect.

'What would Larsson have thought, I wonder, if he'd been told – by one of those fictional clairvoyants that used to crop up in a story – that he, a successful journalist and moderately unsuccessful author, would achieve worldwide fame after he was dead? How would he have reacted if the devil himself had offered to exchange his corporeal life and soul for eternal fame? Larsson might have believed, as some religious people do, that we can all live on, and that we do not die as long as someone somewhere remembers our name. "Stieg Larsson," the devil might have said, "many people will read you, they will hear your voice after you are dead." Might he have settled for that? How might any writer respond to Mephistopheles? It's enough to tempt anyone to kick the hornets' nest.'

WRITERS ON STIEG LARSSON: CHRISTOPHER FOWLER

Christopher Fowler's eccentric investigators Bryant & May couldn't be more different from Larsson's duo, but he has examined the *Millennium* phenomenon in some depth: 'For me the character of Lisbeth is not the most interesting thing about Larsson's trilogy. From the mid-1980s onward, the spiky punk hacker-heroine, tattooed, damaged and afraid to commit, has been a staple ingredient of American comics, although Larsson takes the cliché and fleshes it out beautifully. The film version of *Dragon Tattoo* is forced to turn Salander into a living actress, but succeeds by carefully following Larsson's blueprint. What I most admire is the extraordinary way in which Larsson opens the narrative to include an immense cast, and we can sense that all of them have their own lives, which only intersect at the crossing-point of Blomkvist and Salander. The crime writer's curse is coincidence – one is often driven to coincide characters and situations for the sake of plot, but Larsson avoids this by a system of not-quite-overlapping events. It's how real life works, of course, and makes the account more believable. The result is that when he tells you what a minor character had for breakfast it doesn't feel like a digression. Instead, it's a way of rounding out his world-view into a complex, tangled whole. Writers who have the rare ability to do this often seem to produce trilogies, as if they can see a vast interconnected planet of stories going on behind the main plot. It's a talent that links Elmore Leonard's crime books to Susanna Clarke's fantasies, and for me is the sign of a master storyteller.'

WRITERS ON STIEG LARSSON: FRANK TALLIS

Frank Tallis writes historical crime fiction reflecting his experience as a clinical psychologist (the latest is *Deadly Communion*), so shows acuity in analysing the resonances that exist between psychotherapy and detection: 'For Larsson, crimes are like symptoms and the process of detection is very similar to psychotherapy. We have to dig deep, to find the perpetrator or the traumatic memory. Larsson exploits these relationships in an inspired way. We are presented with a mystery – but embedded within it is another, and perhaps more compelling mystery: that of a violent, antisocial young woman who has been labelled psychotic and appears to have obsessive and autistic personality characteristics. At one point she is described as looking like a half-witted 15-year-old anarchist. As her resourcefulness and impressive talents are revealed, we want to know – more than anything else – the answers to questions that a psychotherapist would ask. Why is she the way she is? What motivates her? What makes her tick? We are as interested in Salander's personal psychology as we are in the overarching plot.

'Although Salander is given various psychiatric labels, an

accurate diagnosis seems impossible. In this respect, Larsson demonstrates his liberal credentials, because, in actual fact, there is nothing "wrong" with her at all. She is not medically ill. One is reminded of stalwarts of the anti-psychiatry movement, renegades like Thomas Szasz and R D Laing, who suggested that a mind can only be sick in a metaphorical sense, and that "madness" is the only sane response to an insane world. It is unusual for a work of genre fiction to address such profound issues. They are at the very heart of the *Millennium Trilogy*, and provide a satisfying philosophical underpinning to a fast-paced, dramatic narrative. Few people have been able to pull this off, but Larsson succeeds with a light touch and without the usual tub-thumping piety.'

WRITERS ON STIEG LARSSON: MINETTE WALTERS

P D James and Ruth Rendell were for many years the joint holders of the title 'Britain's Queen of Crime' – but for quite some time, Minette Walters has been co-opted into this august company with her remarkable series of psychologically penetrating novels. She takes the view that the principal reason Stieg Larsson has been such a global phenomenon is because he's such an extremely accomplished writer: 'It's one thing to have a good idea, quite another to transpose it to the page in such a way that the setting, the characters and the plot come alive for the reader. All the best crime and thriller novels have been written by talented writers and one of the benefits of skilful prose and dialogue is that it's easier to translate.

'Regarding Salander... we tend to have stereotypical ideas about Swedish girls – blonde, beautiful and leggy – so

Lisbeth is refreshingly unusual! You could say that the appeal of Larsson is that he paints the whole of Sweden as unusual. We've become used to the dour Calvinism of Henning Mankell and it was surprising to encounter the eccentric, colourful and more chaotic environment that Larsson inhabits. And his days as a crusading journalist introduced him to the true underbelly of his society, which lends real authority to his fiction.

'I bet that Stieg's dependence on nicotine helped him write his books. Smokers concentrate better and stay awake longer than non-smokers. I wish I'd met him. I'd have enjoyed sharing a fag outside in the cold while the clean-knickered brigade sat in their highly-antiseptic environment inside and discussed their asthma symptoms.'

Does his death at 50 explain to some degree the success of the books published posthumously?

'Not in my opinion,' Minette Walters says. 'He was too good a writer. He would have triumphed anyway.'

Is he a feminist writer – or is there an element of exploitation in the books? Walters' answer to this is less clear cut: 'I'm not sure what feminism is any more so I can't answer this. For me it's always been equality between the sexes and I have no reason to believe that wasn't Larsson's view.

'As for his legacy: if any future crime or thriller writer feels they can only succeed by aping Stieg Larsson then they should put their pen away now and adopt a career that does not require original thinking. The curse of any genre is that 90% of authors piggyback off the originality of the other 10%. It's the originals like Larsson who continue to evolve and develop the art of novel writing.'

WRITERS ON STIEG LARSSON: MARK LAWSON

In the newspaper the *Guardian*, Mark Lawson, one of the UK's leading critics and broadcasters, pointed out that on a French beach he had visited, almost every sunbather of every nationality was reading one of Larsson's novels in the numerous translations: 'This phenomenon is improbable, given the project's many obstacles,' he goes on. 'The author died before the first book even went through the editorial process and, in most such cases, readers are left with a tantalising sense of the polish further drafts might have provided. And while Swedish crime fiction already had a high reputation – through the Wallander novels of Henning Mankell – Larsson has achieved a global level of acclaim and sales which is very unusual for a story that is not originally written in English.'

Lawson has come up with an intriguing analysis of the reasons why the books have done so well: 'My theory for the phenomenon is that Larsson took a genre which has generally sold to men – thrillers turning on technology and conspiracies – and feminised it through a highly unusual central character: Lisbeth Salander, who combines the brain of Sherlock Holmes with the martial arts skills of Lara Croft. It's also likely that the history of Sweden – where an experiment in liberal government was compromised by violence and corruption – resonates with readers in other countries. And the author's sudden death – although family and fans accept that he was killed by smoking rather than a smoking gun – adds to the sense that the novels contain urgent and dangerous truths.

'And yet perhaps the books' triumph should not have been so great a surprise. It is an oddity of Swedish culture that a country often easily ignored suddenly throws up an example in a certain field – Abba, Björn Borg, Volvo – which proves to be a world-beater. Larsson is the latest example.

'The sadness is that the question which always underlies a reader's relationship with a favoured author – what will they write next? – cannot apply here, although suggestions that Larsson's laptop may have contained outlines and notes for many more books are one possible reason why his estate has been so bitterly contested.'

WRITERS ON STIEG LARSSON: YRSA SIGURDARDÓTTIR

Yrsa Sigurdardóttir is the Icelandic author of the *Thora* series. With her knowledge of both the Nordic countries and the UK, how different does she feel the response has been to the Larsson phenomenon in the two countries? She says: 'The success was probably more readily achieved in Scandinavia, Sweden particularly, as these countries are Larsson's home base in the case of Sweden, and his backyard with regards to the others. But it's a remarkable achievement where the rest of the world is concerned.

'It's hard to pinpoint exactly what makes the *Millennium Trilogy* so mesmerising... but I believe it has a lot to do with the feeling of unfairness evoked, followed by justice being served, in an often colourful manner.

'Salander is the quintessential heroine, bent but not broken, a unique fictional character that one cannot help but admire despite her socially irresponsible antics. Her background is tragic and in a more "traditional" novel she would spiral downwards, and most likely come to a heartbreaking end. Instead we are introduced to a spirit that must at times repress the urge to lunge out, biding her time to eke out what she considers the wicked deserve. Her unusual "look" is appealing to me – and I can gauge my drinking with the recurring notion that it would be a great idea to have my nose pierced with a ring in the middle like a bull, telling me it is time to stop. It does show that somewhere deep inside me I have a fascination and respect for those who have the guts to go ahead with such things...

'Larsson was not known at all in Iceland before the *Millennium* books, and possibly this also applies to the other Nordic countries, aside from Sweden. News of fringe politics does not carry over borders.'

And his death?

'The idea that he was assassinated is not one that has many followers although there are always those that believe in conspiracies. I am really tempted to join their ranks, being a chain-smoking workaholic.'

WRITERS ON STIEG LARSSON: HÅKAN NESSER

There is no question that Håkan Nesser – who lives both in London and his native Sweden – is comfortably one of the most adroit practitioners of the Nordic crime novel. He's a man of immense good humour – but possesses a firing-on-all-cylinders readiness to tell it exactly as he sees it: 'People seem to love Stieg's books everywhere, but the worldwide enthusiasm may have more to do with the monotheism connected with all kinds of hype. Everybody reads the same books these days, unfortunately – and seems to need to follow this herd instinct.

'Salander is the key to the success of the Stieg Larsson books, of course. Well, you've got a super-smart underdog, beaten by society, but invincible... it's a formula that's worked before, hasn't it? There is no such thing as a Swedish way of writing crime fiction; that can be said with certainty. My writing differs totally from Stieg's; he's a political action writer with a lot of pathos, and I like his books very much, but the Swedish crime fiction boom is a market phenomenon, not a stylistic confluence.

'Before the crime novels, Stieg was known only to those with an eye on the stuff *Expo* worked with, i.e. neo-Nazis etc. As to his death... well, he died from smoking too much and working too much – there's absolutely no doubt about that. Other theories are just bullshit journalism.

'The first film of his books was very well received. The second one had a cooler reception – in fact, I've only seen the second one, and I'm afraid it was very bad. Everything was reduced and simplified to action and violence. Can anyone fill his shoes? Frankly, I'm simply not interested. I'm responsible for my own writing, and that's enough. A Swedish publishing house has been trying to hype a pen-name writer, and perhaps they have succeeded; he was bought by a number of countries at a book fair last April. The problem is that the book is an unbelievable concoction of speculative shit.'

WRITERS ON STIEG LARSSON: HENRY SUTTON

Henry Sutton, the literary editor of the *Daily Mirror*, is also an accomplished novelist (his most recent book is *Get Me Out of Here*), and is working in the area of crime fiction in writing a continuation of R D Wingfield's Inspector Frost novels. He has a slightly unusual take on the *Millennium Trilogy*: 'Actually, it's in my nature to steer clear of phenomenally popular novels, but one really did have to pay attention in this case. Initially, I have to say, I don't think the book has been brilliantly published in this country. I don't think his publishers capitalised on who he was and the fact that the book was already doing supremely well around the world – I think it was a missed trick there. But you can't argue with the subsequent success of the book. And while we are talking about reservations, I have to say that I did find some of the translations of the books a little clunky – *The Girl Who Kicked the Hornets' Nest*, for instance.

'There are other problems with any kind of translated fiction, but I would have thought it was more feasible to render a translation of a popular genre – such as crime fiction – so that it is more in tune with the original. The same might be said of literary fiction as well, but crime fiction has certain common denominators, even the more innovative examples, which can be accessed in a good translation.

'As for the reasons for the success of books, I'm not sure I agree with the received wisdom that the author's early death is such a major factor in the acclaim. Actually, his death was a tragedy. The books might even have done better had he been alive – he would have been around to promote them, to talk about them – and there would have been a stronger sense of where these books were coming from. In the final analysis, of course, the author really shouldn't matter. The books themselves should stand up, without the need to know anything about their creator – and that's certainly the case with Larsson. It's something of a modern phenomenon, I think, this need to relate the author to his books. This process of scrutinising and examining the author's life to illuminate the books – well, I'm not convinced that it's always particularly helpful.

'Of course in Larsson's case, he was a journalist – and a

very considerable journalist, at that – and the correlation between his work as a journalist and his fiction can't be ignored; of course, there are parallels and echoes. There are his concerns: the feminist issues, the socialist issues and his writing on the extreme Right. Knowing all that, it's hard to disassociate it from the character of Blomkvist in the books – of course, anybody who knows the facts will see the parallels. But this desire to examine the life of the writer – whether it's J K Rowling, Dan Brown or Ian Rankin – well, I understand the impulse, but I'm not really sure that it's illuminating. When I write my own novels, I am asked who a particular character is based on, and although all my characters are, I suppose, extrapolations of fragments of my personality, in the final analysis that doesn't matter – they have to work as discrete entities.

'As for the fact that one of the central characters, Mikael Blomkvist, is clearly a surrogate for Larsson himself – well, I think that's mainly of academic interest. What interests me about Blomkvist – and what amuses me – is that I find him almost ludicrously Scandinavian! The frosty exterior which conceals a warm interior; that studied detachment which is so much a part of his whole rationale – and the fact that he's coming from this morally unimpeachable place.'

Thinking laterally, how would Sutton have reacted to the first book had it been put out under its original title *Men Who Hate Women*, and promoted as a literary title rather than a crime novel? Could the book have functioned with this other identity? After all, much literary fiction has a healthy dose of crime these days.

'I really don't think that the first book could have been sold as a literary novel. Stieg Larsson knew exactly what he was doing. He knew how to get narrative functioning, he knew about the form: short, episodic chapters – and he knew how to shift from scene to scene in a kind of cinematic fashion. And the use of P.O.V. – he knew how to do all the classic stuff; it is as if he'd read the manual, and I don't mean that in any dismissive sense. But it's not great literary fiction.

'In the final analysis, it's Lisbeth who is really the engine of the books. In fact, the aspect of the books that Blomkvist represents is really a little old-fashioned. All the surrounding accoutrements are the new and cutting-edge – and Lisbeth really is a new figure – but there's nothing particularly new in the narrative in relation to Blomkvist. If Larsson is doing something new, it really does relate to the utilisation of cyberspace for the narrative, which he clearly knew about, and that is all really concerned with his heroine. And that notion that science fiction at some point is indistinguishable from magic – well, to a degree, it's true of Lisbeth, whose use of cyberspace gives her this astonishing prescience.'

And Larsson's relationship to his Scandinavian contemporaries and predecessors?

'Oh, he's undoubtedly part of that tradition. And I go back to that suggestion of a slightly chilly exterior, but an underlying moral warmth. I suppose you could say that about the English, which might account for the incredible enthusiasm with which the books are being received in this country. But we are different as nations – for a start, the English are much more ready to moan about things – that's certainly true. Scandinavians just get on with it. Of course, the yardstick by which I judge all Scandinavian crime fiction is the marvellous Martin Beck series by Sjöwall and Wahlöö. There are ten perfect books, with not a wasted word – they are all exactly as long as they need to be. And that was crusading stuff, too, in the form of a socialist conscience – you could say they were progenitors of Stieg Larsson, although he moves much further away from realism.

'I'm not worried by something which is problematical for some readers – the fact that, despite Larsson's feminist credentials, the books are almost pornographically violent and extreme in every sense. And it would appear the majority of his women readers are not worried by this fact. This is striking; apart from anything else, Larsson has a massive female readership. But then so does crime fiction in general, doesn't it? And, of course, pornography is, to some extent, in the eye of the beholder. I'm not sure quite why Larsson wrote the way he did in this area – was it simply commercial imperatives? Or did he think about the effect of this approach – and was fully aware that he would have us musing about exactly where he was coming from in writing about these extremes of sexuality?'

WRITERS ON STIEG LARSSON: JOHAN THEORIN

The prize-winning Johan Theorin (whose *Echoes from the Dead* is another of the seemingly inexhaustible stream of exemplary Nordic crime novels) has reservations about Stieg Larsson – but of a different order from those of Lauren Milne-Henderson. Speaking to him in Göteborg, I found that the *Millennium Trilogy* is the source of much debate in Sweden.

'I never knew Stieg Larsson,' said Theorin, 'but before his novels were published I had noticed his name for many years, since he was working as a journalist and illustrator for the largest news agency in Sweden, called TT, which sent out news articles to the newspapers were I was working. Larsson is a very common name in Sweden, but when his name appeared as a by-line I noticed it because his first name was spelt just like a mystery writer called Stieg Trenter, who wrote stories about Stockholm in the 1950s and 1960s. [Usually, the Swedish name Stig is spelled without an 'e', as was Larsson's when he was born, but he changed it to Stieg to avoid confusion with another author called Stig Larsson.]

'The early death of Larsson was of course very tragic, and his friends and family have my deep sympathies. He was an admirable and brave journalist who worked for *Expo* and *Searchlight* and wrote a ground-breaking book about Swedish neo-Nazi groups, and his commitment would certainly be needed today when these groups have changed their party name, put on a suit and a tie and are ready to get into the Swedish parliament.

'When it comes to the novels of Stieg Larsson, my Swedish friends and I have had big debates about whether they are recommendable or not. I think they are gripping and entertaining as thrillers, but I do have issues with them. They are a bit too long and detailed and preoccupied with computers, for my taste. More importantly, I think their world view is grim and callous, which is a problem I have with many modern thrillers. The world is portrayed as a battleground where there are evil enemies who have to be attacked and destroyed without mercy. I think we have had too many extremists and world leaders preaching that gospel to us lately – we don't need it in our books as well.

'And as for the routine promiscuity which Blomkvist and the women around him practise, please spare me. I've heard that the sex is something Stieg Larsson added to the plot to make it more commercial, but I wish he hadn't. For the last 40 years, after a Swedish film called *I Am Curious (Yellow)* became an unexpected hit in the US, we Swedes have had to live with a wanton reputation. We have tried to persuade Americans that Swedes don't have casual sex any more than anyone else in the world, and just as I think they were starting to believe us, along comes Mikael Blomkvist who routinely beds female colleagues in his stride...'

WRITERS ON STIEG LARSSON: VAL MCDERMID

In some ways, she could be said to be 'The Woman Behind the Man Behind the *Girl with the Dragon Tattoo*'. Val McDermid, one of the UK's most accomplished crime writers, is one of the authors name-checked in Larsson's first novel, and several of the elements that characterise her best-selling crime fiction may be found in the Swedish writer's work – notably in the beleaguered-but-capable female protagonist obliged to confront the darkest extremes of human behaviour, and graphically described scenes of sexuality and violence. Ironically, McDermid has been on the receiving end of some flak for this element of her work herself, unlike many a male practitioner. There is, of course, the element of political commitment which both writers share, and which is the motivating force in the books. To her pleasure and surprise, McDermid says that when reading *Dragon Tattoo* she noticed that Blomkvist's reading progress in the book is from Sue Grafton through Sara Paretsky to McDermid's own work – reflecting, in some way, the darkening tone of the book – as might be seen in the progression of the work of these three best-selling women crime novelists.

'I know it's been said that I was an inspiration for Stieg Larsson,' says McDermid, 'in fact several people have pointed that out to me. It's a flattering idea, but I don't really want to take credit for it. After all, there are only so many ideas out there, and all crime writers are going to end up dealing in that lingua franca of the genre, with all its overlappings. He may have read my books, but then he undoubtedly read a lot of other authors, too. After all, he had an encyclopaedic knowledge of the genre (and not just the crime genre – he knew as much about science fiction as about crime fiction).

'My book *A Place of Execution*, the book that people routinely compare to Larsson, for instance, has been described as having been inspired by *Murder on the Orient Express*, but familiar as I am with that and with the entire Christie canon, I think I can safely say that that was not the case. As I said, there are only so many ideas, and the fact that there is a congruence between *A Place of Execution* and *Dragon Tattoo* doesn't mean that he ripped me off – we're just moving in the same territory, as writers often do.

'It's interesting to me that women like myself have been writing edgy, conflicted, complex and strong female characters for quite some time – often with a feminist slant. But generally speaking, and I know there are exceptions, men do not read crime fiction written by women. So it's salutary that it took a male writer – Stieg Larsson – to move this concept onto a whole new level, in terms of book sales and popularity. I'm not saying I resent it – the fact that he is read by both men and women accounts for the phenomenal popularity – but it is instructive. When a man like Larsson writes a book dealing with misogyny (it's interesting that the original Swedish title of *Dragon Tattoo* was *Men Who Hate Women*) everybody suddenly exclaims "Bloody hell! There's misogyny out there!"

'One of the reasons for his popularity – and it's definitely part of his achievement – is the fact that in several ways, he broke the rules. Certainly in terms of the creation of a totally original protagonist in Lisbeth. Those of us who toil in the crime fiction field usually don't set out to break the rules – my agenda is simply to tell the story which is in my head and if it sometimes breaks the rules, well, that's fine, isn't it? When *The Wire in the Blood* came out, people said you can't have a serial killer whose identity is announced on page 2, and now everybody is doing it! Similarly, Stieg will no doubt be the progenitor of a whole legion of socially challenged (but brilliant) young women heroines.'

Val McDermid, of course, is not the only author who might be said to have influenced Stieg Larsson. There is the American writer Sara Paretsky, also name-checked alongside McDermid in the first book. And as well as being an influence on Larsson, Paretsky certainly had a powerful effect on the author of *A Place of Exclusion.*

'There is no question that Sara Paretsky was an important ground-breaker for many writers such as myself,' said McDermid, 'Although we ended up in different places. Paretsky's protagonist, V I Warshawski, was a strong and capable woman, but was out in the world living out certain feminist values, not living in some little feminist ghetto. She had intelligence, independence and bravery – and a certain foolhardiness (obviously characteristics that also belong to Lisbeth Salander).'

Of course, it could be argued that Larsson is able to deal with some very tricky subject material for a male writer because of his impeccably established feminist credentials – though there are those who have accused him of being somewhat gloating in his treatment of sexual violence.

'I've been accused of being gloating in such matters,' said McDermid, 'And I've been called a misogynist too! But frankly, even a cursory reading of both Stieg's books and mine will show that is hardly a justified accusation.'

While McDermid is clearly an admirer, does she regard the three books as a complete unified achievement?

'I think the first one is really interesting – a really striking book. He's drawn widely upon elements from right across the genre, and synthesised those elements beautifully. He understands the elements of the genre totally, but he is drawn into those elements and interesting positions on feminism and obviously a political position which is left-of-centre and anti-corporatism, as well as, of course, men who hate women. In this regard, I would draw in Sara Paretsky's whole oeuvre, where those elements are crucial plot mechanisms. But it's particularly intriguing to have a male perspective on misogyny – after all, with the best will in the world, a woman will have a certain take on this which will be different from a man, and he is able to articulate this position with great clarity and feeling. As I said, I think that first book is beautifully achieved, but I must admit to having more reservations regarding the second book, *The Girl Who Played with Fire*, which I do feel rather sags in the middle and really is in need of a good edit. For instance, when the superhuman half-brother comes in, alarm bells start ringing. For me, this is similar to the point at which Patricia Cornwell started to go off the rails, introducing a werewolf. A guy suffering from hirsutism! You can't allow the reader to suddenly feel "Come on, this is silly!" It does hurt the book. Larsson never loses the narrative grasp, but for me it's problematical.

'And then we get to the third book, *The Girl Who Kicked the Hornets' Nest*, and he is firmly back on track. This one has a really strong and interesting idea about the individual against the state, and it's particularly interesting for those of us in Britain who had always regarded Sweden as a bastion of liberalism in the best possible sense – it's accordingly more shocking for us to think that the conspiracy like the one described in the book could be possible in Sweden. To be honest, though, I do feel that there are elements in this book – as with its predecessor – which are not really plausible: for instance, the notion that Salander could be controlling events from her hospital bed; for all that we are prepared to accept about her, that really strains credulity.

'She almost becomes a kind of Moriarty figure, although admittedly you don't think such things at the time of reading. I know for a fact that much that she does in the technological sense is actually within the realms of possibility, but Larsson doesn't really quite get us to buy it. When we are enjoying a writer, as here, we don't need much persuasion to take on board a lot of very fairly outrageous premises, but we do have to be given the basic building blocks. In Ian Rankin's novel *The Complaints*, for instance, there is a great deal about surveillance, but Ian allows us to accept everything in the book that he talks about. He gives us enough information and detail to allow us to buy everything we read about. I'm not saying that Stieg Larsson doesn't do that – he's a very persuasive writer – but we are obliged to go some distance with him to take on board premises that he throws at us.

'Frankly, I'm damned sure that if he had lived he would have done some pretty judicious editing himself on the books – after all, he was a respected journalist who knew precisely how to get a point across with concision in his articles.'

But does the author always know what's best for his own work? After all, if Larsson had lived he might, for instance, have insisted that his original Swedish title, *Men who Hate Women*, would have to be used in translated editions (had he had the power to insist on such a thing). And surely the three English language titles beginning with the words '*The Girl...*' are one of the things that so grasped the public imagination? Larsson's original title is surely redolent of something like a Marilyn French book of the 1970s, when feminism was in its most combative and male-hostile period?

'Yes, it's a point worth considering,' Val McDermid continued. 'There is no question that the renaming of the books was a masterstroke. But then there was another masterstroke in Larsson's recipe for success, and it's a rather macabre one: Stieg Larsson dying at 50, before any of his books were published. It is unquestionably true that this sad waste of a life is something that caught the consciousness of readers. And it's one of the first things that people talk about when recommending the books to others – sometimes at the same time as extolling their virtues. It's not a career move that I can say has appealed to me, but it undeniably adds to people's legends. From Mozart to James Dean and Marilyn Monroe – those who died relatively young will always have us speculating what else they might have achieved had they lived. By all accounts, Larsson planned a ten-book sequence – and it's intriguing to think how he might have developed the characters. Having said that, the trilogy – which is what it ended up being – works very well as a trilogy, and who's to say that he might not have lost the elements that make the first three books work so well?

'I suppose I'm luckier than Stieg; what forced me to start looking at my mortality was being diagnosed with osteoarthritis in my knees at the age of 38. I realised I was not invincible, and that unless I changed the way I was living, I was not going to make old bones. By all accounts, Stieg never had that reckoning with himself. Having been a journalist myself, I know that as a profession we're inclined to be careless of our health. That's not to say that novelists can't behave in a similar fashion – Michael Dibdin, who wrote such wonderful crime novels, clearly didn't look after himself, and died at a relatively young age. It's hard not to be annoyed at talented people who are spendthrift of their health – Dibdin, like Larsson, probably had a lot of good books in him which he was never to write.

'There is, of course, another element that one cannot forget where Larsson was concerned: the political. It's something else that we have in common, apart from the kind of books we've both written – I was and am very much a political animal, though perhaps I was more a political pragmatist than Stieg was.

'Like him I was on the fringes of politics for quite a long time – at university I was part of the student and trade union movements. But as I said, I was always on the pragmatist side rather than the theoretical side. My overriding impulse was always: what can we achieve? What practical thing can we do to actually make people's lives better? I'm not sure that this was true of the circles Stieg moved in, but I've always found the trouble with the radical Left was that the women were still expected to make the tea. That's not to say that everyone would not have espoused feminist values, it was just lower down on the agenda: "We'll get to doing things for women when the important things are done..."

'On the other hand, Stieg was very much concerned with attitudes to women in his magazine articles; he'd talk about how (for instance) the far Right would say "feminism was destroying Christianity" – to which I'd say, "Bring it on! What's the problem?" But seriously, it was perfectly obvious that improving the treatment of women in society was an absolutely crucial tenet for him.

'One could say that his change of career from a journalist to novelist – although he didn't live to see the second career flourish – was in some ways a very apposite move. Fiction possibly changes lives more than journalism because of the way it sucks you in emotionally. After all, people who read right-wing newspapers in the UK such as the *Daily Mail* are having their prejudices and attitudes confirmed – that's the *raison d'être* of a paper like that (as it is, I suppose, of left-wing papers such as the *Guardian*). The opinions of readers are confirmed and justified on a day-to-day basis – what they already believe. Whatever our viewpoint may be, I think many of us read novels in a more open state, with political decision-making kept somewhat at bay. And if a good novelist can spring a provocative idea on the reader – within the context of a gripping narrative – it is just possible that attitudes can be changed, or at least confronted. Look, for instance, at how many crime readers – myself included – avidly read the novels of P D James and Ruth Rendell, whose social politics are totally different (in Parliament, they sit on opposite sides of the House).

'And if Stieg and I are political writers, that doesn't necessarily mean that we would alienate readers of other, different political persuasions – at least not in the way that political writing in a newspaper would. If you're about to draw readers into a novel, and you say something nice about something they disapprove of, it doesn't mean that they will stop reading. When I wrote *A Darker Domain,* which dealt with the very divisive miners' strike in Britain in the 1970s, there were people coming up to me in the south of England who were saying "I had no idea things were so bad in the mining communities". And I didn't create a sentimental vision of the miners, I think I painted a warts-and-all picture. For instance, I was very critical of the miners' leaders – you could paraphrase the famous observation about "lions being led by donkeys".

'Important issues can be discussed in the context of the novel – and the novelist can give you all sides of an argument, along with key insights. And to some degree, I think that is one of the things that Stieg Larsson does in his books – he grants us an insight into a society that we think we know – but really have an incomplete view of.

'What really intrigues me is: where was he coming from? I would have loved to talk to him about so many things – something, of course, I can't do now. Often when you find writers who feel almost obsessively about certain issues, there is something about childhood which has provoked or formed that attitude. Stieg lived with his grandparents as a child, for instance, until he was nine years old – that would have affected me, and I would love to talk to him about what he took from that – what his response was as a child, then as an adult. And feminism, of course – I know that there was a lot of suspicion in the women's movement about men who were sympathetic, and who hung around with women. Rather than being applauded, the response sometimes was "Is this the only way you can get laid?"

'Regarding the moment in Stieg Larsson's life when he became the passionate feminist he was, I'm reminded of something involving one of the great crime writers of the past, Sir Arthur Conan Doyle. There was an incident that changed the way he looked at the world. When he was a war correspondent during the First World War, he went with Rebecca West to a factory in the west of Scotland where they made cordite – in fact the factory was nine miles long, the biggest factory of its kind in the world. Most of the factory workers were of necessity women, as so many of the men were at the front. And seeing women working under often hazardous conditions, and being such a key part of the war effort, he said decisively "Women should get the vote. They have a perfect right to say what's what when peace comes." In fact, that is the precise point at which Conan Doyle became a feminist.

'Of course, however radical you think yourself (and I'm sure that Stieg Larsson, like me, would like to think that he would always be an anti-establishment figure) the danger is actually about becoming just the opposite – something, of course, that he never had time to do.'

ACKNOWLEDGEMENTS

I'm immensely grateful to all those who spoke to me for this book, in Sweden, the UK, the US and other points of the compass. Mark Campbell was a rock when I was putting together my *British Crime Writing: an Encyclopaedia*, and he has proved just as Gibraltar-like here (as indeed he has been in all my years of editing *Crime Time*), as was Tom Geddes, Scandinavian translator *extraordinaire,* particularly for this revised edition. An invaluable source was the Bloomsbury Square team of publishers MacLehose Press and Quercus: Lucy Ramsey, Nicci Pracca and Larsson's UK publisher Christopher MacLehose, who gave me crucial help when I first entered the Larssonian world via interviews and articles for various UK newspapers and magazines.

I owe a particular debt to one of Larsson's own favourite writers, Val McDermid, who was generous with her time. *The Rap Sheet*'s Ali Karim, Larsson aficionado extraordinaire, supplied much useful material, and Maxim Jakubowski – who, apart from being the man who commissioned this book, availed me throughout of his usual crime fiction acumen. And I'm particularly grateful to the authors, critics and journalists who gave of their time, along with Swedish friends and professionals (including publishers, agents and members of the Swedish Embassy in London, past and present – with a special mention for Johan Theorin, providing me with invaluable Swedish scuttlebutt); they were – in alphabetical order:

Karin Altenberg, Karin Alvtegen, Marcel Berlins, Ann Cleeves, N J Cooper, John Dugdale, Martin Edwards, R J Ellory, Dan Fesperman, Peter James, Rachel Johnson, Morag Joss, Camilla Läckberg, Mark Lawson, Dan Lucas, Julian Maynard-Smith, Steven Murray, Håkan Nesser, Kim Newman, Heather O'Donoghue, Sofia Odberg, The Rap Sheet, Robert Ryan, Mark Sanderson, Yrsa Sigurdardóttir, Joan Smith, Henry Sutton, Frank Tallis, Andrew Taylor, Boyd Tonkin, Dan Waddell, Minette Walters, Carl-Otto Werkelid, my copyeditor Rodney Burbeck and my inestimable editor John Wordsworth.